The Baudrillard

The Baudrillard Dictionary

Edited by Richard G. Smith

Edinburgh University Press

© in this edition Edinburgh University Press, 2010
© in the individual contributions is retained by the authors

Edinburgh University Press Ltd
22 George Square, Edinburgh

www.euppublishing.com

Typeset in Ehrhardt
by Servis Filmsetting Ltd, Stockport, Cheshire, and
printed and bound in Great Britain by
CPI Antony Rowe, Chippenham and Eastbourne

A CIP record for this book is available from the British Library

ISBN 978 0 7486 3922 9 (hardback)
ISBN 978 0 7486 3921 2 (paperback)

The right of Richard G. Smith
to be identified as editor of this work
has been asserted in accordance with
the Copyright, Designs and Patents Act 1988.

Contents

Acknowledgements

Any edited book is a collective effort, and consequently I would like to thank all the contributors. I am especially indebted to David Clarke, Marcus Doel and William Pawlett for their assistance, enthusiasm and timely participation. Finally, I am also grateful to Máiréad McElligott who helped me launch this project with Edinburgh, and to Carol Macdonald who saw it through to publication.

Introduction: The words of Jean Baudrillard

Richard G. Smith

A dictionary would begin as of the moment when it no longer provided the meanings of words but their tasks. (Bataille, 1995: 51)

Jean Baudrillard (1929–2007) was a visionary French philosopher, sociologist, cultural critic and 'intellectual celebrity' who made a major contribution to theoretical analysis in the social sciences and humanities. In the 1980s, Baudrillard became famous far beyond the narrow confines of academe, especially in North America and the rest of the English-speaking world. The translation of his ideas into English – especially by the publisher Semiotext(e) – meant that he came to be thought of, particularly in the popular press, as the 'guru of postmodernism', closely associated with terms such as simulation and hyper-reality. However, while Baudrillard became well known as the world's leading theorist of simulation – fêted not just in academic circles, but also in the worlds of art, architecture and film-making – the widespread caricaturisation of him as a postmodernist who believed that images had now replaced reality is completely wrong: 'People took "simulation" for postmodernism, and I became a guru of postmodernism . . . [I have] enjoyed undeserved success based on a total misunderstanding' (*UD*, 21). Unfortunately, this misconception was reinforced by the release in 1999 of the movie, *The Matrix*, which, through a visual reference to one of Baudrillard's books (*SS*), sought to align itself to his philosophy when in fact the twist of the film – that the Matrix masks the 'real' – is one that owes its debt to Plato (just like so many other movies: *The Truman Show*, *eXistenZ*, *Total Recall*, *Surrogates* and so on), rather than poststructuralism and the disappearance of illusion (Smith, 2005).

Rather than a 'postmodernist', Baudrillard was, in fact, a trenchant critic of many of the taken-for-granted features of advanced capitalism and western culture – consumerism, the postmodern celebration of pluralism and 'diversity', globalisation, capitalism, modernity, mass communication and the information economy – as destroyers of the act and social relation of symbolic exchange. Throughout his long career, Baudrillard became globally famous for his challenges to received wisdom and the status quo. Most well known in this regard are his works that questioned traditional sociological and philosophical paradigms from Marxism (*MP*), feminism (*S*) and dialectical thought (*FS*), to anthropology, communication studies and structuralism. However, he was also known for his critiques of US foreign policy in connection with the Gulf War (*GW*), Abu Ghraib (*ST*) and the destruction of the Twin Towers (*ST*). He was also a well-known commentator on, and critic of, current affairs, from the HIV-AIDS epidemic to cloning, drugs, reality television and the Rushdie affair, not only in his books and academic articles, but also in such popular publications as the centre-left newspaper *Libération*.

Baudrillard is one of a generation of poststructural theorists – contemporary with such thinkers as Gilles Deleuze, Jacques Derrida, Michel Foucault, Félix Guattari and Jean-François Lyotard – whose writings have both fascinated and bewildered. Baudrillard's writing style, methodology, inventiveness and particular mode of theoretical and critical inquiry require close attention. Indeed, Baudrillard's *oeuvre* employs a technical language and specialised vocabulary of theoretical terms, and is complex in both its form and in the nature of its development. Thus this dictionary has been crafted to serve as an expert guide for Baudrillard's readers as to the jobs, or tasks, that his words perform. The 105 entries are written by thirty-five of the world's leading Baudrillard specialists. By drawing together the expertise of these scholars – from many academic disciplines – the dictionary provides not only comprehensive coverage and lucid accounts of Baudrillard's concepts and themes, it also maps out the impact of Baudrillard's thinking across the world in a wide variety of contexts and in numerous areas of intellectual inquiry and endeavour.

For over five decades Baudrillard wrote with wit and rigour on a multiplicity of diverse topics: architecture, art, anthropology, cultural studies, economics, feminism, film, geopolitics, graffiti, literature, Marxism, philosophy, photography, poetry, semiotics, sociology, structuralism, terrorism. However, Baudrillard's writings as a whole are not a catalogue of unrelated concepts and ideas, but rather constitute a consistent intellectual trajectory and an always developing philosophical position. Consequently, while this dictionary provides a readable synopsis of each concept or theme, it also contextualises how each of them functions within Baudrillard's *oeuvre*. The links between entries are highlighted so that the connections between them can be followed and appreciated. The many elements of Baudrillard's writings – which includes more than forty books – intersect to form a consistent trajectory. Indeed, a rule of thumb for reading Baudrillard is that each of his many books should not just be viewed as an individual work, but rather as a chapter of a single tome that he wrote over some forty years, and consequently, each entry in the dictionary is in a sense the 'same' entry and so beyond the reach of any system of classification.

That said, Baudrillard did not set out to produce a theory that could be deployed and applied in a dogmatic fashion. There is not a Baudrillardian school of thought as such, despite the large number of commentators on his work. Rather, Baudrillard's thought is best considered as an 'attitude' that emerged as he blazed his own idiosyncratic path, ahead of the curve, borrowing, adapting and inventing a constellation of words and concepts to chart the contours of an age that he saw as increasingly impoverished as a consequence of mediatisation and virtualisation. Accordingly, the aim of this dictionary is not so much to produce a portrait of Baudrillard – a task that has been accomplished in other works (for example, Butler, 1999; Gane, 1991a, 1991b, 2000a; Genosko, 1994; Kellner, 1989; Lane, 2009; Levin, 1996; Merrin, 2005; Pawlett, 2007) – or to bury him beneath a welter of words, but rather to offer a multitude of passageways or journeys – from entry to entry – through an *oeuvre* that has no centre.

A list of passage-words ('passwords') is provided at the end of each entry, so that any entry with a significant connection to any other is highlighted. These 'passwords' function as paths, passageways or 'shifters' that enable the reader both to trace specific arguments, concepts, developments, positions and themes back and forth through Baudrillard's *oeuvre*, and to appreciate how Baudrillard's words 'are "passers" or vehicles of ideas' as they 'metaphorize and metabolize into one another by a kind of spiral evolution' (*PW*, xiii). It is through this passing from word to word, from concept to concept, from term to term, from entry to entry, that the dictionary both organises and holds together a seemingly disparate array of materials in an overall configuration, and in so doing, demonstrates the conceptual rigour and integrity of Baudrillard's texts.

In addition to the 'passwords' the dictionary also contains a number of 'link entries'. These linking entries serve as an index to the dictionary: not a concordance like Coulter's (2007) or an exhaustive index of the traditional kind that one might typically find at the end of a book, but rather a specific index of those authors, issues and examples that are commonly associated with Baudrillard. Overall, the link entries have a dual purpose: to serve as additional and alternative entry points into the dictionary's content, and to locate Baudrillard's thought in the context of those wider debates with which he engaged or became associated.

To conclude, it is perhaps worth noting that there is a certain irony in the idea of publishing a dictionary of Baudrillard's thought. The traditional idea of a dictionary is that it 'defines' and 'fixes' the meaning and usage of words. However, Baudrillard's poststructuralist philosophy is both founded and styled on the undoing of that very idea. For Baudrillard, the relation between signifier and signified is not just arbitrary, as Saussure demonstrated, but fundamentally undecidable. In the age of hyper-reality, signifiers float unanchored so that words and images pursue their own trajectories, making their own connections and meanings. As Baudrillard himself noted in his own brief glossary entitled *Passwords* (2003b [2000c]): 'We think we advance by way of ideas – that is doubtless the fantasy of every theorist, every philosopher – but it is also words themselves which generate or regenerate ideas, which act as "shifters". At those moments, ideas intersect, intermingle at the level of the word' (pp. xiii–xiv). In short, this dictionary is not an attempt to present a 'univocal' Baudrillard, but rather it invites the reader to appreciate how Baudrillard's words convey a decentred world of radical uncertainty. Baudrillard has always sought to undermine any confidence we may have in the possibility of establishing an objective knowledge of the world; his non-referential thinking 'does not claim to prove itself, to verify itself' (*PW*, 91), and this dictionary remains loyal to that philosophical position.

A parting anecdote: reflecting on the enigmatic sentence 'I have forgotten my umbrella' written in the margin of one of Nietzsche's unpublished manuscripts, Jacques Derrida (1979) speculates that this fragment is testament to the impossibility of totality and a single coherent outcome; there will always be an unsettling remainder. However, there is maybe another possibility. Perhaps Nietzsche jotted that sentence as a pretext to return to the manuscript, signalling that the manuscript was not finished. Either way, both explanations for Nietzsche's stray sentence are applicable to the task of compiling this dictionary: it can neither be complete (any number of other entries could have been included), nor finished (any number of other passages from Baudrillard's works could have been included under any entry), nor exhaustive (there are undoubtedly many more passages between entries that could have been highlighted). Indeed, dictionaries are never finished totalities, complete with definitive definitions, precisely because the nature of a dictionary is to be excessive: to never be the last word.

A

ABU GHRAIB – see 'reversibility' and 'terrorism'.

ACCURSED SHARE

Paul Hegarty

The numerous but brief references made by Baudrillard to Bataille's concept of the 'accursed share' hardly do justice to the vital role the idea plays in the former's work. The accursed share plays the same role in Bataille as symbolic exchange in Baudrillard. Furthermore, symbolic exchange derives from the Bataillean idea. From *The Consumer Society* (1998a [1970]) on, Baudrillard adopts a position where market exchange is to be criticised, and the tools he uses derive from the French anthropological tradition that comes after Durkheim: Mauss, Hertz, The *Collège de Sociologie* (a group led by Bataille). Bataille argued that the economy as we know it is only a part, the 'restricted' part, of a 'general economy', which would include all types of exchange which had been excluded from the world where 'the economic' has increasingly been taken as the 'real world'. This general economy includes death, waste, expenditure, violence and sacrifice, rather than accumulation, profit, savings, truth and morality. It is first outlined in Bataille's 1933 essay 'The Notion of Expenditure' (Bataille, 1985a), and fully systematised in his *Accursed Share* of 1949 (Bataille, 1991a). The universe is fundamentally about waste, goes the argument (note that this does not provide a theoretical ground or foundation, as waste only exists as it is about to be destroyed), and therefore human society should try to make sure it is not kept away from waste. Like Baudrillard's notion of symbolic exchange, the accursed share in the form of sacrificial behaviour is both a near-metaphysical principle and something that takes place in history. Both have gradually been excluded as undesirable and non-utilitarian, and nowhere more so than in capitalism.

The accursed share is how waste translates into human terms. At a society-wide level, it is best characterised through the practice of human sacrifice. With the advent of Christianity, this is replaced by an impoverished representation. With the 'advance' to capitalism and industrialisation, death and anything that threatens clean, high-performing, moral behaviour is removed (see Bataille, 1991b). Taking Aztec civilisation as the paradigm of a society based on the accursed share, Bataille writes that 'the victim is a surplus taken from the mass of *useful* wealth [. . .] once chosen, he is the *accursed share*, destined for violent consumption' (Bataille, 1991a: 59). The universe is based on destruction, waste and violence and once our sense of this goes, we will have no say in how waste occurs: '[excess] must necessarily be lost without profit; it must be spent, willingly or not, gloriously or catastrophically' (Bataille, 1991a: 21). In modern times, the slightly less bloody version proposed is the redistribution of wealth through an extended Marshall Plan – which might make more sense than a return to human sacrifice, but is a somewhat feeble and contradictory recommendation. At an individual level, the individual should restore his or her connection with 'the sacred' (the realm of waste and excess) through approaching death, in, for example eroticism, drunkenness or any practice where the self is lost, immersed in otherness so that the rational, thinking moral individual slips away, if only briefly. In the second volume of *The Accursed Share*, Bataille concentrates on death as the primordial exclusion performed by humanity. Bataille turns this fearful turning-away into a foundational moment that is deconstructive – that is, only once taken from us, can we recognise this 'outside' that is death.

Without reducing the idea to metaphor, Baudrillard focuses on the critical value of the accursed share, as something 'which refutes all the axioms of economy as usually understood', where the 'target is utility' (Baudrillard, 1991a: 135). Baudrillard is wary of the belief in transgression as a way out that is held by Bataille, and also because late capitalism seems to be working on the basis of ridiculous expenditure and squander. But despite this reasonable critique (which is not indicative of his general position, as the rest of the article is highly positive about Bataille), Baudrillard offers us exactly the same 'flaws' with symbolic exchange in the very year (1976) he points out the limits of the Bataillean accursed share. Symbolic exchange would disrupt the 'system' of capitalism, offers an alternative view of human culture as a whole, and stems from sacrifice and death now lost to the modern West and must be excluded. If anything, Baudrillard's tentative use of Bataille when explicit (for example, the handful of pages in *SED*) indicates the proximity not only in content of the two ideas, not just in the form, but that Bataille's accursed share is the accursed share of Baudrillard's symbolic exchange – excluded as the other that has come too close while going too far. Baudrillard seems fearful of the implications of 'the accursed share' when developed in full, and turns away from it, continually trying to say he has moved on from it when actually it is the pulsating heart at the centre of his own 'system'.

Passwords

Consumption + Affluent society
Death
Excess
Symbolic exchange

ADVERTISING

Malcolm Barnard

Advertising (like fashion (q.v.) to which it is closely related) is a central part of Baudrillard's account of consumption and consumerism. Baudrillard's explanation of advertising begins from the observation that 'Advertising sets itself the task of supplying information about particular objects and promoting their sale' (*SO*, 179). However, he insists that there is no such thing as advertising that is restricted to the supplying of information: rather, advertising exists to persuade and to awaken desires that consumption cannot ultimately satisfy (*SO*).

Advertising persuades through meaning. Baudrillard argues that 'We consume the product through the product itself, but we consume its meaning through advertising' (*SO*, 197). The kind of meaning that advertising provides is 'pure connotation' (*SO*, 178). Connotation is a culture-based form of meaning often described as the feelings generated within us by something or the associations something has for us. It is a function of our individual and cultural identities in that the feelings aroused and the associations things have for us will vary according to which cultural groups we are members of.

Advertising is, in effect, the effacement of any and all 'real' economic experience from consumption and its replacement by meanings, signs and signification. It is the forgetting of the exchange of money for goods or services and it is the occultation of any experience of those goods and services as being things possessing what Marxism calls either 'use value' or 'exchange value'. Baudrillard says that advertising causes goods to be seen not as products, having been produced by labour, but as commodities, or consumer objects (*SO*); the consumer is infantilised by this transformation of a commercial, economic relation into a personal and signifying one as advertising makes us regress to a point before 'real social processes' such as work and production can disturb our 'magical integration' into society (*SO*).

Consumption is experienced and understood in terms of meanings, as a process of communication and social differentiation (*CS*). Advertising is an inescapable (*SO*) and irresistible part of the industrial production of meaningful differences in that it communicates those meanings, or 'significations' (*CS*). These significations are differential; they establish meaningful differences between goods and services so that products become signs or 'social signifiers' of status (*CS*). They also produce meaningful differences between the people consuming those goods and services. These are differences of status and they are meaningful but not real: advertising 'passes over' the 'objective processes of production and . . . the market . . . [as well as] real society and its contradictions' (*CS*, 194). Real differences between people make those people 'contradictory' and set against one another; the differences generated by the advertising and consumption of goods and services are combinatory and cause people to relinquish any real differences. Consequently, we are not alienated or mystified by advertising (*SO*), rather advertising enables us to differentiate and 'label' ourselves, placing ourselves into a social order according to patterns set by the prevailing fashion (*CS*).

Passwords

Consumption + Affluent society
Fashion

AIDS – see 'body' and 'drugs'.

ALTHUSSER, LOUIS (1918–1990) – see 'political economy of the sign'.

AMBIVALENCE

Marc Schuster

Ambivalence is a slippery term whose definition and significance has shifted throughout Baudrillard's career. One constant, however, is that ambivalence always calls into question the legitimacy of value. For Baudrillard, value is the principal illusion behind consumer ideology in that it imputes significance to otherwise insignificant objects and, in so doing, motivates consumers to amass vast quantities of the same. From Baudrillard's perspective, the only way to alter social relations for the better is to reveal all forms of value as illusory. Such a revelation, he argues in his early works, will inevitably trigger the collapse of consumer ideology and, in so doing, allow individuals to regard themselves not as objects but as subjects. While this theory may not explain what ambivalence is or what forms it might take, it does demonstrate what ambivalence should do: serve as a catalyst for the destruction of consumer ideology. Ambivalence, then, represents the incessant potential for the destruction of the illusion of value that is at the heart of consumer ideology.

While Baudrillard's definition of ambivalence gains greater nuance in his later works, he uses the term broadly in *The Consumer Society* (1998a [1970]) to denote a sense of both fulfilment and non-fulfilment, or gain and loss, in relation to the object of desire. The discrepancy between what consumer culture promises with respect to the object and what the object can actually deliver robs the consumer of ambivalence toward the object. Moreover, this lack of ambivalence leads the consumer into an unhealthy relationship with the object. In plain terms, because consumer ideology tells the consumer (via advertising, media images and the like) that commodities will bring absolute fulfilment, the consumer cannot help but lapse into a state of anxiety when those commodities fail to deliver. Because consumer ideology does not allow for ambivalence and, instead, forces the consumer to view the business of consumption only in terms of gain, the consumer cannot help but feel inadequate in relation to the objects he or she possesses. Hence the anxiety inherent in consumerism: the consumer's natural ambivalence toward objects is repressed insofar as consumer ideology insists that the enjoyment of objects should be unconditional. Under these conditions, the consumer has no alternative but to locate the source of dissatisfaction within, and the only option consumer ideology provides to address the resulting anxiety is for the consumer to acquire more objects.

In *For a Critique of the Political Economy of the Sign* (1981 [1972]), Baudrillard argues that the logic of the sign restricts the subject's ambivalence in relation to objects. Building on Ferdinand de Saussure's groundbreaking work in semiotics, Baudrillard notes that the sign is marked by an arbitrary nature. Baudrillard's definition of arbitrary, however, goes beyond that of Saussure. Where Saussure notes that the sign is arbitrary because there is no causal link between the signifier and signified, Baudrillard argues that arbitrariness is rooted in the fact that consumer

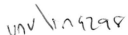

ideology would have us believe that the signifier both equals and is discrete from the signified. So while the signifier is not the signified, it nonetheless 'equals', 'means' or even 'is' in the realm of circulation and exchange that which can neither be spoken nor represented except through the signifier: the signified and the signified only. For the sake of economy, the sign reduces, represses and annihilates 'all that which overflows the schema of equivalence and signification' and eliminates ambivalence in the name of 'a fixed and equational structure' that ultimately denotes value and nothing more (*CPS*, 149). As a result, the subject loses ambivalence toward objects and relates to them only in terms of positive sign value (that is, what the object says to the world at large about the subject's status in relation to all other objects).

In order to restore humanity's potential for meaningful communication, Baudrillard calls for a mode of exchange that operates independently of the arbitrary code of value that regulates consumer culture. This mode of exchange, which Baudrillard calls symbolic exchange, hinges on the concept of ambivalence. According to Baudrillard, ambivalence and symbolic exchange do not confront the discourse of value with an opposing code but with the rejection of codes altogether. That is, because ambivalence is predicated not on the circulation of information and semantic content (which is to say value) but on the negation of these concepts, it can neither be encoded nor decoded and therefore cannot be mass mediated. From a theoretical perspective, however, Baudrillard argues that ambivalence will draw attention to the fact that the object of consumerism 'is nothing, and that behind it stands the tangled void of human relations, the negative imprint of the immense mobilization of productive and social forces which have become reified in it' (*CS*, 196). To be sure, sketching a means of effecting symbolic exchange, even on a personal level, is no easy task. Indeed, to reduce ambivalence to a simple formula is to return to the conundrum at the heart of Baudrillard's theory; doing so would more likely serve than cripple consumerism insofar as the formulaic generally lends itself to commodification. Nonetheless, the concept of ambivalence serves as a theoretical alternative to the illusory value-laden logic of consumerism.

Passwords

Code
Communication + Non-communication
Consumption + Affluent society
Political economy of the sign
Symbolic exchange
Value + Structural law of value

AMERICA

Diane Rubenstein

Baudrillard offers an assessment of the centrality of America for his work in an interview: 'All of the themes that I first examined in my previous books suddenly appeared in America, stretching before me in concrete forms' (*BL*, 135). Indeed, America has been omnipresent in Baudrillard's writings as reference, as model and as 'utopia achieved' (*A*, 77). Baudrillard is perhaps most associated with his polemical Tocquevillian revisitation, *America* (1988b [1986]) and its companion first volume of his memoires, *Cool Memories* (1990b [1987c]), which presented an America that embodied the simulation and hyper-realism characteristic of the *glitzkreig* of the Reagan era. But Baudrillard's engagement with America can be seen in his earliest semiological writings. Both *The Consumer Society* (1998a [1970]) and *The System of Objects* (1996a [1968]) as studies of postwar domestic affluence differ from Roland Barthes' *Mythologies* in their extensive references to American experts, David Riesman (sociologist), John Kenneth Galbraith (economist), Vance Packhard (public relations) and Daniel Boorstin (historian). Baudrillard exemplified his key concepts of the brand name from American labels (Esso gasoline, Marlboro cigarettes). Cinema stars were paradigmatically American (James Dean) as were films (*Citizen Kane*). Baudrillard confessed that he would 'rather see a second-rate American film than a French film' (*BL*, 33). He is a more avid reader of American rather than French fiction (*P*, 82).

The *Consumer Society* (1998a [1970]) also developed an analysis of pop art (that Baudrillard continued in the *The Perfect Crime* (1996c [1995a]) and *Screened Out* (2002 [2000a])), asking whether it was a fundamentally American phenomenon. Focusing on the work of artists such as Robert Indiana and Andy Warhol, Baudrillard resumes the stakes of America for him: 'Pop artists paint objects in terms of their real appearance . . . as ready made signs, fresh from the assembly line . . . this is why they prefer to paint the brand name, slogans . . .' (*CS*, 116). Thus pop art recognises that the truth of objects lies in their brand name: 'If that is Americanism, then Americanism is the very logic of contemporary culture and one cannot fault pop artists for pointing this up' (*CS*, 116). *The Consumer Society* (1998a [1970]) also turned to America to illustrate contemporary anomic forms of 'objectless violence': the Manson killings (*CS*, 179), University of Texas murderer Richard Speck (*CS*, 179), and the Watts riots.

In *America* (1998b [1986]), *Simulacra and Simulation* (1994a [1981]) and *In the Shadow of the Silent Majorities* (2007b [1978]), America becomes less an exemplification of a semiological concept (that is, the brand name) than the paradoxical realisation of a model of simulation, its 'testing ground'

(*P*, 80). It was Baudrillard's key insight that America is 'neither dream nor reality', but hyper-reality (*A*, 28). It is a paradoxical site, disabling or rendering unnecessary European meta-critique or analysis as Americans 'have no sense of simulation. They are themselves simulation in its most developed state, but they have no language in which to describe it, since they themselves are the model' (*A*, 28–9). Moreover, the media is America's message: 'From the outset you're in the transpolitical sphere of the medium and the screen . . .' (*P*, 86). America is described as a 'giant hologram' where the whole can be refracted into any of it parts, whether a desert, a street in a Mid-Western town, Burger King or a California house (*A*, 29).

For Baudrillard, America's reality is profoundly cinematographic. But the cinema is not where you think it is, territorialised into theatres; it inheres in everyday life. Americans 'experience reality like a tracking shot; that's why they succeed so well with certain media, particularly television' (*BL*, 134). Baudrillard provided compelling readings of the first reality television (Public Television's series 'An American Family' documenting the Louds): 'a family who agreed to deliver themselves into the hands of television, and to die by it . . . The liturgical drama of a mass society' (*SS*, 28). He also analysed the phenomenon of the hit American series 'Holocaust' (*SS*, 49–51). In these commentaries and reviews of popular films (*China Syndrome*, *Apocalypse Now*, *Chinatown*, *Three Days of the Condor*), as with his more famous essay on Disneyland (*SS*, 12–14), Baudrillard foregrounds the model of 'cultural deterrence'.

'Disneyland is a perfect model of all the entangled orders of simulacra' (*SS*, 12). Disneyland and other American theme parks may seem to be places of illusion and fantasy. Demographically and in other representative ways, 'everywhere in Disneyland the objective profile of America . . . is drawn.' But this conceals another story. This idealised space works as a dissuasive cover, an 'ideological blanket', which 'functions as a cover for a *simulation of the third order*: Disneyland exists in order to hide that it is the "real" country, all of "real" America that is Disneyland' (*SS*, 12). Disneyland exists to save the reality principle and serves as a sort of 'waste treatment facility' for the imaginary (*SS*, 13). In other words, 'Disneyland is presented as imaginary in order to make us believe that the rest is real . . .' However, 'the rest' is simulated hyper-reality (*SS*, 12). Baudrillard revised his analysis for an era of globalisation and a further radicalisation of simulation in 'Disneyworld Company' (*SC*).

One of the little remarked upon moves in these early essays that will become more discernible in later writings is Baudrillard's delineation between television and cinema in relation to the image. Cinema is a myth and an image as well as 'a screen and a visual form' (*SS*, 51). 'Holocaust' or the American wars in Vietnam, the first Gulf War, the Iraq War, are televisual and not cinematic objects, belonging to the 'social inertia of cold systems' which lack 'stakes, history, investment and speech' (*SS*, 50). Broadcasting and the use of public opinion polls, both prevalent American forms, respond by capturing the 'artificial heat of a dead event to warm the dead body of the social' (*SS*, 50).

If the televisual America is linked to war and abject pseudo events, it is the cinematic America that is lyrically rendered in *America*: 'It is not the least of America's charms that even outside the movie theatres the whole country is cinematic. The desert you pass through is like the set of a western . . .' (*A*, 56). While the desert plays a considerable role in the book, the American city too 'seems to have stepped right out of the movies' (*A*, 56). The emphasis on these cinematic aspects redoubles the theme of simulacral America (under its former actor President Reagan) as contemporary film also attempts 'an absolute correspondence with itself', which is Baudrillard's definition of the hyper-real: 'Cinema plagiarizes itself, recopies itself, remakes its classics, reactivates its original myths, remakes the silent film more perfectly than the original, etc. . . .' (*SS*, 47).

Baudrillard advises those who wish to understand America should move from the screen to the city and not in the reverse order. Similarly, a reader who wishes to understand *America* (1988b [1986]) should remember its construction as fiction. *America* was republished in France in the year 2000 accompanied by seventy-five of Baudrillard's photographs.

Passwords

City
Film + Cinema
Gulf War
Hyper-reality
Model
Simulacra + Simulacrum
Simulation
Transpolitical
Utopia

ANAGRAMS

Mike Gane

Although the anagram and anagrammatisation are a reference point for Baudrillard there are very few actual examples of them in his writings.

As with other key concepts there is considerable latitude in their definition and there is no pretence at pedantry. Nevertheless, along with other
terms such as the aphorism, Baudrillard turns them into 'passwords' and
key concepts. This term is highly significant as it indicates Baudrillard's
search for instances of the key characteristics of symbolic cultures in
poetic reversibility. In much of his early consideration of this thematic
the key target is Freud and psychoanalysis with its depth model of the
psyche, with its parallel in Marx's base–superstructure model of the social
formation, for, as he said in one of his last texts, 'truth, if it exists, can only
show through anagrammatically in the spectrum of thought' (*LP*, 210).
Baudrillard adopted the full force of Saussure's work on classical poetics
which attempted to discover the rules of classical Latin poetics (*SED*; also
see Gane, 1991b; Genosko, 1994). In fact the texts examined by Saussure
went beyond the strict anagram to those which have the elements of a
name, the name of a god for example, dispersed throughout.

Saussure claimed to have discovered the two basic rules which guided
the classical poets in antiquity. The first was the rule of coupling. Here a
vowel was used only with a counter-vowel; there must not be a remaining
uncoupled vowel. The same rule existed for consonants. If, however, there
was a remainder, this must be repaired in the following verse. The second
rule was that of the theme-word, the name of the god, which then was
dedicated and dispersed throughout. In the Latin line *Taurasi Cisanuna
Samio cepit*, for example, we find the god *Scipio*. Saussure refers to the
strict anagram but also to the anaphonic aspect of such texts – referring
to the dispersal of elements based on assonance derived from the theme-
word. According to Baudrillard Saussure himself abandoned and left these
inquiries to one side in order to develop the field of structural semiotics and linguistics. These contributions by Saussure were subsequently
widely taken up as a universal linguistics with the concept of the sign
almost completely effacing that of the symbol. But Baudrillard, in opposition to structural linguistics, sought to radicalise Saussure's discoveries
concerning the anagrammatic character of symbolic cultures and to work
on the transition of symbolic to semiotic cultures.

Baudrillard picks up a number of aspects of this discussion of the anagrammatic character of the poetic. First and fundamental is the evident
parallel of the vowel and counter-vowel to the gift and counter-gift characteristic of symbolic exchange. The second is the problematic character
of the remainder (Genosko, 1994). The third is the fact that the dispersion
of the remainder does not lead to re-establishing an identity or the 'resurrection of the signifier' (*SED*, 199). The poetic is the 'extermination of
value' (*SED*, 198).

Some of Baudrillard's conclusions about Saussure's work on anagrams

(*SED*) are referred to even in his last writings. In one of the final paragraphs of *The Intelligence of Evil or The Lucidity Pact* (2005a [2004]) he wrote:

The secret of the world is in the detail . . . It is through the detail that the anamorphosis, the metamorphosis of forms, passes, whereas the whole short-circuits this becoming by totalization of the meaning or the structure. It is the same with Anagrams in language: the name of God is scattered through the poem; it now appears only fragmented, dismembered. It will never be revealed. It does not even become what it is, in keeping with the ensnaring formula of a finality of being; it simply *becomes*. That is to say, it passes from one form to the other, from one word to the other; it circulates in the detail of appearances. Taken in its detail, the world is always perfectly self-evident . . . In this sense, any image, any act, any event, any detail of the world, is good, provided it is . . . isolated, separated, scattered – anagrammatized, anamorphosed, 'aphoristic'. (*LP*, 209–10)

Passwords

Poetic resolution
Poetry
Psychoanalysis
Reversibility

ANTI-HUMANISM + POST-HUMANISM

Kim Toffoletti

Baudrillard questions the precepts of humanism that declare the subject to be a self-determining, autonomous and rational agent. His writing can be understood as anti-humanist when viewed in terms of his theory of simulation. Following this logic, simulation culture generates the illusion of the human as a liberated individual with choice and agency, in order to obscure the fact that such freedoms have little relevance under the logic of sign exchange. Baudrillard has used the examples of referendum voting and popular opinion polls to demonstrate the way that individuals are presented with the option to choose 'yes' or 'no' and encouraged to freely exercise choice, yet this can only occur with a predetermined set of responses (*CPS*, *SC*). Voting and polling provide the simulation of humanist values and qualities, sustaining the notion of the subject's agency by creating the sense that individuals are empowered to determine voting outcomes, even if the results are unlikely to lead to discernable change. In this regard, the semblance of choice is more important than the actual outcome.

On another level, Baudrillard's anti-humanist tendencies manifest in his writings about human–technology relations. The technical innovations he discusses in *The Ecstasy of Communication* (1988c [1987b]) lead him to conclude that individuals have become 'terminals of multiple networks' (*EC*, 16). He cites the examples of the television screen and the car to illustrate how the human interfaces with electronic systems, and in turn dissolves the neat distinction between 'man' and 'machine'. In the instance of the car, it becomes impossible to fully separate the human from the technological objects s/he uses because they are part of the same system. It is the car

that speaks to you, which informs you spontaneously of its general state and yours (eventually refusing to function if you are not functioning well), the advising, the deliberating car, a partner in a general negotiation on lifestyles; something (or some*one*, since at this stage there is no more difference) to which you are *wired*. (*EC*, 13)

As our lifestyles become increasingly reliant on digital networks of communication and information, Baudrillard observes the emergence of a new modality of the human. The human gives way to the post-human when the virtual replaces the actual as the primary mode by which we conceptualise and experience reality. Humans have become virtualised – immersed within digital circuits of instant and excessive information technologies – to the point where we can no longer maintain a critical distance from the cyberspaces that surround us. Temporal and geographical distance is eradicated in an age of 'real-time' communication via satellites and high-speed digital networks, making it seem as though everything and everyone is instantly accessible, visible and knowable. Yet as Baudrillard's reality principle of simulation would dictate, 'the Internet merely simulates a free mental space, a space of freedom and discovery' (*SC*, 179). As examples of virtual spaces where the self is enacted and realised, online social networking sites like Facebook and MySpace, or programs such as Second Life, demonstrate the post-human moment where

there is no separation any longer, no emptiness, no absence: you enter the screen and the visual image unimpeded. You enter life itself as though walking on to a screen. You slip on your own life like a data suit. (*LP*, 75)

Crucially for Baudrillard, it is the interactive, immersive and instantaneous nature of our digital encounters that erodes the distance between the subject and the screen, and which makes the individual as much a spectacle as they are a spectator.

The erosion of the parameters of the human is also evident in the biological sciences. Baudrillard believes that 'as soon as the human is no longer defined in terms of freedom and transcendence but in terms of genes, the definition of man – and hence, also, that of humanism – is wiped away' (*IE*, 97). This is because increased emphasis on gene manipulation and DNA mapping to explain human existence and motivations remakes the human as the product of genetic expression, resulting in the 'the genetic simulation of living beings' (*IE*, 97). What we are left with is something that is neither human nor inhuman, but a virtual reality – a manifestation of a code signified by the body (*VI*). And if the human can be simulated from a predetermined model (genetic information), this invariably leads to the prospect of cloning. According to Baudrillard, cloning puts an end to the notion of the human as an individuated and autonomous subject. Without a mother or father, it is impossible for the clone to undergo the psychical processes through which the subject differentiates the self from the other. Consequently, we can no longer speak of the human at the point where otherness is eradicated, relying instead on a simulated otherness and humanness (*VI*).

Passwords

Clones + Cloning
Simulation

APHORISM – see 'anagrams', 'cool memories', 'fragments' and 'integral reality'.

APOCALYPSE NOW – see 'America', 'Gulf War' and 'image'.

APPEARANCE – see 'disappearance' and 'production'.

ARCHITECTURE

Francesco Proto

From his early involvement in the French magazine *Utopie*, Baudrillard's commitment to architecture is noticeable throughout his *oeuvre*. Analogous to the third order of simulation, where the model always anticipates the real, architecture stands for Baudrillard as 'the context of a society already experiencing hyperrealism' (*SA*, 4).

This position, which anticipates *Simulacra and Simulation* (1994a [1981]), is already evidenced in *The Consumer Society* (1998a [1970]), where Baudrillard analyses a new type of urban architecture: the hypermarket (Parly 2). Decentred and deterritorialised, the hypermarket is an out-of-town shopping mall that, modelled on traditional downtown shopping areas, is it itself a model anticipating, projecting and decentring a zone that is neither rural nor properly urbanised, the 'metro-area'. By generating a new mode of living and experiencing social spaces, the hypermarket also replaces organised religion in developed countries. Hypermarket shoppers interrogate objects for sale to find an answer to their concerns; yet, shoppers themselves are 'screened' to meet consumer referenda and tests (Lane, 2009). Places for the exchange of object-signs, hypermarkets, therefore, do not attain the role of object-signs.

Written in 1977 immediately after the completion of the Pompidou Centre (Paris), 'The Beaubourg Effect: Implosion or Deterrence' marks a new stage in Baudrillard's writing strategy, one in which different theoretical perspectives – sociological, philosophical, anthropological – are shaped with the frisson of science fiction. Here, the building is identified with a larger-than-life sign, which is later defined as a 'singular object' (*SA*). Hyper-functional like a hyper-commodity or a gizmo, the building is compared to the black monolith from *2001: A Space Odyssey*: simultaneously fascinating and repellent, yet totally useless, it lies like a crushed, geometricised and imploded carcass. Baudrillard provides two explanations for this: first, the very absence of culture, as purveyed by the Beaubourg, produces a vacuum that swallows up all surrounding meaning; second, by flocking 'en masse' to the building, visitors cause it to buckle. Assuming modern culture to be a gift, Baudrillard considers the visitors' presence a 'further symbolic counter-gift' that, 'based on the potlatch-like behavior of the masses', reciprocates the former by 'critical mass' and 'sumptuary hyper-consumption of signs' (Genosko, 1994: xvi). The materialisation of subtler and more abstract indices of social status, the Beaubourg thus epitomises the apotheosis of political revenge: the end of discrimination and privilege after the events of May 1968 (Proto, 2006). As culture is 'a site of the secret, of seduction, of initiation, of a restrained and highly ritualized symbolic exchange' (*SS*, 64), it ends up being simulated by the Beaubourg along with the power by which it has supposedly been generated. Baudrillard makes this position clear in discussing the Duke of Moltefeltro's *studiolo* in Urbino (Italy), a secret room in the middle of the castle where the lack of wall openings is compensated for by the presence of *trompe l'œils* (*S*). Scenic spaces par excellence, the deceptions are here to signify that all the forms of power, such as seduction, are imaginary spaces, for seduction itself is but the ability to deceive or dissimulate (*FF*). Yet the Pompidou does not deceive; it deludes and disappoints; disenchants or, at best, fascinates: real power, like real knowledge, is non-negotiable and therefore under wraps.

To explain this concept Baudrillard resorts to the Watergate scandal of the 1970s as a metaphor for Disneyland: just as the impeachment of the US President Nixon was only meant to rejuvenate a fundamentally empty belief – the principle that moral law regulates politics – so Disneyland is 'a deterrence machine set up in order to rejuvenate in reverse the fiction of the real'. According to Baudrillard, the amusement park only exists to convince us that rationality is out there, that the 'real' America is outside the walls of its childish domain, when in effect rationality has been replaced by childishness everywhere. Disneyland does not belong to the second but to the third order of simulation: rather than blurring the difference between reality and representation, its fairy-tale castles 'hide that it is the "real" country, all of "real" America that *is* Disneyland' (*SS*, 12). Always anticipated by its model – that is, America – Disneyland recalls the Bonaventure Hotel, where the labyrinthine, sanitized, and self-enclosed nature of the building is also a sign of emptiness and death: by simulating the urban environment as perfected, it mirrors the perfection of a society at its end.

Baudrillard's dystopic vision culminates in his analysis of the World Trade Center, where the only possible response to the terrorist attack of 9/11 is for architecture 'to commit suicide' through symbolic death (*ST*). Caught in the middle of a war where what is at stake are not the principles of good and evil but the self-destruction of the West, in Baudrillard's body of work architecture is now placed at the very heart of the symbolic exchange. Indeed, to Baudrillard, the Twin Towers most perfectly mirror the abstract codes (genetic and binary) on which simulation is modelled; yet, paradoxically, their destiny is also anticipated by Hollywood's dark sci-fi genre (Proto, 2006). Given this equivalence between architecture and its symbolic bearing, not only does their destruction implicitly acknowledge the end of US hegemony but their implosion, which recalls the fate anticipated for the Beaubourg, poses again the question that is a hallmark of Baudrillard's thought: 'What are you doing after the orgy?' (*TE*). That is: what happens after 'utopia' is finally 'achieved'?

Baudrillard's position with regard to architecture is therefore twofold. On the one hand, he explains architecture's collusion with the system of objects, with its differential logic of prestige and with the code as a general logic; on the other, he recognises its socio-political relevance within the symbolic domain. Contrary to contemporary art that has, for him, exhausted all means and meaning (*CA*), architecture may still have the capacity to escape its limitations. By setting up a 'new illusion of urban space' architecture can bypass and supersede the 'illusions [that have for so long been generated] about itself' (Baudrillard, 1999: 30).

Passwords

Art
Beaubourg
City
Code
Consumption + Affluent society
Masses
Science fiction
Simulation
Utopie

ART

Gerry Coulter

Baudrillard's numerous references to art and aesthetics span his writings. There are several keys to his approach to art, including: a suspicion of culture, the death of the avant-garde, transaesthetics, the role of art, the relationship of art and the real, and his own photography.

Baudrillard fancied himself, with good cause, to be the contemporary equivalent of the Danube Peasant (*CA*). He denied having any formal training in the arts and admired in himself his brute-like joy of fascination unencumbered by aesthetic, moral, social or political judgements (*ED*). Baudrillard maintained a deep suspicion of culture and the ways in which it is interwoven into structures of the economy (the art world and art market) and political culture. His refusal to promote contemporary culture included a courageous refusal of the celebratory embrace of the New York art world, precisely at the time when accepting it would have led him to greater fame and book sales in the United States of America (*AA*). Baudrillard's thought in this respect constitutes an important challenge to an increasingly promotional art world in which the reputations of curators are staked on keeping alive the idea of an avant-garde. Baudrillard posited that the role of museums and curators in the art market side of the art world was a kind of conspiracy which saw museums and other cultural venues complicit in the generation of speculative values for art in the 1980s (*CA*). In France Baudrillard outraged the arts and cultural establishment by calling Beaubourg a monster which, like other recent architectural monsters, 'testify not to the integrity of the city but to its disintegration, not to its organic nature but to its disorganization . . . they reflect the satellization of urban existence' (*CM*, 105).

Baudrillard realised that the avant-garde died not long after the end of the Second World War and that this had enormous implications for contemporary art. In his view it was still possible to see the subversive remnants of the avant-garde up to abstract expressionism (at least a form of gestural subversion). But after abstract expressionism, and certainly by the time of Warhol, we could no longer talk about the avant-garde. This is not to say that new things did not continue to happen in the arts, but that it was (mainly because of Duchamp's influence on countless young artists since the 1950s) a form of 'posthumous representation'. The result has been what Baudrillard referred to as a confused art world because all forms became simultaneously possible. This meant for him that we had passed through the avant-garde into the age of kitsch (*UB*). Art was no longer art because it had come into too close contact with the real. Art's job, on the contrary, was to negate reality – a power art has at its disposal (*TE*).

In the era of kitsch anything (including relatively unprocessed garbage) can be art. The aestheticisation of everything removes what is special about art and it dies. With Duchamp's ready-mades Baudrillard felt that we passed into an order of transaesthetics, or a kind of aesthetics of banality. Before long he felt this would overtake our entire culture and is well into the process of doing so by the early twenty-first century (*CA*).

Baudrillard did like some contemporary art if, like Olivier Mosset's, it deeply problematised the role of the creator in the contemporary art world (*UB*). He was also fond of Enrico Baj (*UB*) who he said succeeded admirably in resolving the monstrosity of our social existence. The only art that interested Baudrillard in recent years was that which 'succeeds in being itself a monstrous act succeeds in resolving and in reabsorbing the monstrosity of our lives' (*UB*, 142). For him a medium like painting can succeed in becoming such a mythic operator. This does not mean that we have an avant-garde but we do have some art that stands against the effort to subsume the art world into the promotional culture of late capitalism.

Passwords

Artists
Beaubourg
Culture

Photography
Real
Transaesthetics

ARTISTS

Richard G. Smith

Baudrillard commented on artistic movements – Hyper-realism, Pop Art, the Velvet Underground – and the work of artists such as Enrico Baj (*UB*), Sophie Calle (*PFM*), Barbara Kruger (*UB*), Charles Matton (Baudrillard, 1991b), Olivier Mosset (*UB*) and Andy Warhol (Baudrillard, 1995a) throughout his career. He wrote substantial essays on art in some of his earliest books (*CS*, *CPS*), an interest that spans his *oeuvre* (*AA*, *CA*). Several essays by Baudrillard (for example, Foster, 1983) and interviews with Baudrillard (for example, Baudrillard et al., 1991) appeared in art books, exhibition catalogues (for example, Baudrillard, 1988) and numerous art magazines (*Art in America*, *Artforum*, *Art Papers*, *Art Press*, *Art & Text*, *Block*, *Eyeline*, *Flash Art*, *Galleries Magazine*, *Parachute*, *Paragraph*, *Tate Magazine*, *World Art* and so on). Furthermore, he gave several invited lectures in the United States, perhaps most notably at the Whitney Museum of American Art in 1987 where he spoke about Andy Warhol. That said, it is also worth noting that Baudrillard's own theoretical writings had a considerable influence on artists and the art world, and he was the subject of numerous articles in the art press (for example, Carrier, 1988; Foster, 1986; Hughes, 1989; Kester, 1987). However, this influence had far more to do with the power of Baudrillard's name and fame for lending intellectual cachet to certain artists than a truly artistic engagement with Baudrillard's ideas about simulation, hyper-reality and art as disappearance. Indeed, Baudrillard appeared to be quoted by many artists rather than understood by them.

Richard Vine (1989) noted that in the 1980s the name 'Baudrillard' had become a password of tribal identification, a buzzword, in New York's contemporary art scene among both critics and artists alike. At that time a generation of abstract geometrical artists known as 'Neo-Geos' (Geometrists of New York) or 'Simulationists' had emerged, who described and discussed their art as simulation and hyper-reality as they tapped into the hype around Baudrillard's ideas. Baudrillard became required reading, footnoted, cited and most quoted by artists such as Ashley Bickerton, Ross Bleckner, Jenny Holzner, Jeff Koons, Sherrie Levine, Simon Linke, Robert Longo, Allan McCollum, David

Salle, Haim Steinbach, Philip Taafe and Meyer Vaisman. However, it was perhaps Peter Halley who most explicitly appropriated and publicly announced his enthusiasm for all things Baudrillardian, on one occasion commenting that 'Reading Baudrillard is the equivalent for me of looking at a painting by Andy Warhol' (cited in Baudrillard et al., 1991: 9), while elsewhere he confessed that 'it was Baudrillard who allowed me to understand what I was doing with those day-glo colours I had been using. All of a sudden I began to see them as hyperrealization of real colour and I don't think I could have conceptualized that without Baudrillard' (Halley, 1986: 33).

It was in the context of such enthusiasm for his work that, in 1987, Baudrillard embarked on a speaking tour in America sponsored by the Whitney Museum of American Art, Columbia University, and the School of the Art Institute of Chicago. However, the artists were in for a surprise when in a lecture at Columbia University he delivered his verdict on those artists who had appropriated his work: 'I cannot get involved in explaining this new art of simulation . . . In the world of simulation, there is no object. There is a misunderstanding in taking me as a reference for this work' (Baudrillard, in Heartney, 1987: 18). Indeed Baudrillard pronounced 'the end of art' in an era of simulacra and simulations, and so he was hardly going to endorse and praise those artists who were now claiming their art to be simulacra.

Finally, Baudrillard's influence on the art world was not simply one of American admirers and one-way unquestioning adoration. In 1987, White Columns in New York organised and sponsored an 'Anti-Baudrillard' exhibition and panel discussion (organised by the artists' collective Group Material), which 'disputed the primacy within the art world of the theory of Jean Baudrillard' (Miller, 1987: 49). The irony was that Baudrillard himself sided with the 'Anti-Baudrillard' camp, because in the art world at this time the excitement around Baudrillard was to do with the logo 'Baudrillard', not with Baudrillard's actual philosophy. In short, in the art world 'Baudrillard' became a logo, a gesture and a signature, and so ironically came to be, not a singularity, but merchandise, a part of art as the simulation of the act of disappearance.

Passwords

Art
Disappearance
Hyper-reality
Simulation
Transaesthetic

B

BALLARD, J. G. (1930–2009) – see 'literature' and 'science fiction'.

BARTHES, ROLAND (1915–1980) – see 'America' and 'photography'.

BATAILLE, GEORGES (1897–1962) – see 'accursed share', 'excess', 'gift', 'gnosticism', 'modernity', 'obscene', 'radical alterity' and 'symbolic exchange'.

BEAUBOURG

John Armitage

The Centre Georges Pompidou (constructed 1971–7) is a building complex in the Beaubourg area of Paris, France. Exhibiting a postmodern, high-tech, architectural design, the Centre houses a *bibliothèque* (library), the Musée National d'Art Moderne and a centre for cultural research. Owing to its location, the Centre is known to Parisians as Beaubourg. It is named after Georges Pompidou, President of France (1969–74), and was officially opened on 31 January 1977 by the then French President Valéry Giscard d'Estaing. The Beaubourg has had millions of visitors since its opening.

The Beaubourg project was awarded to a creative team led by the Italian and British architects Renzo Piano and Richard Rogers in an architectural design competition in 1971. The design of the Beaubourg revolutionised the architecture world, with Rogers especially securing a global reputation as a high-tech iconoclast on its completion, particularly given the Beaubourg's exposed frame of coloured pipes and automated systems. The Beaubourg thus transformed the city museum, converting former privileged monuments into popular sites of culture and leisure. All the operative structural elements of the Beaubourg are colour-coded: green for plumbing, blue for climate control, yellow for electrical networks and red for circulatory elements and safety mechanisms.

Baudrillard's 'The Beaubourg Effect: Implosion and Deterrence' (*SS*) contributed to the postmodern architectural revolution by critiques of the Beaubourg 'machine' or 'thing', of this anonymous mystery, this corpse of fluctuation, symbols, systems and circuitry. Baudrillard argues that the mission of the Beaubourg is to enable 'the final impulse', which is not simply the transformation of a nameless structure but the individualisation of social life and its irretrievably bottomless implosion. He sees little hope for social relations when the Beaubourg is devoted to information and surface aeration, simulation, media and self-supervision.

The impact of Baudrillard on architecture fluctuates, but the effect of the Beaubourg on Baudrillard was prolonged. For the Beaubourg is a shrine to mass simulation. He defines its three functions: incineration, monumentalism and convection. The Beaubourg consumes cultural energy; it is the black monolith of Stanley Kubrick's *2001: A Space Odyssey*; it is the mad convection of its merely apparent substance. These annihilations also affect the neighbourhood. The Beaubourg is purely a defensive precinct, resolutely postmodernised and sanitised by means of its condescending design. Figurative industrial terms dominate Baudrillard's Beaubourg: it is a 'machine for making emptiness' similar to nuclear power stations manufacturing menace. Or it is a system of maximum security, a radiant shield, a sector of comprehensive control and slow-moving territorial deterrence. Technology and ecology, economics and geopolitics are the constituents of this cultural colossus. It is a totalitarian model of security and prevention, a nuclear inflected station whose matrices encompass the social field. Yet this model of deterrence also offers a space to challenge global control, to interrogate the symbols of peaceful coexistence, to consider atomic risk and to contemplate the Beaubourg's cultural fission and political prevention measures.

For Baudrillard, then, the Beaubourg's flow of liquids is uneven. Certainly, high-tech aeration, cooling, electrical systems and the customary fluids surging there indicate perfect functionality. But the transfer of people through the Beaubourg is uncertain and the outdated escalators inside synthetic sheaths must be questioned. Why do we think of this ornate drama in terms of fluids? What is the basis of innovation at the Beaubourg? The question of the Beaubourg is thus the question of propulsion. The Beaubourg in its immobility is a fabricated cultural factory, of objects, of books and of internal spaces. Baudrillard is therefore engrossed in the Beaubourg's movements and incoherence, in its fluids and its modes of transmission. In *The Conspiracy of Art* (2005b) he criticises the consequences and contradictions of the Beaubourg through the activities of its personnel, its assignment to absolutely circulatory interior spaces and its lack of private work stations. Baudrillard questions the movements of Beaubourg's personnel, its exaggerated fashionable mannerisms and its lithe adjustment to the structures of this postmodern space rather than its stationary or existential condition.

Critics of Baudrillard's Beaubourg might ask what the demand for an architectural analysis of the building's personnel and structural postmodern spaces alerts other commentators to. Sat in their non-existent space, Beaubourg's personnel are perhaps an analogy of Baudrillard's philosophy. Does his concentration on Beaubourg's personnel, on its tiredness, simulated isolation and its spaces, offset the building's immense ploy of deterrence? For Baudrillard, Beaubourg's personnel employ cultural energy as a means of personal resistance. Remarkably, very similar contradictions typify the Beaubourg 'thing'. Is the Beaubourg 'thing' purely a movable exterior that substitutes modishness and postmodern architecture for a static interior that continues to uphold modern cultural values? How are the Beaubourg's spaces of deterrence and dogmas of visibility related to the translucent and polyvalent, to the consensual and the tangible? Baudrillard argues that we must move beyond our contemporary obsession with security if we are to re-establish genuine social relations. He proposes that the whole of social discourse is embodied in the Beaubourg, a discourse that permits the treatment of 'culture' and its contradictions, its precise intentions, to shift into possibilities not controlled by Beaubourg 'things'. Baudrillard contends that no Beaubourg 'thing', in thought or in steel and glass, is as monumental as postmodernity would have us believe. Indeed, the Beaubourg's postmodernity is produced by entrenched modern ideas, logics and orders that are lacking critical thought. There is no evading this truth at the Beaubourg for Baudrillard, but this truth must be considered, constructed and experienced from the perspective of the Beaubourg's process of developing into an uncontainable apparatus, which, by way of its own achievements, somehow manages to flee from modern thought and the rules of the established order.

Baudrillard's reflections on the contradictions and state of the Beaubourg have been prominent in postmodern cultural theory, but efforts to utilise them on similar buildings are neither many nor entirely successful. However, Baudrillard's account of the empty interior of the Beaubourg can usefully be compared with Fredric Jameson's description of the Bonaventure Hotel in Los Angeles (see Gane, 1991b).

Passwords

Architecture
Art
Masses
Postmodernism/Postmodernity

BENJAMIN, WALTER (1892–1940) – see 'clones + cloning', 'culture', 'real' and 'simulation'.

BODY

Kim Toffoletti

Across a number of his books and essays Baudrillard reflects on the changing status, role and perception of the body in contemporary western society. He has conceptualised it variously as a consumer object (*CS*), a fetishised marker of sexual difference (*SED*) and a genetic code (*EC*). He has considered it in terms of pornography (*S*), cloning (*SS*), obesity (*FS*), (trans)sexuality (*TE*), fashion (*SED*) and torture (*CA*). Each of these instances represents a 'mode of disappearance for the body' and demonstrates Baudrillard's preoccupation with the body as a fatal form.

Under the influence of Marxist thinking, Baudrillard argues that the body is being manufactured into a sign for consumption. In *The Consumer Society* (1998a [1970]) he proposes that the body, in particular the female body, is produced as a consumer object though investments of labour, time and money toward the maintenance and presentation of one's bodily 'property'. Baudrillard uses the examples of the fitness, beauty and diet industries to illustrate how the body is mobilised as a commodity-sign, form of capital or asset: 'one manages one's body; one handles it as one might handle an inheritance; one manipulates it as one of the many *signifiers of social status*' (*CS*, 131). As a sign of ourselves projected to the world, our bodies become our chief mode of display, objects through which we proclaim our health, wealth, happiness, satisfaction and success. This model of the 'functional body' replaces the religious notion of the body as 'flesh' and the capitalist view of the body as labour power.

It is in the context of the fashion system that the body's remaking as image is fully realised. No longer defined by its reproductive function and biological capabilities, or viewed as innate and unchangeable (unlike the clothes and accessories we wear), the body is transformed through sign-exchange into an object of fashion in its own right. In this sense, it is not only clothes but the body itself that is assessed as 'fashionable' or 'unfashionable' according to the preferred look for any given season (*SED*). As is the case with catwalk models, body types (the waif, the supermodel, the ethnic model) are as much fashion trends as the garments and accessories that adorn the body. Plastic surgery procedures also enable the remodelling of the body as a sign, as appears to be occurring with the tendency toward emulating the features and traits of popular celebrities. Fashion functions to give the appearance that the body has been 'liberated' from class constraints and the corporeal limitations of sex, race and disability. Baudrillard uses the example of androgenous dressing to suggest that gender identity manifests via the play of signs of gender difference, rather than through the experience of difference tied to a fixed, bodily 'reality' (*SED*).

In subsequent writings Baudrillard observes a change in the way that bodies are experienced and understood in the age of computer culture and digital media. He understands bodies to be manifestations of information codes that can be replicated and transmitted. Baudrillard, who cites the AIDS virus, cloning technologies and DNA mapping as examples of the 'miniaturisation' of the body, questions traditional conceptualisations of the body as a biological entity or cultural construction. As pure information the body is an effect produced by the code rather than the source of selfhood. We can see this in the way Baudrillard speaks about the possibilities of cloning bodies:

The DNA molecule, which contains all information relative to a body, is the prosthesis par excellence, the one that will allow for the *indefinite extension of this body by the body itself* – this body itself being nothing but the indefinite series of its prostheses. (*SS*, 98)

Inverting common understandings of the body/prosthesis relationship, whereby the prosthesis augments and extends the (bounded) biological body, Baudrillard instead views the cloned body as the prosthesis – the residue or extension of the genetic code (*IE*).

It has been suggested that Baudrillard's theorisation of the body as sign and code neglects a focus on the embodied experiences of corporeality (Sobchack, 1991). His remarks about the body as 'useless' and 'superfluous' have been interpreted in some instances to mean that bodies no longer matter in conceptualising selfhood (*EC*). For social justice movements like feminism, his statements seem to deny the pain, suffering and discrimination often associated with corporeal difference. Yet what distinguishes Baudrillard's take on the body from materialist paradigms is his focus on the conditions under which the reality principle functions to uphold the notion of 'real' bodies in an era of airbrushed magazine pictures, genetic manipulation and cosmetic surgery. In this respect, Baudrillard is not denying embodied experience inasmuch as he identifies a set of circumstances (simulation and hyper-reality) whereby bodies have 'disappeared' as they come to be mediated through models, codes and images.

Passwords

Clones + Cloning
Consumption + Affluent society
Fashion
Feminism/Feminine
Sex/Gender
Transsexual

BONAVENTURE HOTEL – see 'architecture' and 'Beaubourg'.

BORGES, JORGE LUIS (1899–1986) see 'globalisation', 'literature', 'modernity' and 'poetic resolution'.

C

CALLE, SOPHIE (1953–) – see 'art', 'artists', 'double', 'following', 'photography', 'radical alterity' and 'seduction'.

CAPITAL/ISM – see 'code', 'consumption + affluent society', 'political economy of the sign', 'production' and 'value + structural law of value'.

CHANCE – see 'destiny'.

CHINA SYNDROME – see 'America', 'film + cinema' and 'image'.

CITY

Richard G. Smith

While a great deal has been written about architecture by poststructuralists such as Derrida, relatively little has been written about cities and urbanism. This is also true in the writings of Baudrillard, who – with the exception of a section of text in *Symbolic Exchange and Death* (1993a [1976]), a few paragraphs in *The Consumer Society* (1998a [1970]) and *Simulacra and Simulation* (1994a [1981]), and reflections on visits to cities such as Istanbul (Baudrillard, 2001), New York, Los Angeles (*A*) and Las Vegas (*CM2*) – has said remarkably little about cities or urban issues per se when compared to his numerous writings on architecture (*SA*; Proto, 2006).

Baudrillard's lack of specific attention to the urban world – what he has written tends to be highly fragmented and undeveloped – is perhaps more notable given three strong urban influences in his early academic career. First, a close friend of his was Roland Barthes who wrote an urban semiology of Tokyo and outlined a broad framework for the development of an urban semiological approach. Second, his doctoral supervisor was Henri Lefebvre who was one of France's most influential urban thinkers. Third, he was on the directorial committee of *Utopie*, a journal that was in part a forum for debate about the format of the urban landscape. Nevertheless, while Baudrillard did not focus on writing about cities in a sustained manner, what he did write (*SED, CS*) is highly original as he extends his theorisation of the political economy of the sign to conceptualise cities as zones dominated by signs, media and the code.

The city is made in the image of the political economy of the sign. Thus, urban space is coded to be dominated by signs, media and advertising so that the system reproduces 'itself not only economically and spatially, but also in depth by the ramifications of signs and codes, by the symbolic destruction of social relations' (*SED*, 77). For Baudrillard, the city – the space of the code – is now the model of socialisation, an operational semiology, as 'multiple codes assign a determinate space-time to every act and instant of everyday life' (*SED*, 77). The layout and life of cities are, says Baudrillard, dominated by simulation models so that everyone, all social relations, are commutable within a combinatorial urban matrix.

To resist the homogeneity and differential logic of the city what is needed, says Baudrillard, is a 'reversion of the code according to its own logic, on its own terrain' (*SED*, 78), hence Baudrillard focuses on graffiti as an insurrection of signs against an urban political economy of the sign: *empty signs against full signs*. According to Baudrillard the outbreak of graffiti across New York City in the spring of 1972 (across its trucks, walls, subway trains, buses, elevators and so on) was not mindless vandalism, but rather a form of symbolic riot, a guerrilla action against the terror of the code 'where all sociality is invested, covered and dismantled by signs' (*SED*, 77). Thus Baudrillard contends that graffiti represents 'a new type of intervention in the city', a reaction and form of retaliation against the hyper-real city that is produced by the political economy of the sign.

Baudrillard argues that the strength of graffiti is that it operates at the level of the signifier, avoiding every reference and origin, so turning the city into a body: 'graffiti turns the city's walls and corners, the subway's cars and the buses, into a *body*, a body without beginning or end' (*SED*, 82). In other words, graffiti is an act that runs counter to the dominant process whereby general political economy is always turning the 'urban body' into an 'urban organism'. That is to say that graffiti runs against the way in which, through political economy, the 'urban body' (alive with living social relations and symbolic exchange) is always being dissected and differentiated into functional organised zones, 'branded with functions and institutions' (*SED*, 82), to become an 'urban organism' whose meaning can be entirely reduced to the structure that accounts for it.

The contemporary city is destructive of social relations and symbolic exchange because it is cast in the image of the political economy of the sign to be no more than a 'cut-up space of distinctive signs' (*SED*, 77). However, the orgy of graffiti scrawled across New York in the early 1970s upset the urban political economy of the sign because it was empty of content and had no message. Neither political or pornographic, the strength of the New York graffiti was that it consisted of names (and variations on names) from comic books, and so escaped the principle of signification: 'SUPERBEE SPIX COLA 139 KOOL GUY CRAZY CROSS 136 means nothing, it is not even a proper name, but a symbolic matriculation number whose function it is to derail the common system of designations' (*SED*, 78). Thus, for Baudrillard, graffiti is politically significant as with no meaning or message it contests what is now the real strategic terrain: 'the total manipulation of codes and significations' (*SED*, 80).

Passwords

Architecture
Code
Hyper-reality
Model
Political economy of the sign
Semiotics

Sign
Simulation
Utopie

CLARKE, ARTHUR C. (1917–2008) – see 'literature'.

CLONES + CLONING

Richard J. Lane

At first cloning appears to be the end: the end of totality (clones are built from parts, which contain all of an individual's genetic code); the end of sexual difference (since clones do not need male and female parents); the end of psychoanalytical theories of developmental stages, such as Freud's Oedipal stage, or Lacan's mirror stage (since both rely on relationships with one's now absent parents). Cloning becomes a final solution to an enduring human fantasy: the desire for immortality. The cloned individual will live forever in the endlessly reproduced copies of his or herself. Is this liberation (from death and disease) or nightmare? The clue lies in Baudrillard's main analogy for the process of cloning: the metastasis of cancerous cells. The clone, then, is like one of those cancerous cells, endlessly proliferating, and in the process going beyond what it currently means to be human. Human beings have long dreamt of entities similar to clones: witness the tradition of the double, which Baudrillard calls an 'imaginary figure' (*SS*) just like the soul, the shadow or the mirror image. But all of these entities are phantasmatic, merely having power via the imagination and its dreams and fantasies. We might think that these entities are like the clone, but in fact Baudrillard argues that the material reality of the clone exorcises them – they belong to a prior age, one in which humanist and transcendental notions held sway. Along with this exorcising of metaphysical ghosts goes the banishment of one's parents and of the Other. A clone is not a double: it is the iterative reproduction of the same. Baudrillard also points out that the construction of a vast information network that is currently underway in western society is like the cloning of the entire world. He concentrates, however, on the monstrous and frightening cloning of the individual. What replaces our parents? For Baudrillard, they are replaced by the matrix – or – the code (here, more specifically, genetic code). Cloning in this sense is not productive: it produces nothing extra or additional so to speak, it merely reproduces itself; the genetic code thus precedes and takes priority over the body. With reference to Benjamin (2008) Baudrillard suggests that with cloning an analogous situation occurs: we witness a shift from the external technologies of the industrial age (the exotechnical), to the soft technologies of the information age (the esotechnical) (*SS*). This shift is not celebrated by Baudrillard; rather he perceives the new technologies that facilitate cloning as being a form of 'revenge' on mortal beings. In other words, the new cybernetic technologies which are often portrayed in the media as a revolutionary progression (in science, technology, rationality) are regarded here as an 'involution', which nullifies difference and differentiation. This 'involution' is a return to a primitive state of 'incest' and 'entropy' (*VI*). Banishing death, one's parents, the Other and even sexual difference (or at least the reproductive functionality of sexual difference), the clone lives an 'undifferentiated' life of 'non-individuated existence'. Maybe future clones will need to pay for simulated acts of sexual difference or even of 'dying'? Baudrillard ponders future 'cyberdeath' or the luxury of simulated mortality. Cloning can be thought of as a vast test whereby we attempt to discover if there is some human essence or remnant that survives the 'artificialisation' of all human beings, that is something that escapes or exceeds the technologies of genetic code manipulation. But what if we fail this test? What if there is no essence, no remnant, after the Final Solution of cloning? Perhaps what the test will reveal is that all along human beings were already their own simulations. But surely social and cultural achievements are a permanent marker of humanity? Perhaps this once was the case, but in our information age Baudrillard takes the pessimistic view that social and cultural systems are code-driven, and that the dumbing down of society proceeds via the very realms that should liberate us. Thus education, the media and other cultural forms all produce 'monothought' (*VI*), in other words they prepare us for cloning, or they are the very grounds for the technological process of cloning and the concomitant desire for revenge on the mortal. If we fail the cloning test by becoming the non-human, the immortal or infinite series of clones, then what do we care that we were already our own simulations?

Passwords

Anti-humanism + Post-humanism
Body
Code
Double
Psychoanalysis
Simulation

CODE

William Pawlett

The concept of the code (*le code, la grille*) is an important term in Baudrillard's early work. It is used in two related senses: firstly, to understand and critique consumer capitalism, suggesting that it is a system of control that functions by conferring illusory 'freedoms'; and secondly, to deconstruct modern critical theories – particularly Marxism, feminism and psychoanalysis. Such theories, Baudrillard argues, cannot challenge the capitalist system because they are structured, at a fundamental level, by the code; their arguments are easily assimilated because they do not question the system's 'logics of value' – the interlocking network of use values, economic exchange values and sign exchange values that constitute the code (*CPS*, 123). The code can be challenged, Baudrillard asserts, only by symbolic exchange, by the 'counter-gift' of anti-value (*SED*, 40). The notion of 'the code' is notably absent from Baudrillard's later work; DNA 'code' is discussed at length (*TE*, 120) but the concept of the code seems to have been rejected because it remained within the orbit of modern critical theory. Nevertheless, many of the themes discussed through the concept of the code reappear in Baudrillard's later arguments concerning 'integral reality'.

Baudrillard's notion of the code suggests that we, as consumers, live within a far more complete form of social control than anything conceived under the rubric of ideological analysis. The code is a system of 'manipulation', 'neutralisation' and assimilation which 'aims towards absolute social control' (*UD*, 98). Though this is never achieved, the code constitutes 'the fundamental, decisive form of social control – more so even than acquiescence to ideological norms' (*CPS*, 68). This is because the code operates, fundamentally, at a preconscious level. For Baudrillard, 'the code itself is nothing other than a genetic, generative cell' (*SED*, 58). The term code is used interchangeably with 'the structural law of value', that is as a feature of the third order of simulacra dominated by simulation (*SED*, 50). The code then is the grid or 'generative core' from which social signification is produced or simulated. The medium of the code is the abstracted sign; torn from symbolic relations, drained of all ambivalence and intensity, the sign becomes a 'dead' unit of information. The code can assimilate any meaning, idea, emotion or critical gesture by reproducing it as an abstract sign or code position within an ever-expanding field of options and possibilities. All signs are, at the fundamental level of the medium, equivalent or commutable; abstract signs enable a 'universal equivalence' through the 'de-sign-ating' of everything as a term within the code. Marginal or simulatory differences are injected into the code, feeding consumption and sustaining the illusions of choice and diversity.

It is a mistake to think of the notion of the code as exclusively semiotic. As simulation becomes prevalent, conceptual oppositions are simplified into binary code, zeros and ones are no longer meaningful oppositions but, for Baudrillard, merely tactical modulations. The code absorbs the first and second orders of simulacra (in which signs work referentially and dialectically) with a system of signs that refer only to preconceived simulation models. With the third order 'the code's signals . . . become illegible', units or 'bits' of information replace signification (*SED*, 57). Indeed, the code is 'the end of signification'; social control by ideology, characteristic of the second order, is supplemented by 'social control by means of prediction, simulation, programmed anticipation and indeterminate mutation, all governed . . . by the code' (*SED*, 60). For example, any radical potential of Marxist, feminist or 'green' politics is defused by the code; they are designated as coded 'lifestyle' positions, feeding consumption and so presenting no fundamental challenge to the system. The code maintains a system of social relations through the 'obligatory registration of individuals on the scale of status' (*CPS*, 68) and functions covertly 'to better prime the aspiration toward the higher level' (*CPS*, 60) enforcing the competitive individualism of the system of consumption. The code simulates choice, difference and liberation, pacifying the deep divisions in consumer society by allowing the privileged term of binary oppositions to switch tactically or 'float', for example by simulating equality between terms (male/female, black/white, adult/child), so containing critical opposition. The code is 'indifferent' and 'aleatory'; it controls through tolerance, solicitation and incorporation.

The code encompasses far more than consumption; it includes the construction of knowledge and information through the conversion of thought into coded information flows. With the advent of DNA and genetic sciences, the code, according to Baudrillard, absorbs life itself, eliminating it as symbolic form and reproducing it as code (*SED*). The notion of DNA, Baudrillard suggests, was made possible by modernity as it is a social system dedicated to control. By providing a virtual map or code of life the concept of DNA reduces life to a copy or clone, destroying its 'destiny' and enabling the elimination of certain 'undesirable' traits such as 'criminality' before a person is born (*LP*, 29). For Baudrillard the code, in all its forms, must be defied:

[Y]ou can't fight the code with political economy, nor with 'revolution' . . . can we fight DNA? . . . perhaps death and death alone, the reversibility of death, belongs to a higher order than the code. Only symbolic disorder can bring about an interruption in the code. (*SED*, 3–4)

For Baudrillard only suicidal death, hurled against the system as 'counter-gift' and so countering the simulatory gifts of liberation conferred by the consumer society, can defy the code. This argument is further explored in Baudrillard's work on the 9/11 attacks (*ST*).

The term code largely disappears from Baudrillard's writings after *Symbolic Exchange and Death* (1993a [1976]). Is the code still operational in the 'fourth order', the 'fractal stage' of 'haphazard proliferation' (*TE*)? Baudrillard is clear that the previous phases continue to function alongside the fourth order, indeed they function even better. The concept of the code might be dead but it functions more effectively than ever, expanding, becoming virtual, producing 'integral reality': the complete and final replacement for the world as symbolic form.

Passwords

Ambivalence
Consumption + Affluent society
Double spiral
Integral reality
Simulacra + Simulacrum
Simulation
Symbolic exchange
Value + Structural law of value
Virtual

COMMODITY-SIGN – see 'code', 'consumption + affluent society', 'political economy of the sign', 'production', 'sign' and 'value + structural law of value'.

COMMUNICATION + NON-COMMUNICATION

Paul A. Taylor

The key to Baudrillard's theory of communication is the notion of symbolic exchange, the idea that authentic communication requires a truly reciprocal interaction grounded in a cultural context that is capable of spontaneity and relationships based upon 'unbreakable bonds of reciprocity' (*S*) rather than the abstract, mediated signs that constitute pre-encoded categories designed to circulate within the socio-technological system of advanced capitalism – the 'totalitarian semiotic order' Baudrillard's work opposes.

For Baudrillard, the notion that communication between two or more parties requires meaningful content has been supplanted in such a semiotic order by excessive emphasis upon the mere technical efficiency of the transmission rather than the content itself: 'The mass media are anti-mediatory and intransitive. They fabricate non-communication – this is what characterizes them' (*CPS*, 169). This results in a contemporary media society in which consumers/citizens have access to numerous technical forms of transmission that are labelled 'interactive' but which in fact reduce the act of communication to an essentially one-way process. The outcome is an ersatz form of communication that is a simulated, etiolated abstraction of more substantive, symbolic encounters.

We are all quite familiar with this immense process of simulation. Non-directive interviews, call-in shows, all-out participation – the extortion of speech: 'it concerns you, you are the majority, you are what is happening.' And the probing of opinions, hearts, minds, and the unconscious to show how much 'it' speaks. The news has been invaded by this phantom content, this homeopathic transplant, this waking dream of communication. A circular construction where one presents the audience with what it wants, an integrated circuit of perpetual solicitation. (*S*, 163)

The mainstream's misapprehension of the essence of communication and its subsequent fetishisation of transmission and artefacts of transmission leads to an unwarranted glorification of the empowering and enabling qualities of new communicational technologies: 'As if owning a TV set or a camera inaugurated a new possibility of relationship and exchange. Strictly speaking, such cases are no more significant than the possession of a refrigerator or a toaster' (*CPS*, 171).

The clearest manifestation of Baudrillard's theory in practice has been the rise of reality TV. Having mentioned in *Simulacra and Simulation* (1994a [1981]) the pioneering Australian reality TV filming of the Louds family, in his later work, Baudrillard engaged with the French equivalent of the Big Brother franchise, 'Loft Story', which he described as 'the mirror and the disaster of an entire society caught up in the rush for insignificance and swooning to its own banality' (*CA*, 190). In stark contrast to the largely positive analyses of active audience theory and cultural populism, Baudrillard was scathing about the non-communication represented in such shows: 'this existential micro-situation serves as a universal metaphor of the modern being enclosed in a personal loft that is no longer his or her physical and mental universe but a tactile and digital universe

. . . of digital humans caught in the labyrinth of networks, of people becoming their own (white) mice' (*CA*, 193).

An essential paradox in Baudrillard's approach is that non-communication results from superficially highly communicative events that from a symbolic point of view are merely non-events in events' clothing. Mainstream media theory's innate conservativism results from its unwillingness to engage with this communicational paradox. Frequently, it uncritically provides a legitimating eulogy for non-communicational mega-spectacles. It fails to heed Debord's warning that 'When *analyzing* the spectacle one speaks . . . the language of the spectacular itself' (Debord, 1983: 11). Baudrillard's sensitivity to the communication/non-communication dynamic problematises conventional media theory because, by comparison, it shows how it chooses to privilege the examination of social forms over the particular media forms that make those social forms possible in the first place.

Just as Baudrillard paradoxically claims that communications technologies are designed to 'fabricate non-communication', so at a theoretical level, the very disciplines designed to illuminate the role of media technologies in the act of communication have facilitated the overlooking of Baudrillard's theoretical significance. This failure has occurred at a conceptual level with the consistent ignoring of Baudrillard's crucial distinction between symbols and signs. In mainstream media studies, both tend to be conflated, thus removing a major element of those critical perspectives like Baudrillard's that identify technology's role in the hollowing out of symbolic substance. At a stylistic level too there has been a failure to appreciate the significance of Baudrillard's particular style of writing. Baudrillard's various McLuhanite 'probes' and 'mosaic' style are geared to questioning, at the most fundamental level, the communicational assumptions of the contemporary mediascape.

Baudrillard's innovative approach allowed him to grapple with the implications of Heidegger's famous paradoxical assertion from his essay 'The Question Concerning Technology' that 'the essence of technology is nothing technological'. The mediation created by Baudrillard's deliberately evocative, allusive and, at times, poetic writing style allows the reader to be reflexive about his communication about the act of mediated communication. It is ironic that Baudrillard, the postmodern, nihilist bête noire of empirical social 'sciences' was in fact much more concerned with examining the actual felt phenomenological communicational experience of the mediated life than his empiricist detractors, trapped as they are by the insufficiently acknowledged levels of abstraction required by more 'scientifically legitimate' methodologies.

Baudrillard's imbrication of form and content allowed him to do what other great French thinkers before him (Lacan, Derrida and so on) also did – something that Žižek describes in terms of creating a 'parallax view' and 'looking awry' – namely, to produce a critical perspective in the midst of the dominant, uncritical celebration of the 'empowering' possibilities created by the flux and flows of new media technologies. Baudrillard's poetic quality was a fundamental feature, rather than an optional by–product, of his writing. It marks his particular mode of communication premised as it is upon a willingness to speculate and find the truth that inheres within exaggeration: 'All that remains for us is theoretical violence – speculation to the death, whose only method is the radicalization of hypotheses' (*SED*, 5).

Passwords

Media
Symbolic exchange

CONSUMPTION + AFFLUENT SOCIETY

David B. Clarke

A society in which 'an ever-accelerating procession of generations of products' results in a 'luxuriant growth of objects' (*SO*, 3) calls for the kind of taxonomical effort normally reserved for flora and fauna, Baudrillard suggested – not least because such an abundance of goods marks 'something of a fundamental mutation in the ecology of the human species' (*CS*, 25). Baudrillard's initial forays into the prosperity and pro-fusion of the affluent society sought to take stock of the brave new world of consumerism, capturing the sense in which we now live 'beneath the mute gaze of mesmerizing, obedient objects which endlessly repeat the same refrain: that of our dumbfounded power, our virtual affluence, our absence one from another' (*CS*, 25). While ours is far from the first society dedicated to excess, as Georges Bataille revealed, it is nevertheless a striking development in capitalist society, one detected in Thorstein Veblen's study of the leisure class, but now extended to the masses in a manner unanticipated by Marx: 'The bourgeoisie negated itself as such (and capital along with it), engendering a classless society' (Baudrillard, 1992a: 237). Accordingly, Baudrillard's analysis of consumption incor-porates an appreciation, critique and extension of Marx's analysis of the commodity, and a radical retheorisation of our relation to objects. In a quasi-structuralist vein, Baudrillard refuted conceptions of consumption defined in terms of individual pleasure, insisting on the importance of a system of objects as a means of grasping consumption's increased centrality to the reproduction of capitalism.

The 'fundamental theorem of consumption', Baudrillard proposed, is 'that the latter has nothing to do with personal enjoyment . . . but that rather it is a restrictive *social institution* that determines behavior before even being considered in the consciousness of the social actors' (*CPS*, 31). This does not, therefore, entail that perennially unlikely scenario whereby capitalism reduces consumers to dupes. Rejecting 'simplistic ideas like "the manipulation of needs" and denunciations of "artificial needs"' (*CPS*, 136) as naive conceptions that assume the existence of 'real' needs in some idealised social arrangement elsewhere, Baudrillard argues that the very notion of 'needs' – and the corresponding conception of 'use-values' geared to their satisfaction – arises from a peculiarly modern relation to the world, one Marx failed to do more than reflect in naturalising use-values and needs rather than recognising their role as alibis of the system of exchange-value. Thus 'consumption does not arise from an objective need of the consumer, a final intention of the subject towards the object' (*CPS*, 75), which would be analogous to explaining language in terms of an individual need to speak, nor from an intrinsic finality of concrete objects in their ability to serve as use-values, which would be analogous to the pre-Darwinian argument that eyes have the properties they do because people need to see with them. Just as Marx demonstrated that 'production is no longer in its present finality the production of "concrete" goods, but the expanded reproduction of the exchange value system' (*CPS*, 134), for Baudrillard consumption has become '*the most advanced form of the rational systematization of the productive forces at the individual level*' (*CS*, 75). Hence his insistence that, '[f]ar from the individual expressing his needs in the economic system, it is the economic system that induces the individual function and the parallel functionality of objects and needs' (*CPS*, 133). Because 'needs are not produced one by one, in relation to the respective objects, but . . . as a *consumption power*, as an overall propensity within the more general framework of the productive forces' (*CS*, 74–5).

Whereas Marx distinguished productive from unproductive consumption, a consumer society marks 'no fundamental difference between "productive" consumption (direct destruction of utility during the process of production) and consumption by persons in general' (*CPS*, 133). The latter was classically regarded as the 'reconversion of economic exchange value into use value' (*CPS*, 113). However, insofar as Baudrillard demonstrates that use-value accords to a logic of equivalence in precisely the same manner as exchange-value – use-values are not the natural properties of objects but emanate from a system – the Marxian distinction breaks down: 'no more "productive" or "unproductive" consumption, only a *reproductive* consumption' (*SED*, 28) to which even conspicuously unproductive consumption contributes. In demonstrating that use-values, like exchange-values, have 'no more meaning than a phoneme has an absolute meaning in linguistics' (*CPS*, 64), Baudrillard shows that consumption involves not only the reconversion of exchange-value into use-value but also 'the conversion of economic exchange value into sign exchange value' (*CPS*, 113). To recognise only the functional aspect of the object, as a use-value and a source of individual satisfaction, is to fail to recognise the priority of the system of objects. Rather than its meaning deriving from its use-value (functionality) in relation to the subject, '[the object] finds meaning with other objects, in difference, according to a hierarchical code of significations' (*CPS*, 64). As such, the object is 'reified into a sign' (*CPS*, 65): we should speak of 'sign-objects' rather than 'objects'. And 'sign-objects exchange among themselves' (*CPS*, 66), possessing the structural properties common to all sign systems. The 'functionality of goods and individual needs only follows on this, adjusting itself to, rationalizing, and in the same stroke repressing these fundamental structural mechanisms' (*CPS*, 75).

The repression entailed by the naturalisation of use-values and needs simultaneously disavows that dimension of consumption detected in Marcel Mauss's and Bataille's accounts of archaic consumption practices – the gift, potlatch, sacrifice: the 'accursed share'. For the 'act of consumption is never simply a purchase (reconversion of exchange value into use value); it is also an expenditure . . . it is wealth manifested, and a manifest destruction of wealth' (*CPS*, 112). Such profligate expenditure once served to symbolise an ambivalent social relation – for example, in the inalienability of the gift and the giver – whereas the sign-object 'only refers to the absence of relation itself, and to isolated individual subjects': 'it is no longer the mobile signifier of a lack between two beings, it is "of" and "from" the reified relation (as is the commodity at another level, in relation to reified labor power)' (*CPS*, 65). The alienation achieved in commodity production is thus paralleled by 'a labor of expanded reproduction of use value as an abstraction' in the sphere of consumption (*CPS*, 134). And so the mythology of consumerism prevails: 'Affluence *does not exist*, but it only has to make us believe it exists to be an effective myth' (*CS*, 193). Only the *consummation* expressed in expenditure 'escapes recycling in the expanded reproduction of the value system – not because it is the destruction of substance, but because it is a transgression of the law and finality of objects' (*CPS*, 134).

Passwords

Accursed share
Gift
Symbolic exchange
Value + Structural law of value

COOL MEMORIES

Richard J. Lane

Baudrillard does give his own paradoxical definition of the five texts (*CM*, *CM2*, *CM3*, *CM4*, *CM5*) gathered under the title of *Cool Memories*: 'They are multiple fragments of a nonexistent hypothetical continuity which can only be rediscovered beneath these notes like a watermark, after death' (*CM*, 63). Fragments, notes, journal entries, travel writing, aphorisms, insights, performance pieces, meditative musings, poetic musings – all these, and more, have been used to describe the writings that fill the five volumes. Baudrillard's own definition, paradoxes aside, points to the graphical surface that makes these books so striking: the layout, the blank spaces, the poetic stanzas of gnomic observations, even the traces of some underlying watermark, the systems-thinking that the texts both work with and resist. 'Each thought is the last' writes Baudrillard, 'each note the final touch' (*CM*, 62), but then another thought appears, another 'final' final touch is made, and so they go on, these memories that resist closure.

If the *Cool Memories* are aphorisms, why are they often written with the certainty and force of dicta? As Gary Saul Morson (2003: 416) writes, 'Unlike aphorisms, dicta see no mystery. They precisely resemble the solution to a riddle . . . The dictum announces the discovery and specifies its essential nature. Its sense is: the mystery is over'. Reading *Cool Memories* one is struck by the certainty, the insight, the solutions to the riddles of postmodern society, such as the following: 'Anamnesis, exegesis, diegesis, catachresis – a load of meaningless Greek! The wise man who wishes to know the state of his soul looks at the half-moon of his fingernails' (*CM*, 132). The certainty of the dictum is used here to undermine certainty itself, revealing the paradox that in asserting how the complexities of postmodernity can be analysed and revealed in a schematic form, a mysterious remainder baffles us further. So Baudrillard writes aphorisms with the clarity of dicta, which by their close, have usually imploded. As Morson (2003: 423) writes of the aphorism: 'They are momentary probes, or flashes that die out before we have quite made out what they reveal'. In the first volume of *Cool Memories*, Baudrillard does indeed do a lot of patriarchal probing, juxtaposing Nietzschean aphorisms concerning seduction and 'women' with a range of observations concerning postmodern society, place, travel and so on. How far the act of juxtaposing undermines the patriarchal comments is not always clear: does it create an ironic distance? Baudrillard's language even takes on theological overtones here: 'Seduction plunges us into discrimination as it plunges us into predestination' (*CM*, 62), or, 'Every man has an intense fear that he will no longer be taken in charge by some woman or female image. No one can live without the absolution of a female image' (*CM*, 44). What does this pseudo-theological discourse signify? Perhaps that the aphorism digs deeper into the mysteriousness of the world: Oedipus proclaims his superior knowledge in that he solved the riddle of the Sphinx only to later discover that this is hubris and that the gods always win. Baudrillard's strategy is to utilise the power of the Symbolic to deconstruct the apparently impervious surface, or continuum, of the code, or the Semiotic. The aphorism appears to assert some truth, only the more we read it, the murkier it gets; the aphorism uses the language of the gods – of mystery, paradox, transcendence and the sacred. The language of rationality, science and technology asserts and explains; the language of *Cool Memories* ultimately resists such apparent clarity: 'Science and technologies could have become extensions of our human faculties, as McLuhan wanted. Instead, they have devoured them' (*CM*, 110). So Baudrillard resists the production of 'metalanguages' – language that rises above the world and claims the ability to explain the world, what Baudrillard calls 'Hegemony of the commentary, the gloss, the quotation, the reference' (*CM*, 25). As Lyotard notes in *The Postmodern Condition* (1986), we now regard metalanguages as merely different types of narrative: stories that claim to tell the truth but use rhetorical strategies to do so. Baudrillard regards metalanguages as totalising, hegemonic and anti-democratic. Thus he favours 'the ellipsis, the fragment, the quip, the riddle, the aphorism' (*CM2*, 25), all examples of 'fragmentary' or 'democratic writing'. Fragmentary writing resists expressing a hierarchy of value, whereby the most banal fragment 'finds its exceptional reader. Each, in its turn, has its hour of glory' (*CM3*, 8). Every fragment has the potential to be logically developed in a book-length account, but Baudrillard resists this because of his notion that 'the ellipse is superior to the straight line' (*CM3*, 8).

The *Cool Memories* depict then not so much conventional philosophical ideas as they do situations, thought experiments, 'microscopic ideas' that originate in the intensity of 'cerebral electricity' (*CM5*, 8); the cool memories are ephemeral traversals of the physiological and perceptual field of consciousness and the unconscious: thus Baudrillard refers to dreams, fantasies, desires and taboo thoughts. His aphorisms thus have an affinity with Freud's *Interpretation of Dreams*: 'Exactly like the shaft of wit, the character trait or facial features, the fragment is made up of contradictory lineaments of meaning and their happy coincidence' (*CM5*, 10); resisting both Lacan's mirror stage and notions of perceptual or cognitive reflection, Baudrillard argues that 'The fragment is like a broken mirror – ideas don't have the time to reflect themselves in it' (*CM5*, 17). And so the *Cool Memories* – affect based, resisting metaphysical and rationalist speculation – are the perfect vehicle for the intense image-based technological society of the hyper-real. Will it be Baudrillard who guides us through this new society, or the 'immortal' Claude Lévi-Strauss: 'From the depths of his academic immortality he is awaiting the return of the societies with no writing. Perhaps he does not have long to wait. For the coming society, computerised and illiterate, will also be a society without writing. It is our future primitive society' (*CM4*, 65).

Passwords

Anagram
Poetic resolution
Postmodernism/Postmodernity

COPPOLA, FRANCIS FORD (1939–) – see 'film + cinema' and 'image'.

CULTURE

Richard J. Lane

Consumer, postmodern, popular or mass-media culture: all these are synonyms that describe the same phenomenon, one that Baudrillard calls 'cultural consumption' (*CS*, 99). If culture is thought of simply as 'an inherited legacy of works, thought and tradition' (*CS*, 101), one which undergoes dynamic and productive self-reflective critique, cultural consumption is something quite different: it is the resurrection through caricature and parody of that which has been lost or destroyed. Culture may be defined in the traditional sense as 'the creation and use of meanings' (Tester, 1994: 128); in comparison, cultural consumption is a 'consummation' of meaning – the completion of meaning and the movement to something new. Cruising America, Baudrillard goes in search of this newness; with the flattening of hierarchies in popular culture, where everything is perceived as having equal value, the result is akin to the beauty of the Californian desert (*A*), or 'the fascination of the very disappearance of all aesthetic and critical forms of life in the irradiation of an objectless neutrality' (*A*, 124). European cultural theatricality gives way here to the flat desert or city surface (television screen rather than theatrical stage), upon which an endless play of signifiers can circulate. In other words, Baudrillard discovers in the desert cities of California a culture that has replaced the real with signs.

Mass culture is constituted as such through the process of mass 'communication', the irony being that in the process nothing is communicated at all. In consuming the fashionable, up-to-date signs of mass culture, Baudrillard argues that the one thing not present is culture itself; instead, an immense process of cultural recycling takes place, whereby one's knowledge of culture – its latest fashionable manifestation – stands in for actual content. Culture (with a large 'C'), in effect, has been replaced for Baudrillard with culture (with a small 'c'), where the latter is cyclical, produced by the medium (television) rather than autonomous human subjects. Mass culture follows the same logic of the hyper-real, where the authentic gives way to the simulation. Baudrillard's apparent nostalgia for content is apparent in his term 'lowest common culture' or LCC, a minimum quotient of knowledge lacking in intrinsic value but required to pass entry into contemporary society, engaged via media quizzes or, in our time, 'reality' television shows. Starkly, Baudrillard asserts that 'Mass communication excludes culture and knowledge' (*CS*, 104). He suggests that this is so because 'There is no question of real symbolic or didactic processes coming into play' (*CS*, 104) during the preordained answer-and-question response of the quiz or other testing arenas, such as the shopping mall. The LCC rules, and as McLuhan suggests, the medium is now the message/mass(age). LCC is available on instalment plan, and this fragmentation and dumbing-down of Culture follows the pattern suggested by Benjamin (2008); parodying Benjamin's Angel of History, Baudrillard writes that 'A great democratic wind has blown through the heavenly Jerusalem of culture and art' (*CS*, 105). What Benjamin's Angel sees, of course, is 'one single catastrophe, which keeps piling wreckage upon wreckage and hurls it at his feet' (Benjamin, 2003: 392). And this catastrophe is our notion of 'progress'. While it is true that Baudrillard follows this mode of thinking, he also simultaneously recoils from such linearity, arguing that with the implosion of meaning a new fascinating, non-linear culture emerges, one where the masses are not so much controlled by the media, but gain autonomy through their lack of response to the media.

This fascination with the culture that has destroyed Culture pervades Baudrillard's work, leading to an awareness of points of resistance against the hyper-real: 'sending back to the system its own logic by doubling it; to reflecting, like a mirror, meaning without absorbing it' (*SSM*, 108). Mass culture, then, does have political force, but such force is fragile, fleeting and temporary. Baudrillard argues that 'All the repressive and reductive strategies of power systems are already present in the internal logic of the sign' (*CPS*, 163). Turning that logic back upon itself can lead to implosive outcomes – witness 9/11 – but whether turning culture against culture leads to a return to value remains to be seen.

Passwords

America
City
Communication + Non-communication
Hyper-reality
Masses
Postmodernism/Postmodernity

DEATH

William Pawlett

Death is a vital term in Baudrillard's theoretical vocabulary, used in a number of different but interrelated senses. According to Baudrillard the system of power and control is founded on a particular construction of the relationship between life and death, one which separates and opposes them, making death the absolute termination of life. Baudrillard explores an alternative understanding of death in 'symbolic' or 'primitive' cultures: death as a social, cyclical and reversible position in symbolic exchange ritual. Death, understood as a stake in an ongoing cycle of symbolic exchanges, is never fully eliminated by rationality, Baudrillard asserts. Indeed, he contends that the symbolic exchange of death, in sacrificial or 'suicidal' form, constitutes the 'ultimate weapon' against the capitalist system because it strikes at the very foundation of its organisation. His work on the 9/11 suicide attacks explores this difficult idea (*ST*).

Baudrillard also discusses the (attempted) elimination of death as symbolic form through the technology of cloning, and his final works suggest ways of thinking about life and death as 'parallel', inseparable and 'complicit' symbolic forms.

For Baudrillard death is the most vital stake in social organisation – for both modern and 'symbolic' societies. He claims that a fundamental reversal in the nature of social organisation has taken place: a shift from the symbolic order where 'what cannot be symbolically exchanged constitutes a mortal danger for the group' (*SED*, 131), to capitalist modernity where 'everything which is symbolically exchanged constitutes a mortal danger for the dominant order' (*SED*, 188). Modern society functions only by dismantling and preventing the cycles of symbolic exchange, specifically by disallowing the moment of response or 'counter-gift'. The system creates a fundamental 'symbolic debt', showering consumers with (simulatory) gifts of culture, education, medical technology, communication and 'liberation'. This unexchangeable debt constitutes 'the social relations of symbolic domination'; capital is a form of 'domination over life and death' (*SED*, 31). We are constructed as 'wage-consumers' who must work for a wage and must spend that wage on 'dead signs' supporting the system of consumption, 'a man must die to become labour power . . . [he dies] by his definition as a productive force' (*SED*, 39). Baudrillard refashions Hegel's master/slave dialectic arguing, 'The master confiscates the death of the other while retaining the right to risk his own' (*SED*, 40); the power structure is thus 'a structure of death' (*SED*, 40). For Baudrillard immediate death is the ultimate weapon against this system: 'you will never abolish this power by staying alive . . . only the surrender of this life, retaliating against a deferred death with an immediate death . . . the only possibility of abolishing power' (*SED*, 40). Baudrillard insists 'the revolution can only consist in the abolition of the separation of death, and not in equality of survival' (*SED*, 129).

For Baudrillard, death is 'ultimately nothing more than the social line of demarcation separating the "dead" from the "living"' (*SED*, 127). In symbolic cultures death is affirmed and marked by elaborate ceremony. Through ceremonial forms of symbolic exchange death is understood as part of a symbolic and reversible cycle, not merely as the biological endpoint of the individual's life. For example, initiation rites are a kind of social 'death' followed by a rebirth with transformed status – indeed all 'death' is social because it is part of a process of the transformation of social status. '[T]he initiation consists in an exchange being established . . . the opposition between birth and death disappears' (*SED*, 132), 'Symbolic exchange is halted neither by the living nor by the dead' (*SED*, 134). By contrast in modernity the dead are 'thrown out of the group's symbolic circulation

. . . no longer beings with a full role to play' (*SED*, 126). Increasingly, death is separated from life; it is medicalised and 'confined'. The symbolic exchange of death is ruptured as the dead are removed further and further away from the living, no longer buried in village churchyards but banished to out-of-town cemeteries or 'ghettos', increasingly inaccessible to their kin. Death becomes 'anormal', '*it is not normal to be dead, and this is new*. To be dead is an unthinkable anomaly: nothing else is as offensive as this' (*SED*, 126). Separated out from symbolic ritual death is devoid of meaning, an 'unprogrammable' horror, an 'unthinkable anomaly'. Yet life too, separated from death, loses its meaningfulness, reduced to 'the indifferent fatality of survival' (*SED*, 127).

With the technology of cloning the separation, confinement and control of death reaches a new level: death can finally be eliminated. For Baudrillard cloning would eliminate radical otherness, death, sex and the Other (the 'singularity' of other people). In cloning the individual is 'reduced to his abstract and genetic formula' to be 'nothing more than a message' (*TE*, 118). For Baudrillard death is inseparable from, and runs parallel to, life: death 'does not . . . await us at the end of life, but accompanies us faithfully and implacably in it . . . one is dead in one's lifetime itself; multiple deaths accompany us' (*LP*, 199). Liberation from death is a far more terrifying prospect than is death, and, Baudrillard asserts, death as symbolic form will always haunt us leading to the possibility of new ritual forms of death. He conjectures 'clones of the future may well pay for the luxury of dying and become mortal once again in simulation: cyberdeath' (*VI*, 12). A further possibility is that 'original' humans may desire to 'Kill your clone, destroy yourself with no risk of actually dying: vicarious suicide' (*VI*, 27). Where previous generations have suffered alienation, future generations face an infinitely worse prospect: the horror of 'never knowing death' (*CM5*, 55).

Baudrillard often wrote of cancer as a condition caused by cells that forget how to die (*VI*) and proliferate wildly, killing the host. With cancer, as with civilisation, the loss of death prefigures the loss of life. Developing the theme of double lives and 'parallel universes' in *The Intelligence of Evil or The Lucidity Pact* (2005a [2004]), Baudrillard suggests that we have a life of biological existence and a second life of destiny; the two rarely intersect: 'Double life entails the notion of double death' so that 'in one of these two lives you may already be dead, doubtless without knowing it' (*LP*, 198). Cloning technology represents a terrible violence because it threatens to eliminate both forms in an 'absolute death', yet this 'perfect crime' can never take place because life and death, are symbolic forms, 'complicit . . . parallel and indissociable' (*LP*, 200). People – 'original' and cloned – will fight, to the death, for their death.

Passwords

Clones + Cloning
Destiny
Modernity
Perfect crime
Symbolic exchange
Terrorism

DEBORD, GUY (1931–94) – see 'communication + non-communication', 'simulation' and 'situationism'.

DERRIDA, JACQUES (1930–2004) – see 'Foucault + dead power', 'nature + animals', 'radical alterity', 'singularity' and 'terrorism'.

DESTINY

William Pawlett

Destiny is intimately linked to some of the most difficult ideas in Baudrillard's vocabulary, in particular seduction, the object and fatal strategies. Baudrillard is not interested in the notion of individual destiny (you will meet a handsome stranger, and so on), but the destiny of the object, its cycles of appearance, disappearance and reappearance. Indeed, for Baudrillard, '[destiny] comes to us from the other. Each is the destiny of the other. There is no individual destiny' (*IEx*, 84). There are a number of exchanges, experiences or spaces where what we might ordinarily call the 'subject', person or individual, becomes, according to Baudrillard, an object. This notion of becoming-object is crucial to Baudrillard's understanding of destiny.

For Baudrillard destiny is rarely sensed in the 'indifferent spaces' of modern life (*FS*) where people (as 'subjects') are confined by instrumental rationality, purpose and time constraints. Yet where action is governed by a set of 'entirely arbitrary rules', rather than by norms or laws, in spaces such as those of ceremony and ritual, games and traditional dance, destiny, Baudrillard contends, is given free reign. Ceremonial or ritual space is enchanted not indifferent: time/space relations are altered, ceremonies unfold in their own time, 'the ceremony contains the presentiment of its development and its end . . . [Time] must have the time to disappear'

(*FS*, 207). Further, the rules of the game or ritual leave no place for legal, moral or psychological considerations; indeed, all that holds together 'the subject' is suspended, returning only when the game or ritual is over.

Baudrillard's oft-repeated example of the play of destiny is based on the old Iraqi folk tale known as 'Death in Samarkand'. A soldier, on his way to market, sees the black-cloaked figure of Death apparently beckoning him. Terrified he flees and begs his king to lend him his fastest horse so that he may escape to the distant city of Samarkand. The following day the king asks Death why he frightened his soldier. Death replies 'I didn't mean to frighten him. It was just that I was surprised to see this soldier here, when we had a rendez-vous tomorrow in Samarkand' (*S*, 72). The soldier is destined, inevitably, to meet Death, who is himself 'an innocent player in the game' (*S*, 73).

There is a direct line of development from Baudrillard's positions concerning ritual initiation, his arguments on seduction and his thinking on destiny: 'the initiatory fact of seducing and being seduced . . . consists in giving you a destiny, and not only an existence' (*FS*, 165–6). Destiny then comes into play as a dual or 'double life' that unfolds beyond biological existence. That which reappears or returns signals a double life of destiny; 'each individual life unfolds on two levels, in two dimensions – history and destiny – which coincide only exceptionally' (*IEx*, 79). Baudrillard seems to derive this thinking from Nietzsche's notion of the Eternal Return (*IEx*), though this influence is allusive not formative. Freed from biology, from historical change, from social norms and moral laws that define the 'subject', the double life is one of becoming object, becoming other, metamorphosing not by choice but by the hands of fate.

The opposition between chance (randomness) and determination (causal connection), Baudrillard argues, is a modern construction built on the denial of sacred and ceremonial social forms; he insists 'the truth is that *there is no chance*' (*FS*, 182), 'Nothing is dead, nothing is inert, nothing is disconnected, uncorrelated or aleatory. Everything, on the contrary, is fatally, admirably connected – not at all according to rational relations [. . .], but according to an incessant cycle of metamorphoses, according to the seductive rapports of form and appearance' (*FS*, 185). Games of chance such as gambling involve, for Baudrillard, a passion 'to upset the causal system and the objective way things proceed and *re-engage their fatal linkage*' (*FS*, 189). But how can events be 'fated'? Writing on the death of Princess Diana, Baudrillard states 'if we assess all that would have had not to have happened for the event not to take place, then quite clearly it could not but occur . . . no Dodi and no Ritz, nor all the wealth of the Arab princes and the historical rivalry with the British. The British Empire itself would have had to have been wiped from history' (*IEx*, 136).

And we prize such fated events, such spaces of destiny; for Baudrillard 'each of us secretly prefers an arbitrary and cruel order, one that leaves us no choice, to the horrors of a liberal one where . . . we are forced to recognise that we don't know what we want' (*FS*, 206). Our fundamental passion, he asserts, is to be drawn out of the (hyper-)reality of rationality and causality and to be placed within a 'pure unfolding' of destiny. Further, with causal, temporal and subjectivist illusions suspended, there is, for Baudrillard, renewed potential for symbolic relations with the other: 'if I am inseparable from the other, from all the others I almost became, then all destinies are linked . . . being is a linked succession of forms, and to speak of one's own will makes no sense' (*IEx*, 84). 'There is in this symbolic circulation, in this sharing of destinies, the essence of a subtler freedom than the individual liberty to make up one's mind' (*IEx*, 85).

According to Baudrillard, the processes of writing poetry and (radical) theory, like ritual, impose a set of rules of the game that must be followed and so can suspend the illusory opposition between a causal determined universe and one of freedom and choice. Words, signs, and things seduce each other with the subject reduced to their conduit, forging connections through 'chain reaction'; this is the 'order of destiny'. In both language (wit, slips of the tongue, poetry, theory) and in material, 'socio-political' registers destiny appears 'where events attain their effects without passing through causes' (*FS*, 192), moving in a predestined linkage. In 'chance' meetings and encounters and in 'socio-political' events things sometimes seem to happen in a flash, 'in advance of the unfolding of their causes' so that 'reasons come after' (*FS*, 198). We are seduced by the rapid flashes of appearance and disappearance, sometimes following them without thinking. Rationality, by contrast, seeks to invent causes to dispel this play of appearance and disappearance, to make them more 'solid'. However 'no event can put an end to the succession of events, and no action can definitively determine what follows' (*IEx*, 87).

Ultimately, Baudrillard suggests that both the world of destiny and the world of reason and causality are 'equally groundless' (*FS*, 206), but while the former seduces and links us to the Other, the latter bores and frustrates.

Passwords

Death
Fatal
Object
Seduction

DIALECTICS – see 'duality', 'fatal', 'hyper-reality', 'Manichaeism', 'modernity', 'orientalism', 'simulation', 'terrorism', 'translations', 'transaesthetics', 'transpolitics' and 'value + structural law of value'.

DICK, PHILIP K. (1917–2008) – see 'drugs', 'literature', 'science fiction' and 'singularity'.

DISAPPEARANCE

Mike Gane

To appear and to disappear might appear at first glance to be simple everyday processes. This is not so for Baudrillard who takes these terms and subjects them to the most subtle examination. The key discussion of the issues involved here concerns the way death is confronted in different cultures. Our culture treats death as a biological reality, but this way of dealing with death is relatively recent. With the eclipse of the symbolic by the semiotic (and the ontologies of the 'real' that underpin it), biological death becomes the first, the dominant criterion for the end of life, and then at a subsequent stage with cloning technology, death 'ceases to be an event' yet returns as a 'singularity that assumes its full force as a symbolic stake' (*LP*, 197). In any case the issues associated with the 'soul' become highly problematic and remain so. For Baudrillard all the issues of appearance and disappearance belong to the symbolic and thus to an order that cannot be reduced to physical processes. However, this is difficult in contemporary cultures because mastery in the symbolic order, mastery over disappearances – that is passing 'from one form to another is a means of *disappearing, not of dying*' (*EC*, 47) – has been lost. Contemporary cultures have lost the ability to see things as they 'inscribe themselves in advance in their disappearance' (*FS*, 194). Baudrillard draws on anthropology for these ideas, especially the work of Marcel Mauss, to suggest that 'symbolic exchange is halted neither by the living nor by the dead . . . this is an absolute law: obligation and reciprocity are insurmountable.' For 'death is nothing other than this: [being] taken hostage by the cycle of symbolic exchanges' (*SED*, 134).

The general theory that Baudrillard develops here locates disappearance in the process of metamorphosis. This is not the order of meaning, metaphor, psychology, but rather the order of the generation of the symbolic in relation to metamorphosis – 'forms which slip directly from one to the other' – thus 'it is only when this transfiguration of forms from one into the other comes to a halt that a symbolic order appears' (*EC*, 46 and 47). The modern notion of the primacy of the body in its material existence is, he suggests, a reduction, a 'materialist precipitation' capable of being the reduced object of verification on the condition of it having become 'the scene of a single scenario' (*EC*, 48). This reduction is accomplished by the elimination of the whole range of rituals that previously dominated the symbolic sphere. The culture of myths and practices that dealt with birth and death and linked the human with other species and the stars – where 'the sign of the apparition of things is also the sign of their disappearance' (*FS*, 193) – is also displaced and abandoned. Baudrillard does not romanticise here. This primordial symbolic was rigorous but also cruel and in this there is a certain ironic easing of the human condition – this primordial 'subjectivity has dissolved (and we joyously accept it) because it has been absorbed into the automatism of events' (*FS*, 197). Yet the symbolic order of fate and destiny haunts the universe of chance and the random that has replaced it.

Clearly Baudrillard's conception of disappearance has long been associated with processes of life and death. But his use of this term has been far more general and used to examine a range of phenomena. A key one of these is modern art, since becoming indifferent to the world merges with it and lives on as a prolonged process of the disappearance of art as art. Another is photography. Even his series *Cool Memories* (*CM*, *CM2*, *CM3*, *CM4*, *CM5*), fragmentary entries of a journal kept over the years from 1980, he said, was to let 'phenomena appear . . . grasp them as they appear, hardly giving them time to make sense, then steer them immediately into the director of their disappearance' (*BL*, 179).

Baudrillard's last paper was 'On Disappearance' (in Clarke et al., 2009). Here he outlines situations in which the real disappears behind the appearance of the concept and the way the concept can disappear into the real. But these examples are given only to set the scene for a discussion of what he sees as the dramatic disappearance of the human itself – for humanity may even have produced an 'art of disappearance' of itself (*PC*, 39). Hypothesised is the idea that this disappearance of the human might be a fatal strategy, one that pushes technology to the limit so that death itself is overcome (disappears), becomes post-human (disappearing in cloning or genetic modification). Here the apparent aim of technology might be 'to create an autonomous, a fully achieved world, from which we could at last withdraw' (*PC*, 39). But no less problematic is the disappearance of the inhuman within the domain of the human – for example the humanisation of animals by genetic modification (*VI*). Perhaps Baudrillard suggests there is a secret strategy here: 'if I can see the world after the point of my disappearance, that means I am immortal' (*PC*, 38). Technology becomes the art of producing a new artificial post-humanity in which each can 'expel himself from himself into an artificial orbit in which he will circle forever' (*PC*, 39).

In the writings of the later Baudrillard further surprising hypotheses on these themes are developed. One of these is the possible existence of two parallel universes for each individual: one is the actual lifeline and the other is the order of potentiality. Birth is then the appearance of the order of the ego into one of the existential lines, but 'all the possibilities set aside at birth continue to run parallel to the ego' and these unrealised potentialities 'from time to time make a foray' into to the lived lifeline. Any individual life is thus never reducible to biology or to the lived experience, since there are 'two parallel dimensions of any existence' (*LP*, 198).

Passwords

Anti-humanism + Post-humanism
Art
Clones + Cloning
Cool memories
Destiny
Fatal
Photography
Singularity

DISNEYLAND – see 'America', 'architecture', 'Foucault + dead power', 'hyper-reality', 'imaginary', 'model', 'politics' and 'real'.

DOUBLE

Graeme Gilloch

From earliest times, human beings have imagined themselves to be accompanied by the double, be it as a shadow, a spirit, a namesake, a reflection or a totem. But while 'the primitive has a non-alienated duel-relation with his double' (*SED*, 141) based on reciprocity, dialogue and exchange, this figure has taken on a sinister aspect in modern times. A commonplace in nineteenth-century Gothic and Romantic literature as well as in the modern thriller genre, the doppelgänger constituted for both

Otto Rank (1914) and Sigmund Freud (*SE XVII*) the definitive figure of the uncanny, of the *unheimlich*, of the strangely familiar. Perhaps not surprisingly, it is also one of Baudrillard's favourite and most frequent motifs. Appropriately, the double appears in his writings in a number of different incarnations and guises: as mirror-image (as Narcissus in *S*; as the 'mirror people' in *PC*), as shadow (*SV*), as twin (see *CM2*, and see also the discussion of the Twin Towers in *ST*) and, finally, as clone (*S*; *SS*). As a disquieting manifestation of both identity and non-identity, of ambiguity and anomaly, the double serves as a recurrent trope for so many of those conventional binary oppositions and antitheses beloved of dialecticians that Baudrillard eagerly sets in play and subverts through ironic inversion and sudden reversal: 'reality' and representation, essence and appearance, soul/spirit and body, subject and object, self and other, original and copy, authenticity and (dis)simulation, good and evil, absence and presence, surface and depth, secret and obscene, critique and complicity.

The figure of the doppelgänger poses such questions as: which of these is which? how can we tell them apart? which of these takes precedence and priority over the other? which of these is to be believed? who is to be trusted? who is haunting whom? The double challenges epistemological certainties and ontological securities, and in so doing becomes a key agent and instrument of Baudrillard's critically subversive fatal theory.

The double may be understood as the double, so to speak, of the Möbius strip. Both tropes suggest the singularity of the dual and the duality of the singular. In the single-sided looping mathematical construction, there is the seemingly impossible dissolution of one surface into another; with the sinister figure of the doppelgänger, that which seemed individual and indivisible, the human subject, becomes duplicated in some way: through bisection, bifurcation, distillation, reflection, mimesis, separation, polarisation, (re)generation, reproduction, replication and/or artificial fertilisation. And, importantly, this double appears not as something wholly different and other (good old-fashioned dialectics!), but as an embodied being both radically contrary yet seemingly and simultaneously identical.

Here, it would seem, the double belongs to the realm of seduction, those in finite and involuted games of appearances and illusions that Baudrillard so relishes. And indeed, the double figures prominently in an exemplary instance of seduction, the act of following in *Suite vénitienne/Please Follow Me* (1988a [1983]). The intriguingly inexplicable pursuit of Henri B. sustained over many days by the photographer Sophie Calle, tailing him in his banal meanderings around the streets and across the bridges of Venice, is characterised by Baudrillard as the most perfect art of shadowing, as the act of becoming another's shadow, of the mimetic doubling of a life.

But, perhaps more surprisingly, Baudrillard's most developed discussion of the double is in relation to the order of production, specifically in the rather curious Conclusion to *The Consumer Society* (1998a [1970]) where Baudrillard offers a distinctive reading of the old silent film, *The Student of Prague* (Paul Wegener/Stellen Rye, 1913; remade by Henrik Galeen in 1926). In this Expressionist historical drama, the eponymous and impecunious young man Balduin makes a rash bargain with a sinister magician Scapinelli (in the later version the Devil himself) in which a fortune in gold is exchanged for whatever the conjuror chooses to take with him from the student's humble abode: to the astonishment of the unfortunate student, his own mirror image. Baudrillard sees this tale as an allegory of capitalist exchange relations, alienation and commodity fetishism: commodity production involves the worker investing and selling him/herself in the labour process of objectification and the extraction of surplus value. Removed by the capitalist, the object produced appears to take on an independent existence, a life of its own. The student has lost his shadow. And worse. For the benign companion of the 'primitive' becomes the malevolent tormentor of the modern subject. Freed from the mirror, the doppelgänger, does not leave Balduin in peace but rather murders the cousin of his beloved, sabotaging the very romantic aspirations for which the newly acquired riches were necessary. The student is haunted by his doppelgänger, cannot escape him or the increasing disgrace that follows his every crime. Finally, Balduin hunts him down, confronts him, fires at him with a duelling pistol and collapses. He has shot, not his double, but himself. He dies. Scapinelli reappears and tears up the contract, the shreds of papers falling like confetti on Balduin's corpse. Baudrillard's point is that if commodity production involves the self-estrangement of the worker, consumer culture is that moment when the object returns as an alien thing, not casually and contingently, but persistently, insistently, compellingly. The worker is haunted by the commodity. Marx, then, exposes the deception of 'formally free' labour in the capitalist production process; Baudrillard reveals the myth of 'individual choice' in the system of consumption.

The significance of *The Student of Prague* for Baudrillard's conception of seduction must be stressed. The film dramatically envisions a plethora of key motifs: the importance of the pact/bargain as a ritual form in contrast to the contract of capitalist exchange relations; the notion of the duel and irresistible logic (however illogical) of the challenge; the act of reversal when the haunting of first one by another (of the student by his likeness) gives way to the hunting down of the double by Balduin; destiny, fate and fatality.

Baudrillard insists that one cannot survive the encounter with one's double. This is the moral of Balduin's death; it is also that which gives

Calle's ludic pursuits their tension and frisson. She must remain disguised; she must keep her distance; she must not be discovered. Can she elude detection? This is what makes her shadowing fascinating.

Nor can the double and doppelgänger survive today. For Baudrillard, these figures, too, have encountered their own fatal double, their own likenesses, their destiny. The double is a figure of the imaginary reliant on distance, fascination and the possibility of reversal. The advent of scientific cloning (with its own double helix of DNA) has realised the planned production of the replica. The double becomes the treble, the quadruple in an infinite mass proliferation. All this reproductive technology is banal, obscene, lacking any secrecy, any charm, any aura (see 'Clone Story' in *SS*). Cloning is cancerous metastasis. It is without interest, without seduction. The double has had its day. The mirror people have deserted us in this age of mechanical reproduction. And who can blame them?

Passwords

Clones + Cloning
Double spiral
Duality
Fatal
Following
Mirror
Photography
Seduction

DOUBLE SPIRAL

Richard G. Smith

Once upon a time there was a general consensus among the Anglo-American Left that Baudrillard's writings could be separated into those that are Marxist and those that are postmodern. Reminiscent of Althusser's famous separation of Marx's *oeuvre*, the story told by many early Baudrillard commentators was that there is a watershed (an 'epistemological break' or 'critical disjuncture' (Gottdiener, 1994: 25)) in Baudrillard's *oeuvre*: that those books published before 1976 broadly fall within a neo-Marxist paradigm, while those after, and including, *Symbolic Exchange and Death* (1993a [1976]) fall under the aegis of postmodernism. However, following the translation of *The Ecstasy of Communication* (1988c [1987b]) it became quite apparent to many (for example, Gane,

1991b) that to understand Baudrillard he must not be broken in two but, rather, that the rhythm of his writings as a whole must be understood as a 'double spiral'. Indeed, after Baudrillard had explicitly pointed out the double spiral (*EC*) in his philosophy it quickly dawned on many specialists that he had first spelt out this opposition of forms in considerable detail in *For a Critique of the Political Economy of the Sign* (1981 [1972]), some four years prior to when many commentators (for example, Kellner, 1989) had identified a divide in his writings, and in *The Mirror of Production* (1975 [1973]) and *Symbolic Exchange and Death* (1993a [1976]).

It was Baudrillard himself who likened his thought and *oeuvre* to that of a Möbius strip, a double spiral like the DNA double helix or Giuseppe Momo's famous double spiral staircase in the Vatican:

The double spiral moves from *Le Système des Objets* to the *Fatal Strategies*: a spiral swerving towards a sphere of the sign, the simulacrum and simulation, a spiral of the reversibility of all signs in the shadow of seduction and death. The two paradigms are diversified in the course of this spiral without altering their antagonistic position. On the one hand: political economy, production, the code, the system, simulation. On the other hand: potlatch, expenditure, sacrifice, death, the feminine, seduction, and in the end, the fatal. (*EC*, 79)

In other words, the double spiral traces the destruction of the symbolic by the semiotic and the ironic eruption of the former in the latter, as both spirals are always in fact one, like a Möbius strip. As such, the double spiral is a figure that captures not only the opposition of the symbolic (ambivalence and so on) to the semiotic (the code and so on) in Baudrillard's philosophical system, but also, as with a Möbius strip, refers to the inseparability of the symbolic and the sign; ambivalence always haunts equivalence in Baudrillard's thought, thus allowing for the possibility of reversibility.

The double spiral is present from Baudrillard's first book (*SO*) all the way through to his last book (*CC*). The semiotic appeared as the 'code of social standing' in 1968, the 'code' in 1970, the 'political economy of the sign' in 1972, the 'structural law of value' in 1976, 'hyper-reality', 'simulation', 'simulacra' and 'simulacrum' from around 1981, and the 'virtual' and 'integral reality' from the mid-1990s onwards, whereas the symbolic appeared as the 'gift' and 'ambivalence' in 1972, 'symbolic exchange' and 'death' in 1976, 'seduction' in 1979, 'fatal strategies' in 1983 and as 'evil' and 'terrorism' more recently. However, it is important to note that the double spiral is not the structure of Baudrillard's *oeuvre*, but rather is best understood as its rhythm (*BL*). For while two forms are in opposition across Baudrillard's writings – between production and seduction, political economy and death, hyper-reality and symbolic exchange, the fatal and the banal, appearance and disappearance, and so on – one must not take the double spiral metaphor too literally (Smith with Doel, 2001). As Baudrillard himself says: 'What is interesting is that notions and concepts criss-cross each other, slide into each other, melt into each other' (*BL*, 202). In other words, the double spiral is not a fixed structure that 'explains' Baudrillard, it cannot be precisely because 'there is no static opposition, no binary system that functions *ad libitum* from beginning to end. It means that polarization is in movement, in a rising upward curve' (*BL*, 202). In short, the double spiral follows a non-equilibrating logic of escalation and potentialisation, not a dialectical logic of sublation and resolution, for it is 'sworn to radical antagonism, not to reconciliation or synthesis' (*FS*, 25).

Passwords

Hyper-reality
Political economy of the sign
Reversibility
Symbolic exchange

DRUGS

Richard G. Smith

According to Baudrillard, a 'perverse' logic (*SC*, 97) drives consumer societies. A logic that fuels, not just the use and abuse of drugs, but also the growth of other phenomena: terrorism, violence, depression, fascism and so forth. These phenomena are all, says Baudrillard, the product or outcome of 'an excess of organization, regulation and rationalization within a system' (*SC*, 97). In other words, those societies which are defined and 'saturated' by their system of consumption tend to suffer from an excess of systemic rationalisation (logic and rationality, surveillance and control), which perversely leads to the emergence – for no apparent reason – of 'internal pathologies', 'strange dysfunctions', 'unforeseeable, incurable accidents', '*anomalies*' (*SC*, 97), which disrupt the system's capacity for totality, perfection and reality invention.

It is the logic of an excessive system to fuel the growth of anomalies, which along with AIDS and cancer are pathologies in that they have not come from elsewhere, from 'outside' or from afar, but are rather a product of the 'over-protection' of the body – be it social or individual.

The system's overcapacity to protect, normalise and integrate is evidenced everywhere: natural immunity is replaced by systems of artificial immunity – 'hygienic, chemical, medical, social and psychological prosthetics' (*SC*, 98) – in the name of science and progress.

In Philip K. Dick's (1977) novel *A Scanner Darkly* the use of a highly addictive illegal drug, Substance D., has reached epidemic proportions across California's Orange County. The lead character Brian Arctor is both an undercover police officer (Agent Fred) and a Substance D. addict, a narcotic he began to take to 'feel good' and escape the monotony of his daily life (nuclear family, suburban house and so on) in a consumption-driven authoritarian society of surveillance. However, Baudrillard risks a more shocking and obverse interpretation of such 'escapist' drug-use, namely that it is a defence by dependents against the 'syndrome of immunodeficiency' (*SC*, 99) endemic to consumer societies: a 'vital, symbolic reaction – though an apparently desperate and suicidal one – to something even worse' (*SC*, 99). Thus Baudrillard posits a significance to drug addiction that exposes a paradox at the heart of the issue of substance abuse in modern consumer societies: 'It is society which produces this perverse effect and society which condemns it. If it is not going to stop producing the effect, then it should at least stop cursing it' (*SC*, 101).

Passwords

Consumption + Affluent society
Excess
Terrorism

DUALITY

Ashley Woodward

Duality is one of Baudrillard's most central ideas, with which many of his other concepts and contentions have an integral relation: reversibility is an applied form of duality (*PW*), seduction is always a dual relation (*BL*), duality governs the principle of evil (*LP*), in impossible exchange duality replaces exchange (*PW*), thought is in a dual relation to the world (*PW*), and so on. According to Baudrillard, 'everything is in the play of duality' (*IEx*, 90). Duality is a fundamental metaphysical principle which governs the operation of the world. He develops this principle in contrast to the metaphysical principle of unity, which, he contends, has been dominant in the history of religious and philosophical thought and continues to pervade thought today. The principle of unity asserts that everything is fundamentally reducible to the One. Systems of thought predicated on unity frequently involve dualisms or theories of the Many, but all varieties are, in the end, reducible to a single principle.

Baudrillard contends that most 'dualisms' evident in modern thought rest on a principle of unity insofar as the two terms posited are opposed to each other and exist in a dialectical relation. That is, they are subject to reconciliation in a higher synthesis. Typically, one of the two terms is given a metaphysical and moral privilege and subordinates the opposed term to itself: although two terms are posited, one embodies the unitary principle into which the other is ultimately incorporated. According to Baudrillard, this dialectical, oppositional relation is in fact what governs most contemporary philosophies of otherness and difference. Duality, however, posits terms which are in a relation of radical otherness: they do not share any commonality which would allow them to be initially opposed or subsequently reconciled. Nevertheless, the two terms exist in a dynamic, antagonistic relation, and take part in a shared destiny.

Baudrillard frequently develops these ideas through the metaphysical and moral duality of Good and Evil. In most traditional forms of philosophy and theology, Good is posited as the single, fundamental principle of reality, while Evil is given a subordinate position in dialectical relation to Good. Typically, the world is posited as originally existing as a unified whole governed by the principle of Good, before Evil erupts. Evil retains a subordinate role and will eventually be subsumed back into the unity of Good. Baudrillard defends an alternative, dualistic hypothesis: Good and Evil are primordial and immortal principles which will always exist in an antagonistic relation. He points to examples of this dualistic hypothesis in certain minor religions – in particular Manichaeism – which have typically been persecuted as heretical. Paradoxically, he insists on the one hand that neither Good nor Evil should be thought as primary; rather, it is duality itself which is primary. On the other hand, he states that the principle of duality is itself Evil (since Good predicates itself on unity).

Baudrillard offers at least two arguments for why we should think that duality, rather than unity, is the more fundamental metaphysical principle. First, only duality can explain the genesis and transformation of living things and the existence of variety in the world. He argues as follows:

By definition, the One is One, and can only repeat itself to infinity. But by what strange combination, then, does life transform itself? Why would it chose to differentiate itself, metamorphose and die, rather than persevere in its being by irrepressible totalization? . . . If you assume a single term at the outset, it is not clear what would interrupt its running on in perpetuity. (*IEx*, 99)

Second, only duality can explain the existence of chance and uncertainty in the world. He contends that 'if the world were not the inextricable manifestation of two opposing principles . . . we would have only absolute certainties' (*IEx*, 100).

Duality is the basic form of relation underlying Baudrillard's attempts to theorise alternatives to capitalist and semiotic exchange, such as symbolic exchange and seduction. While terms in exchange are equivalent, substitutable and governed by a basic law, terms in a dual relation are asymmetrical, reversible and engaged in a game of challenge and one-upmanship governed by arbitrary but reciprocally binding rules. Duality involves an essentially antagonistic relation, to which Baudrillard alludes by playing on the ambiguity inherent in the French term *duel*, which means both 'dual' and 'duel'. While exchange operates in the rational universe, in which everything is comprehended and homogenised, duality governs the symbolic universe of dynamic relations where radical otherness inevitably persists.

Passwords

Evil
Impossible exchange
Manichaeism
Metaphysics
Other + Otherness
Reversibility
Seduction
Symbolic exchange

E

EVENT – see 'singularity'.

EVIL

Paul Hegarty

The world of simulation is entirely bound up with 'Good' – the real, the true, the safe, the hygienic, the politically correct, and the notion that we can all be part of a global community under the perceived Good of western liberal capitalism. Simulation, or hyper-reality, is relentlessly positive and positivist – everything 'is', and its realness is a test of its goodness (hence the hyper-realism of the Gulf wars, hence the misunderstanding of Baudrillard's critique thereof). Baudrillard consistently argues that we live in a sanitised world, where all that is threatening, unpredictable, genuinely new, non-real, mysterious or other must be reduced, ignored or destroyed. Gradually, he introduces the idea that Evil is something other than the system of simulation, this principally in *The Transparency of Evil* (1993b [1990a]). Evil is not moral but structural – with simulation we already inhabit a world 'beyond good and evil'. But this condition of being beyond is not the ferocious opening of possibility envisaged by Nietzsche – instead it looks something like that, it seems to have been realised, visualised, modelled, mapped out (alternatively, it has failed to come to be, because Good and Evil merged (*F*)). So for there to be any radicality, there must be an Other, and this can be thought of as Evil. Given Baudrillard's take on Islamist terrorism as something that breaks through simulation, we might imagine his position to be a perverse rethinking of Samuel P. Huntington's 'clash of civilisations', but this is where we need to note that the terms 'Good' and 'Evil' are not attributes of one side or another. Good and Evil are not moral, and Evil is not just a way of dramatising attacks on the West, it is a structural critique of anything all-pervasive that emanates from simulation and a hygienised reality. Commenting on the title *Transparency of Evil*, Baudrillard clarifies that it is not about the visibility or obviousness of Evil, rather it is about Evil appearing everywhere, just where it is most excluded (*PW*). For a concrete example we can look to the overuse of antibiotics which allows the possibility of new bacterial evolution, or how excessively clean environments heighten vulnerability to infection. But it is also 'transparency itself that is the Evil' (*PW*, 36). Here the complexity of the idea of Evil begins to appear: transparency is of course 'good' – who can refuse transparency, openness, *glasnost* – or best practice, excellence, quality? Goodness and transparency meet up in a mutually reinforcing spiral, and all else, all that would be secret, or must now be done away with (things deemed inefficient, no longer desirable), will be seen as Evil. Simulation flattens, 'makes good' continually, and this is 'another world in which things no longer even need their opposites' (Baudrillard, in Clarke et al., 2009: 25). Baudrillard is in fact using Evil as a deconstructive term, one that restores duality, and through confrontation, the duel. At the same time, Evil is fundamentally caught up with simulated versions of goodness that are actually the thing that is bad. 'Evil' is the more positive force, though: 'the principle of Evil is not a moral principle but rather a principle of instability and vertigo, a principle of complexity and foreignness, a principle of seduction, a principle of incompatibility, antagonism and irreducibility. It is not a death principle – far from it. It is a vital principle of disjunction' (*TE*, 107).

Baudrillard returns to the idea of Evil, this time relating it to unhappiness. Instead of Evil (*le Mal*), we have its reduced, curable form, unhappiness (*le malheur*) (*F*). Even better than being cured, it can be managed, prolonged – misery as a perpetual precursor to happiness – as seen in the hyper-realism of 'misery memoirs', but also at the international level, where every nation wants to be someone else's victim (*F*). The past is recast as the unhappiness underpinning today's shiny happy real, tinged with a halo of moral superiority for either being a victim or apologising for having made someone a victim. As the phrase has it, 'it's all good'. Attempts to resuscitate Evil fall into the cheapest simulation – like the low-budget special effect of the 'Axis of Evil' idea. When individuals, such as paedophiles, are deemed evil, they have a greater utility, which is to reinforce the sanitised goodness of everyone else, as we all agree that Evil exists, but not here, not me, not us. Meanwhile, the victims can 'rebuild their lives' according to one of many models available in the media or in psychological advice in general. As for national victims (or victimisers) of slavery, colonialisation and so on, they can work out the value of unhappiness as *malheur* is part of an economy where all can be bought, exchanged and traded, just so long as nothing interrupts that virtuous circle (*F*) – and for Baudrillard, all economic value is not only a mystical supplement, as it is for Marx, but is a replacement for the thing valued. The thing itself need never have been there, and valuing is an exact equivalent of de-valuing.

Overall, unhappiness replaces Evil, because for all the rhetorical value of, say, the 'Axis of Evil', the attempts to extirpate that Evil can only bring the Evil more to the fore, and in a world where 'it's all good', there is no Evil, only *malheur*, and this is the slow living death of Evil as a creative principle. Baudrillard's hope is that the drive to render all transparent, good and clean can only encourage the possibility of disruption, of Evil.

Passwords

Duality
Gulf War
Hyper-reality
Simulation
Terrorism
Viral

EXCESS

Ashley Woodward

Baudrillard's treatment of the theme of excess varies over the course of his writings, and it appears as both a positively and a negatively valued idea. Baudrillard's early understanding of excess is significantly indebted to Georges Bataille. Excess plays a crucial role in what Bataille terms 'general economy', an economy of natural forces opposed to the restricted economy of capitalism. While capitalist economy is predicated on utilitarian principles of good use and maximum profit, Bataille contends that all systems produce excesses of energy that need to be consumed in useless expenditures, examples of which in human culture are sacrifice, waste, death, luxury and eroticism (Bataille, 1991a, 1991b). What most interests Baudrillard is the way Bataille's general economy suggests a transgression and disruption of capitalism through excess. In *For a Critique of the Political Economy of the Sign* (1981 [1972]), symbolic exchange is reminiscent of Bataille's vision of excess: it involves excessive forms of social behaviour (such as gift-giving and the wasteful expenditure of goods), and promises to transgress the order of capitalist political economy.

From *Symbolic Exchange and Death* (1993a [1976]) onward, however, Baudrillard moves away from the theme of transgression and correspondingly alters his understanding of excess. In these later works, excess plays a double role. On the one hand, it continues to name an Other to the system of capitalist political economy; on the other hand, it indicates the extremes of the contemporary capitalist system itself. As the latter, excess is a key idea underlying Baudrillard's analysis of contemporary culture in terms of hyper-reality, the implosion of meaning in the media and so on, as the following passages from *The Vital Illusion* (2000) well indicate:

Let us be clear about this: if the Real is disappearing, it is not because of a lack of it – on the contrary, there is too much of it. It is the excess of reality that puts an end to reality, just as the excess of information puts an end to information, or the excess of communication puts an end to communication. (*VI*, 65–6)

. . . Everywhere we see a paradoxical logic: the idea is destroyed by its own realization, by its own excess. (*VI*, 47)

As the former, excess indicates all those things which continue to resist incorporation into the systems of reality, information and communication: seduction, the fatal, destiny and so on. Thus in Baudrillard's mature works excess indicates both the tendency of contemporary systems to exceed their proper bounds and attempt to assimilate everything, and the excessive remainder which refuses to be assimilated. In these later works, far from seeing excess as a transgression which would lead to a liberation, Baudrillard stresses the non-distinction of two, oppositely valued, forms of excess:

In a way there is no difference between the excess that represents the saturation of a system and that leads it to a final baroque death by overgrowth (*excroissance*) and the excess that stems from the fatal, from destiny. Basically, today, it is impossible to distinguish between good and bad excess . . . that is precisely what makes the present situation original and interesting. (*BL*, 37)

Passwords

Accursed share
Culture
Destiny
Fatal
Gift
Hyper-reality
Media
Seduction

EXTREMES

Ashley Woodward

In a way, all of Baudrillard's work is an exploration of extremes. Extremes pertain both to the subject matter of Baudrillard's reflections – the extreme phenomena of contemporary culture – and the form these reflections take – the adoption of an extreme vantage point, an extreme form of thought, in order to take stock of an extreme situation. Baudrillard's critical diagnosis of contemporary culture rests on the contention that the animating ideals and values driving the West – in particular, those deriving from the Enlightenment dream of perfecting the world through the progressive development and application of reason – have been pushed to extremes. In this extreme state, the Enlightenment dream has not been realised. To the contrary, the extreme realisation of these values and ideals has in fact destroyed them.

For Baudrillard, 'extreme' is to be understood in the specific sense of that which occurs 'beyond the end'. According to him, extreme = *ex terminis* (*VI*). Thus extremes are what occur beyond (*ex*) a boundary or limit (*terminis*). Baudrillard insists that this movement to extremes is not simply a change in quantity, an increase in degree. Rather there is a real qualitative change in systems once they achieve extreme points: 'It's not a matter of being more expanded or extensive – it's more *intensive* in gradation. It's a kind of power, an upgrading of power – a movement to extremes, an increase in power of effects . . .' (*BL*, 84). Systems move to extremes by pursuing their own perfection, attempting to incorporate or eradicate everything which limits them. The qualitative change in extreme systems involves 'a state of unconditional realisation, of total positivity (every negative sign raised to the second power produces a positive), from which all utopia, all death and all negativity have been expunged (*VI*, 46–7). The equation 'extreme = *ex terminis*' also suggests a link between 'extreme' and 'extermination'. For Baudrillard, when systems move to extremes, the very attempt at perfection leads to destruction.

Extreme phenomena are explored in Baudrillard's work through many of his critical concepts, but are perhaps most evident in the various permutations of the formulae 'more x than x' and 'trans-x'. Examples of the former include the masses (more social than the social), simulation (truer than true), hyper-reality (more real than real) and so on (*VI*). The latter is explored in Baudrillard's book *The Transparency of Evil* (1993b [1990a]), which is subtitled 'Essays on Extreme Phenomena' (*TE*). Here Baudrillard characterises contemporary culture as a vast orgy in which every sphere of value moves to extremes insofar as it attempts to incorporate everything into itself, to make everything exchangeable in its own terms. The political becomes the transpolitical (everything is political), the economic becomes the transeconomic (everything is economic), the aesthetic becomes the transaesthetic (everything is aesthetic), and so on. According to Baudrillard, this movement to extremes leads to a generalised confusion of categories and a breakdown of distinctions in all spheres of culture. Thus, through seeking to extend its form of value to everything, each sphere in fact destroys its value because it no longer has a clearly delimited, coherent domain of application.

Baudrillard's own theory is deliberately extreme, both in its propositions and its style. At times he argues for the necessity of extreme theory by asserting that theory must correspond to the world in order to speak meaningfully about it: 'why are people going to those extremes, if you don't suppose that at some point the world, and the universe, too, is in the grips of a movement to extremes' (*BL*, 115). In this sense, he suggests, theory cannot just be fiction; it must offer something like an objective, rational hypothesis, and there must be a point in the real to which it can stick (*BL*). At other times, however, the justification he gives for extreme theory rests on a more radical hypothesis about the relation between theory and the word. In this sense, the role of theory is to push itself to extremes beyond, or in a contrary direction to, states of affairs in the world. Speaking of the Gulf War, he asserted that: 'If the war doesn't go to extremes, then writing must be allowed to, one way or another. That is its role . . . a transfiguration brought about by writing' (*BL*, 180). As such, theory engages in a duel, or an antagonistic relationship with, the world. The aim of extreme theory is then not simply to describe the world, but to change it.

Passwords

Culture
Excess
Gulf War
Hyper-reality
Masses
Simulation
The end
Transaesthetic
Transpolitical

F

FASHION

Malcolm Barnard

Fashion (like advertising (q.v.) to which it is closely related) is a central part of Baudrillard's account of consumption and consumerism: it encompasses and includes the commodities that we consume and our bodies, as well as the things that we wear (*SED*). Fashion exists only in modernity and it begins with the decline of feudalism and the development of capitalist economy and society (*SED, SS*). This is because fashion requires arbitrary signs that are not possible in a society in which mobility between classes is impossible or in which members are fixed in a particular caste. In pre-modern, feudal or caste societies, signs are 'obligatory' or symbolic: they refer inevitably to class or caste identities and to the positions of those classes and castes in social structures or hierarchies. Meanings here are fixed. Consequently, the objects individuals buy and wear in a feudal or caste-based society identify those individuals as members of particular classes or castes and locate them at a particular place in a social structure or hierarchy. With capitalism, however, there is the possibility of social mobility, of moving between classes, and signs are no longer tied to such identities and positions. Signs that are not tied to designating genuine identities and prescribed meanings are said to be 'free' or arbitrary and they may signify any identity and mean anything. In a capitalist economy, fashion and counterfeiting, or pretending and signifying an unreal identity, become possible (*SED*). Consequently, individuals living in a capitalist society can use objects and clothing to make themselves look like members of a higher (or lower) social class and to suggest a status other than they 'really' are.

Baudrillard (*CPS*) uses two rings to explain what he means by fashion and to illustrate the various different logics that objects conform to. The first is a wedding ring and the second is an ordinary ring. The wedding ring is not fashion because it obeys the logic of symbolic exchange. This ring is unique and symbolic of a couple's enduring relationship; one would neither change it nor wear more than one. The ordinary ring is fashion and, freed from any symbolism, it follows the logic of sign value. This ring is simply an accessory and part of the 'constellation of fashion'. The logic of fashion is, for Baudrillard, one of differentiation, a logic he explores in order to develop and critique Thorstein Veblen's account of the function of fashion. Veblen argued that fashion was about conspicuous consumption and the way in which fashion was used by individuals in order to signify prestige and success: Baudrillard argues that the conspicuous consumption of fashion is the way in which social classes differentiate themselves from each other.

Using the example of short and long skirts Baudrillard explains fashion as the endless return of differences where meaning, even beauty, is the product of these differences. Long skirts and short skirts are not meaningful in themselves and they are not symbolic of some other realm, morality or gender politics, for example. The move from wearing long skirts to wearing short skirts will have 'the same distinctive and selective fashion value as the reverse' (*CPS*, 79): it is only the difference between the skirts that generates any and all meaning the skirts are said to have. Difference here can account for the perception of the new, different, skirt as fashionable, but also for the perception of beauty. Even beauty is a product, or 'effect' of difference.

Finally, for Baudrillard, there is no simple alternative to fashion, there is no escape from fashion and there is no way to resist or subvert it (*SED*). It is impossible to step outside fashion because there is no outside or beyond to step into: modernity means that all objects obey the logic of fashion. Even if one tries to refuse fashion by wearing items that are not themselves fashion (Baudrillard proposes blue-jeans as an example (*SED*)), fashion makes the refusal of fashion into a fashion feature. The logic of difference means that whatever item one wears, being different from other items, is inevitably drawn into fashion. The non-simple alternative to fashion as an endless proliferation of different signs and of signs of difference is the deconstruction of the very form of the sign and of the principle of signification.

Passwords

Advertising
Body
Code
Consumption + Affluent society
Modernity
Sign

FATAL

Andrew Wernick

The notion of fatal strategies is most associated with Baudrillard's book of that title (*FS*). But the idea, interwoven with what he called 'the turn to the object', can be traced in his work from the mid-1970s onwards, a journey reflected on in *The Ecstasy of Communication* (1988c [1987b]). Though he drops the language of 'the fatal' it also provides a key for understanding much of his subsequent *oeuvre*.

In its guerrilla-like provocativeness, pataphysical extremism and aspiration for a form of theorising that would be performative rather than descriptive, analytic or (in its various senses) critical, Baudrillard's espousal of 'fatal theory' remains distantly marked by his earlier sympathies for Situationism (of the kind that flowered at Nanterre in 1968). But it also marks his exit from leftism, as well as from Frankfurtian negative dialectics, towards a kind of irony in which he swims in, mirrors and exaggerates the excesses he describes, provocatively drawing them to their limit. All takes places after the 'dead point' at which 'things have found a way of avoiding a dialectics of meaning' (*FS*, 25). He had already moved from situationist contestation (minority action to unconceal the contradictions and provoke a 'situation') to its reinterpretation in terms of the gift, the counter-gift and the move to 'the symbolic' (*SED*). He now abandons the terrain of oppositional/emancipatory politics altogether in favour of perversely embracing the vertiginous movement of what he continues to call 'the system'. As with Nietzsche, he will push the nihilism actually in train to the limit. However, this 'theoretical terrorism' – fatal theory – is not thought of as wilful or unlitateral but, on the model of gift giving, as a duel. It is a duel, moreover, between unequal contestants, in which the aim of the weaker is to throw judo moves in which the object's power turns against itself.

Fatal, it should be noted, carries a double sense. Like the moment of death in his story about the 'soldier at Samarkand' (*FS*) the fatal is that which is both mortally destructive and pertaining to fate. Fate or destiny is counterposed both to the order of causation (Newtonian or dialectical) and to that of probability and chance, and it works amorally against both. The fate and fatality in question are those of the system, as one of general exchange, simulation and metastatic proliferation in every direction, and of the system considered as 'object': an object that has wholly vanquished (its) subjects, and incorporated them as relays and as agent-supports.

Fatal as opposed to banal strategy (any strategy of the subject; politics as project or calculus) takes the side of the object. In doing so, such a strategy presupposes that the object can always outwit the subject, but that it can also outwit itself. That is the game that fatal strategies enter into. In the first instance, indeed, the agents of such strategies are not human subjects, individually or collectively, at all. They are strategies, if that is the right word, deployed blindly and ironically by the system/object itself. They result from the system's excrescent growth, in combination with the rule that a challenge must be answered by a challenge, by an overbidding, or suffer defeat. As Baudrillard puts it: 'This is no longer the irony of the subject faced with an objective order, but the objective irony of things caught in their own devices – no longer the historical workings of the negative, but the workings of reduplication and the rising stakes' (*EC*, 83–4).

Just as the more real than real, the hyper-real, makes the real disappear, the obscene (the more visible than visible) puts an end to the scene – and so puts an end also to illusion which, following Nietzsche, Baudrillard takes to be vital for life. Likewise, sex, individualised and normatised as the right and duty of liberated desire, is eclipsed by the more sexual than sexual. Whence porno – a half step which neutralises desire by removing all prohibitions except that of its code – and the transsexual which volatilises sex as signs, but restores a form of seduction in the play and challenge of appearances. In similar terms, politics disappears behind the transpolitical, and the social is sucked into the black hole of the mass, polled incessantly for yes/no opinions on rigged questions, yet evincing an abstentionism and 'refusal of meaning' that challenges the whole electoral game by rendering it weightless.

Altogether, after general exchange has suppressed symbolic exchange, the fractal multiplication of simulacra exterminates the real in all its forms – all of them essentialist illusions and projections of the code – and reinstates reversibility.

At the catastrophe point implosive growth is checked by redundancy – the abundant becomes the obese – and entropy sets in. Baudrillard's wager is that even so, the symbolic, reversibility and a kind of cosmic uncertainty principle precipitated by these same developments offer the possibility of a metamorphic challenge. In an initial formulation (*SED*) self-death is offered to the system as a way to get it to suicide. Notoriously, what fascinated Baudrillard here were 'terrorism' and hostage taking. But he also highlights passive and abject forms of fatal counter-gifts, such as over-obedience, and political apathy as the defiance of meaning. After the turn to the object such examples fall away, leaving fatal theory itself – of the kind Baudrillard was pursuing – as the only clear instance of a fatal strategy from the side of the subject.

Passwords

Double spiral
Gift
May 1968
Nihilism
Situationism
Symbolic exchange

FEMINISM/FEMININE

Victoria Grace

Baudrillard has been an arch-critic of feminism, of movements for women's liberation and sexual liberation, and yet he would be (and has been) the first to say that there have been some genuine and problematic misunderstandings as a result. From the point of view of many feminists, both in continental Europe and the Anglo-American contexts, Baudrillard has been viewed as the ultimate defender of the very patriarchal values and politics that feminism confronts and seeks to overturn. This is even more galling when Baudrillard is categorised as a postmodern, critical thinker within the general terms of the radical 'Left'.

Baudrillard is concerned to challenge feminism's relentless insistence on instantiating female subjectivity, or women's identity. From Baudrillard's point of view not only is this a project inevitably doomed to reincarnate the feminine in the very terms that constitute the masculine, but it also turns its back on the strength of the transformational potential of the feminine: that of seduction. While the sexual order is predicated on a division of bodies into male and female, on an axis of masculine and feminine, the female-feminine body is effectively annexed to the phallic order and condemned to non-existence. Within the structural logic of identity/difference, the structural bar of exclusion opposes the masculine to that which it is not, the feminine. This opposition of masculine and feminine is a masculine one (S). Where feminists expose the politics of this logic and critique this binary form, Baudrillard finds no cause to object. But when feminists then oppose this logic with a demand for women's autonomy, identity as difference, specificity of desire, of pleasure, of speech and writing, then he takes up a very different stance. Baudrillard incites feminism instead to oppose this logic with seduction. According to Baudrillard, the idea that sexual liberation lies in the securing of rights, status and pleasure is a manifestation of an enduring Enlightenment humanism that assumes the liberation of a servile sex, race or class in the very terms of its own servitude.

When Baudrillard was asked if feminism had influenced his thought in any way, he said that it had never influenced him 'a great deal' and that in fact 'it is truly one of the most advanced forms of *ressentiment*' (*BL*, 209). By demanding the right to be an autonomous subject, to wish to take up the definitional mantle of identity with its apparent existential security, is illusory. In Baudrillard's terms, there is nothing gained or achieved by the feminine attempting to somehow pass through the structural bar to set up camp on the other side, to 'cross terms' (*S*, 6). Either the structure will stay the same and the impossibility of this attempt will fuel renewed *ressentiment*, or the structure will collapse to mean there is no longer male and female, masculine and feminine. It is this latter that Baudrillard claims is evident today as we witness the rise of the transsexual position in the context of a polyvalent non-differentiation, trending to complete neutralisation of sexual difference. As he writes in *The Perfect Crime* (1996c [1995a]), 'what is "liberated" is precisely not their [the sexes'] singularity but their relative conflation and . . . their respective indifference' (*PC*, 118).

Baudrillard invokes the figure of the feminine, not as one subjected to a position of the excluded and 'different', but rather as an agency of seduction. This is 'her' strength, and as Baudrillard sees it, the very strength that feminism does not see, repels through a certain *ressentiment*, or regrettably misunderstands. A feminism that celebrates a triumphant mastery within the structure of identity/difference encloses the feminine within the structure that condemns it.

The feminine, however, is, and has always been, somewhere else. That is the secret of its strength. Just as it is said that something lasts because its existence is not adequate to its essence, it must be said that the feminine seduces because it is never where it thinks it is, or where it thinks itself. (*S*, 6)

The feminine neither 'is' nor 'is not' ('is neither a marked nor an unmarked term' (*S*, 7)); it enacts the indeterminism of things; it operates as a kind of uncertainty principle that eludes the phallic, or any other, exchange standard. If the sexes are not opposed, if they are incomparable, then the feminine is not of the order of identity/difference but rather is that which seduces this structure.

Passwords

Seduction
Sex/Gender
Transsexuality

FILM + CINEMA

Laurence Simmons

In an early scene of *The Matrix* (Wachowski and Wachowski, 1999), hacker Thomas Anderson (a.k.a. Neo played by Keanu Reeves) opens a copy of Baudrillard's *Simulacra and Simulation* (1994a [1981]) to a chapter entitled 'On Nihilism'. But we see that the book is hollow for it serves as Neo's hiding place for the computer programs he sells on the black market. While it seems that Baudrillard's theory of simulation provided much of the inspiration for the film, according to Baudrillard the film-makers have fundamentally misread his work: they have taken 'the hypothesis of the virtual for an irrefutable fact and transformed it into a visible phenom-enon'. This produces the irony that, he goes on to note, '*The Matrix* is surely the kind of film about the matrix that the matrix would have been able to produce' (Baudrillard, 2004a: unpaginated). The film-makers have thus ended up domesticating the concept of simulacrum in the face of what they believe to be a higher reality.

Nevertheless, the moment signals the importance of film for Baudrillard and Baudrillard for film. While there exists no systematic theory of cinema as such in Baudrillard there do exist repeated confessions of personal pleas-ure in the medium when, for example, he declares himself to be an 'unre-strained film buff' (*ED*, 28) who is 'very much in love with [the cinema]'

(*BL*, 23) as 'really the place where I relax' (*BL*, 23). Cinema, then, does not merely provide examples that illustrate or make Baudrillard's theories accessible but it forms and constructs insights, critiques and extends his work. At the heart of Baudrillard's attraction to cinema is its participation in the third order of simulacra and Hollywood film's hyperfidelity to the real that is paradoxically achieved at the expense of its own cinematicity. It is the consequences of this third order of simulacra, as we will see, that involve a significant reversal of the apparent position of Baudrillard's cameo citation in *The Matrix*. For Baudrillard, any attempt to preserve or recreate the real is always doomed to failure and so cinema's attempt to achieve a correspondence with the real through 'its naked obviousness, in its boredom . . . in its pretension to being the real' (*SS*, 46) simply results in a perverse hyper-reality. The result is hypotyposis and specularity: cinema cannibalises itself in remakes and retroactivations: '*the cinema is fascinated by itself as a lost object as much as it (and we) are fascinated by the real as a lost referent*' (*SS*, 47). Cinema becomes lost in itself.

An early chapter of *Simulacra and Simulation* (1994a [1981]) describes how history no longer 'takes place'. Baudrillard lights on *The China Syndrome* (Bridges, 1979), the film which anticipated the events of the accident at Three Mile Island nuclear power plant near Harrisburg, to show how playing out a scenario before an event occurs empties the real event of its significance (*SS*, *EDI*). *The China Syndrome* is an uncanny and disquieting case of the 'strange precession of a film over the real' where 'the real arranged itself, in the image of the film, to produce a *simulation* of catastrophe' (*SS*, 54).

Francis Ford Coppola's *Apocalypse Now* (1979) is another example of the third order of simulation. It is the case, suggests Baudrillard, that because of its testing of technological 'special effects' the Vietnam War was like a film before it was filmed. So Coppola's film 'is really the extension of the war through other means, the pinnacle of this failed war, and its apotheosis. The war became film, the film becomes war' (*SS*, 59). *Apocalypse Now* operates retrospectively on a war itself enacted as 'a succession of special effects' (*SS*, 59). War and film thus implode (the war becomes the film, the film becomes war) – finally providing the US with a simulacral victory in Vietnam and erasing the historical truth.

If the Wachowskis' reading of Baudrillard is hollow (like Neo's book), ultimately delivering its audience domesticated truths about human freedom from machines, and representing in their computer-generated form exactly the process of virtualisation he discusses, Baudrillard in *The Evil Demon of Images* (1987 [1987a]) continues to explore 'the perversity of the relation between the image and its referent' (*EDI*, 13) employing many film examples. The virtual is not that which will become actual or exist parallel to the real but is that which 'takes the place of the real' and is 'the final solution of the real in so far as it both accomplishes the world in its definitive reality and marks its dissolution' (*PW*, 39–40).

In one of Baudrillard's favourite locations, the American desert, Wim Wender's *Paris, Texas* (1984) employs the road movie as a powerful symbol of an American way of life, a society that is constantly moving on and scoring out the traumas of its past. *Paris, Texas* plays, as the title suggests, on the division between Europe and America. In America, Baudrillard responds almost breathlessly, 'you *are* in a film. In California, particularly, you *live* cinema' (*BL*, 34). '[T]he whole country is cinematic' (*A*, 56). But film is a cultural mirage generated by third-order simulation that will eventually evaporate to leave only the desert, 'an ecstatic critique of culture, an ecstatic form of disappearance' (*A*, 5). As the now famous line from *Simulacra and Simulation* (1994a [1981]) in *The Matrix* invites, welcome to 'the desert of the real' (*SS*, 1).

Passwords

America
Hyper-reality
Science fiction
Simulacra + Simulacrum
Simulation
Time + History
Virtual

FOLLOWING

Graeme Gilloch

Of the many possible meanings of the term 'following', two seem to be of particular significance for an understanding of Baudrillard's work. 'Following' may be understood firstly in a spatial/active sense as the conscious pursuit of someone or something by another person or thing, and, secondly, in temporal/relational terms, wherein something occurs subsequent to and is entailed by something else, as logical consequence or necessary conclusion, as an instance of cause and effect.

In his essay 'Please Follow Me' (1988a [1983]; see also *FS* and *TE*) Baudrillard provides an insightful reading of *Suite vénitienne*, a work combining photographs and text by the French conceptual artist Sophie Calle (*SV*). After spending the day tailing people randomly around the streets of Paris, Calle meets a man, Henri B., at a party and learns that he is leaving for Venice the following day. Calle travels to Venice herself, phones around the hotels to discover his whereabouts, and then, disguising herself with wig and make-up, spends the next few days following him around the labyrinthine streets and alleyways of the city. As she follows, she dispassionately documents Henri B.'s wanderings and encounters with photographs (of him, of where he has been, of what he himself has photographed) and jots down her own prosaic diary-style entries and musings. After a couple of days of this urban hide-and-seek (and it is Calle that is doing the hiding), Henri B. recognises her and confronts her. The game is over. Calle cannot follow any longer but instead contrives to arrive back in Paris at the same time but by a different route. She takes one last photograph of Henri B. on the platform in the Gare de Lyon.

This is not, Calle stresses, some sexually motivated stalking. Calle has no particular interest in Henri B., let alone any erotic aspirations or expectations. Indeed, it is this very disinterest, this determination to follow in the apparent absence of any banal motive, of any identifiable psychological or pathological compulsion, that is striking and intriguing. Accordingly, Baudrillard interprets Calle's following as an example of the wholly irrational and utterly irresistible game of appearances, challenges, stratagems and reversals that is seduction (*se-ducere*: literally 'to lead astray').

For Baudrillard, the ludic, mimetic act of following constitutes a form of shadowing. This is no mere metaphor: Calle becomes Henri B.'s shadow, his double. In copying his movements, Calle creates a 'double life' for the man, not in the mundane sense of a secret existence led by him, but in the profound sense of an existence that remains a secret to him.

The notion of reversal is also an essential aspect of this seduction. True, he leads and she follows. But it is not Henri B. who is a mystery for the reader, but Calle; it is not he who fascinates but she. While her attention is directed to him, Baudrillard's is focused on, follows, her. The reader is on her trail. It could not be otherwise. And, of course, it is she who must take care to stay unobserved, to remain undetected. The game is ever open to inversion. Eventually, inevitably, he turns on her, turns the tables on her, challenges her. The hunter becomes the hunted.

Baudrillard himself is an expert exponent of such spatial and, importantly, temporal reversals. That which comes first, which takes logical priority, is displaced and the order of things is reversed. That which follows takes the lead. After all, shadows can as easily come before as after. Consequence becomes contra-sequence; succession becomes precession. The most obvious instance of this is Baudrillard's vision of the 'precession of simulacra' (*SS*). Today, that which conventionally and logically follows (the copy, the reproduction, the fake) is no longer to be found in the wake of the original, the authentic, the real, but rather it precedes it, outdoes it. In the age of simulation and the hyper-real, it is the 'original' that now 'follows'. The object takes precedence over the subject, a central insight for Baudrillard's conception of fatal theory.

Passwords

Double
Photography
Reversibility
Seduction
Simulacra + Simulacrum

FOUCAULT + DEAD POWER

Rex Butler

In a superb memoir published in *October* magazine, Sylvère Lotringer (2008) recalls the circumstances surrounding the original French publication of *Forget Foucault* (2007a [1977]). Baudrillard, who at the time was a relatively minor figure on the French intellectual scene, was to publish his essay, which in an obvious sense was critical of Foucault, in the prestigious journal *Critique*, along with a reply by Foucault. But Foucault, apparently advised by his friends, withdrew from the agreement, so that Baudrillard for his part felt free to publish his essay alone. The consequences for Baudrillard were dramatic. He reported to Lotringer that he was ostracised by the French intellectual community for many years. It is even possible to argue that the change in style in Baudrillard's work that occurred afterwards – *Symbolic Exchange and Death* (1993a [1976]) was the last of Baudrillard's books to be written in an orthodox academic manner – was caused by this enforced break with intellectual respectability. Indeed, it is rumoured that Baudrillard had originally intended to publish, along the lines of *Forget Foucault*, an attack on Deleuze and Guattari and their notion of 'desiring production' but subsequently abandoned it. In an abstract sense, this shows Baudrillard moving beyond the project of critique; but, on a personal level, it points to Baudrillard moving beyond the entire French intellectual scene and towards the English-speaking reception that would increasingly occur from the late 1970s on.

In writing *Forget Foucault*, Baudrillard was not only criticising a powerful external figure, but also – as with all authentic critiques – himself. In Baudrillard's work leading up to the essay, such as the chapter 'The

Orders of Simulacra' from *Symbolic Exchange and Death* (1993a [1976]), he is heavily indebted to Foucault's 'genealogical' method. In a later interview with Lotringer, Baudrillard attempts to deny this debt, stating that 'For a time I believed in Foucauldian genealogy, but the order of simulation is antinomical to genealogy' (*FF*, 76), but he is being slightly disingenuous here. Foucault in his *The Order of Things* (1970) is closer than Baudrillard would care to admit to his own *Symbolic Exchange*: at the bottom of Foucault's own genealogy there is also the figure of death. In fact, *Forget Foucault* does not obviously understand itself as a critique of Foucault, and the essay is as much as anything about the limits of critique. Read carefully, it starts off with almost the opposite presumption: that Foucault's analysis is perfect and there is nothing to say against it. Baudrillard's essay, that is, is not about the conceptual limits of Foucault's work, but about the fact that it has no limits, that the 'very movement of the text gives an admirable account of what it proposes' (*FF*, 29). Indeed, one of the methodological issues at stake in Baudrillard's text is the extent to which any critique of Foucault can merely repeat him. Baudrillard is aware of this problem, but it is an open question whether he entirely avoids it. This is not to disqualify Baudrillard's analysis, however, but paradoxically to confirm it. In part, Baudrillard's repetition of Foucault results from certain 'limits' to Baudrillard's analysis; in part, it is unavoidable, the inevitable result of the status of Foucault's analysis as simulation.

What exactly is the problem with Foucault's analysis of power and sexuality, as Baudrillard outlines it in *Forget Foucault*? Baudrillard at this point in his career was in the middle of the development of his theory of simulation, which was to reach its climax with 'The Precession of Simulacra' (Baudrillard, 1978), which formed part of the book *Simulacra and Simulation* (1994a [1981]). In that essay, Baudrillard elaborates a so-called third stage of simulation, which he had previously identified in 'The Orders of Simulacra' (*SED*). In this stage, the various systems of control and reason do not work directly but only by positing an other to themselves. The famous example of this is Disneyland, which through its fantasy would imply a contrasting reality (*SS*). And so it is with Foucault. Baudrillard's point is that Foucault's argument for the inseparability of power and resistance in *Discipline and Punish* (1977) is only to go towards a power that would be proved by its resistance. The same thing can be seen with Foucault's brilliant inversion in *The History of Sexuality* (1978), in which it is not sex that is repressed but sex that represses. Here too, for all of Foucault's distance from any liberatory hypothesis, his argument implies that there remains some natural body and its pleasures that would be proved by its repression by sex. Foucault has still not broken with the idea that there is some reality of the body or use-value to pleasure.

What does Baudrillard oppose to this? Here is where the real complexity and interest of his text arises. Against that aporetic logic in which power is proved by its resistance and the body by its repression, Baudrillard puts forward what he calls at this stage of his work 'seduction', which is the reversibility or exchangeability of power or the effects of domination so that the one in power can never be separated from the one who is dominated. As Baudrillard puts it: 'The one-sidedness of a force relation never exists, a one-sidedness upon which a power "structure" might be established' (FF, 53). But, of course, the question might be asked: why is seduction in its opposition to power not another extension of it? Why does it not constitute another limit that it will inevitably leap over? Indeed, at certain moments in his discourse, Baudrillard does appear to speak of seduction as opposed to production, a seduction that simply comes before or resists power (FF). And yet, in another way, Baudrillard does not do this. Seduction is not a limit or an outside to power. It is not opposed to it and does not arise as result of it. Rather, it is that reversibility between power and its other without which there would not be power in the first place. It allows that aporia between power and its other which means that power has no limit. Seduction therefore is a kind of 'void' (FF, 54), both an imaginary catastrophe that cannot occur without falling back into power and a 'revolution' (FF, 58) that has already taken place insofar as there is power. In a certain 'double strategy' – Derridean echoes intended – Baudrillard at the same time speaks of the limits to power and sexuality and of the fact that they have no limits. Paradoxically, the 'absolute beyond' (FF, 89) of seduction would be 'absolute' only in not being 'beyond'.

Passwords

Body
Death
Production
Seduction
Simulacra + Simulacrum

FRACTAL – see 'fragments', 'globalisation', 'singularity' and 'transsexuality'.

FRAGMENTS

Mike Gane

In his studies of the double spiral of the symbolic and the semiotic (*EC*) Baudrillard includes the spiral of the fragment and the fractal (*F*). The fragment belongs to the symbolic order, but the fractal belongs to the semiotic or networked order. There is a whole range of phenomena that Baudrillard identifies as fragments – including the aphorism, the witticism, the joke, the anagram, the singularity – that contrast fundamentally to those in the category of the fractal that include the video-clip, the advert and the news alert. Baudrillard's consideration of this dual thematic is marked by two contrasts therefore – one is between the fragment and fractal, but this is developed against a wider context which is the opposition between the symbolic order considered as a culture and the networked system considered as an order of simulacra.

Baudrillard emphasises the fact that although there might be some characteristics that are shared between the fragment and fractal, such as ephemerality and instantaneity, the difference is fundamental in the sense that a fragment 'creates a whole symbolic space around it' (*F*, 26). Yet fragments can be put together to form a whole as he remarks several times in his series of notebooks (*CM*, *CM2*, *CM3*, *CM4*, *CM5*) called *Cool Memories*: 'each fragment could become a book. But the point is that it will not do so, for the ellipse is superior to the straight line' (*CM3*, 8). In fact he did collect all the fragments he had written on America and published them together (*A*). He said in preparing *America* (1988b [1986]) that the material 'is secretly ordered by the same thinking' (*CM*, 219). Again in such an enterprise 'there must be a poetic resolution which encompasses and integrates all the fragments of a finite whole – one merely has to find the rule which organizes the reversibility of the slightest details' (*CM3*, 61).

Fractals, but not fragments, on the other hand, are networked into the system. These terms are used as very loose categories, what Baudrillard suggests would include any element and any whole which is modular and totalising or detotalising where subdivision might be endless. In this sense Baudrillard takes considerable licence with his concepts. Totalities here include both ends of the spectrum of high and low integration. What is key is the fact that the fractal as an element is part of a continuity, a matrix, whether or not it is a cell, a node, a module, a value, a vote or even an object without such coded systemic regularity; whatever the nature of the element it is by nature something that will fit, or be capable of being absorbed into a networked totality. Such is the power of the modern order

of simulacra, he suggests, even an alternative 'form of continuity, whole-
ness or totalization . . . will be immediately obliterated by the system itself'
(*F*, 26). What happens is that each absorbable element becomes coded
with positive value and thereby becomes exchangeable or interchangeable.
There is then a reduction, so that the essential space or symbolic void
around the fragment is annihilated (*P*). The fragment becomes a fractal.

There is, therefore, a strategic aspect to Baudrillard's idea of the
fragment. In order to counter the hegemony of the system it is necessary to break out of system thinking itself, break out of thinking that is
dominated by the idea of working progressively towards a final end. He
says 'we have to break all that down by saying that at each moment each
phase is perfect in its incomparable singularity' (*F*, 26). In this sense
there is a certain ambiguity in the idea of the symbolic order itself. As
his writings progressed it seems that the idea of the symbolic became
less system-like; indeed, he was led to present it at some points as being
characterised as having 'no scale of measure in the symbolic chain. No
species is inferior to any other. Nor is any human being. All that counts
is the symbolic sequence' (*CM3*, 131). This chain is essentially one of
the metamorphoses of forms. Each form is not an element or unit or cell
that has a univocal value derived from an exchange system, and here
Baudrillard emphasises that gift exchange is not an exchange system
in the modern sense – in his terminology it is, paradoxically, more like
'impossible exchange'.

The term 'fractal' therefore should not be taken too literally in
Baudrillard's usage and it is possible to find alternative formulations such
those he uses to define contemporary individualism. This he maintains
arises out of a '*liberalization* of slave networks and circuits, that is, an individual diffraction of the programmed ensembles, a metamorphosis of the
macro-structures into innumerable particles' (*IE*, 107) so that the 'neo-
individual is . . . an interactive, communicational particle, plugged into
the network, getting continuous feedback' (*IE*, 106). The logic here is the
same: it is the system functioning that produces the place for the particle
or 'fractal' and networks that element into the totality. It seems superfluous to note that Baudrillard is not using fractal theory as a mathematical
technique, yet the whole development of fractal mathematics is profoundly
linked to the semiotic logics of contemporary orders of simulacra. As the
theory of fractals develops he even claimed that it did produce a new situation in which a new kind of singularity could be identified.

Although Baudrillard develops an interest in fractals and singularities, it is clear that the significance of the primordial features of symbolic
order remain paramount: 'exactly like the shaft of wit, the character trait
or facial features, the fragment is made up of contradictory lineaments of

meaning and their happy coincidence. The aphorism is like the starry sky, the blanks in it being the intersidereal void' (*CM5*, 10).

Passwords

America
Anagram
Double spiral
Impossible exchange
Poetic resolution
Reversibility
Semiotics
Simulacra + Simulacrum
Singularity
Symbolic exchange

FREUD, SIGMUND (1856–1939) – see 'anagrams', 'clones + cloning', 'cool memories', 'double', 'hysteresis', 'Manichaeism', 'mirror', 'modernity', 'perfect crime', 'psychoanalysis', 'sex/gender' and 'simulation'.

GEOPOLITICS

Richard G. Smith

In the 1990s, Baudrillard became especially well known outside of academic circles because of his analysis of the Gulf War (*GW*), which was published as a series of articles in the French daily newspaper *Libération*, not retrospectively, but as the war was still unfolding 'live' on the world's television screens. His reputation as a high-profile public intellectual and insightful commentator on world affairs was further enhanced by his analysis of terrorism and the events of 9/11 (*ST*). However, it is perhaps less well known that Baudrillard also wrote on numerous other geopolitical issues and events: the Cold War, state terrorism, the Algerian War, the 'end of history', Chechnya, Chernobyl, Islam, the Bosnian conflict, the Vietnam War, the Rushdie fatwa, Holocaust revisionism, the fall of the Berlin Wall, the defrosting of Eastern Europe, the New World Order and western military impotence, to name but a few.

A short but prescient essay concerning the revolutions across Eastern Europe as the event of the end of the twentieth century typifies Baudrillard's approach to interpreting geopolitical events. In 1989 Francis Fukuyama famously proposed that with the fall of the Berlin Wall history as a contest of ideologies was effectively over, that liberal democracy would now be triumphant and universalised as the model of choice. However, also writing during the events of 1989, Baudrillard (*SC*) presented an 'end of history' thesis quite different to Fukuyama's. Baudrillard's thesis was one of reversibility, history in reverse, not the triumph of a linear and unidirectional history. Baudrillard's thesis is not a celebration, but rather a compelling critique of the West's desire to whitewash history:

We are in the process of wiping out the entire twentieth century, effacing all the signs of the Cold War one by one, perhaps even all trace of the Second World War and of all the political or ideological revolutions of the twentieth century. The reunification of Germany is inevitable, as are many other things, not in the sense of a leap forward in history, but in the sense of a re-writing in reverse of the whole of the twentieth century, a rewriting which is going to take up a large part of the last ten years of the century. (*SC*, 43)

The task of the 1990s will not be in making history, but in undoing history, in commemorating history, in purging history. All the geopolitical events of the 1990s fall into this cathartic logic: 'we are into a gigantic process of *revisionism* – not an ideological revisionism but a revisionism of history itself' (*SC*, 44).

On the whole, Baudrillard's geopolitical writings are a critique of both globalisation and universality. In other words, more often than not, Baudrillard writes about wars, conflicts or other geopolitical events in order to highlight the hypocrisy of the West's interventions in the affairs of others whereby, while promoting the right to difference and singularity, the West simultaneously and tirelessly works toward the exact opposite: 'a bloodless, undifferentiated world' (*SC*, 65). For example, in 1993 Baudrillard argued in a discussion of the Bosnian conflict that the ethnic cleansing of the Serbs marked a 'new frontier' in the construction of Europe. That is to say that while, on the one hand, Europe condemns the Serbs, on the other hand, the foundation of a white Europe (the New European Order) is reliant upon the success of the Serbs: 'For it *is* being constructed, the "real" Europe: a white Europe, a white-washed Europe, integrated and purified morally as much as economically or ethnically' (*SC*, 49).

Passwords

Globalisation
Gulf War
Reversibility
Terrorism
Time + History
Universality

GIFT

Paul Hegarty

Marcel Mauss's *The Gift* (1966) is a central influence on Baudrillard. In this book, Mauss outlines the many ways in which exchange can be based on gift-giving rather than profit extraction. His conclusion, that the residual gift economy within capitalism could be reinvigorated, is not one shared by Baudrillard's or Mauss's key mediators for Theory: Bataille and Lévi-Strauss. Nonetheless, the gift offers Baudrillard the basis for an alternative to sterilised, hyper-capitalised society, if only temporarily and more aggressively than Mauss would have liked.

There are two key forms of gift-giving in *The Gift*, the kula, where gifts are in continual circulation rather than being swapped directly. In this form, gift-giving structures not only individual Melanesian societies, but also how they interact as a wider social group. From the kula we get the idea that exchange does not have to involve commodities, least of all the commodity of money, and that a system of exchange can be permanent rather than momentary (as in the exchange of a money commodity for a different commodity) and not result in accumulation. Even more central to theorists is the potlatch, typified in societies original to the northwest of North America. Here the exchange is one of escalation, as one leader offers objects, slaves, a banquet, or indeed anything, to a rival leader. The latter is obliged to accept, then to return the gift through exceeding the gifts given him in the previous exchange. Leaders could also destroy their own property (often ceded them only to be immediately exchanged, rather than actually owned by them). Relations between peoples and structures within them are defined through these periodic exchanges. So, for all Mauss's optimism, what he also highlights is the aggressive nature of gift-giving, identified as the 'counter-gift', and it is this aspect, as mediated by Bataille, that Baudrillard picks up on.

Bataille took the potlatch as the inspiration for his model of a universe based on waste, destruction and death, where the counter-gift becomes the initial principle (that is, the counter-gift and its possibility are there from the start in the very first gift). The gift in Bataille is only ever violent, erotic, wasteful – and it creates a situation where any involved in the exchange lose their identity – not in communion, but in absence. The universe itself gives destructively, or demands destruction in return for its gifts (for example, human sacrifice to make sure the sun rises). Baudrillard comments that Bataille has '"naturalised" Mauss', but that this is a properly vital move, as it is 'in a metaphysical spiral so prodigious that the reproach is not really one' (Baudrillard, 1991a: 137). Both Bataille and Baudrillard focus on the counter-gift, but do not fully lose the utopian character of Mauss's argument, maintaining that some sort of gift can still offer disruption of capitalism, if not a resolution of its problems – this would be too useful for either writer. For both, the unanswerable gift is the strongest possible force, and Baudrillard proposes very different ways in which this works: the first is in the form of labour established by capitalism, the second is death as resistance, and ultimately this occurs in the form of violent terrorism.

In *Symbolic Exchange and Death* (1993a [1976]), Baudrillard argues that capitalism inflicts a symbolic violence on us all, reducing all humans to the status of things, in 'offering' us work – the prospect of work must be accepted, as must consumerism. This largely unanswerable gift can be met only by suicide – the capitalist society that brings us into simulation can only be thwarted by returning the gift of death to the system that forcibly gives you life in the form of living death. As well as the literal version of this, the key counter-gift being offered by those who presumably have become aware of the simulatedness of their existence is that of the challenge [*défi*]. The challenge is that the system comes to recognise the possibility of the reversal of its gift.

The ultimate statement of this challenge – or impossible exchange – is to be found in Baudrillard's controversial reading of the attack on the World Trade Center (9/11). In *The Spirit of Terrorism* (2003c [2002]) and also *Power Inferno* (Baudrillard, 2002), he argues that the towers crumbled under the weight of the gift of death presented by the planes – become missiles – and their pilots. The choice of object is perfect as the towers encapsulate simulation (*SA, SED*). The media impact of the event (and most 'events' are non-events for Baudrillard) is a heightened reality in, paradoxically, a simulation so strong it is no longer caught within the orbit of the world we imagine to be real (but is totally simulated): 'a death which is far more than real: a death which is symbolic and sacrificial' (*ST*, 17). Ultimately the potlatch concludes not with a return gift, but a concession of defeat in the towers mirroring the suicide of the pilots (*ST*). Subsequent attacks on Afghanistan and Iraq were clumsy attempts to return the gift, but are merely utilitarian and aimless. The gift, in the form of the counter-gift, is the restoration, however briefly, however violently, of symbolic exchange.

Passwords

Architecture
Death
Impossible exchange
Symbolic exchange
Terrorism

GLOBALISATION

Paul Hegarty

In the story by Jorge-Luis Borges, mapmakers make a map so perfect it covers the whole territory, but it is not solid, and it falls apart, with scraps floating around in the winds. Baudrillard reverses the story, somewhat approximately, so that the map displaces the territory, and it is the real that tears, only surviving in small, displaced fragments. This is the world of simulation, and simulation *is* the world – or, rather, what we have instead of the real world: a total system that is ultra- or hyper-real. Globalisation and simulation do not have a relationship of neat causal priority: simulation brings about globalisation, through the mass media, but is itself brought about by the totalisation of the financial system since the Crash of 1929. The 'more real than the real', or a real world that knows only copies without originals, cannot but be total. Unlike others deemed postmodernist, Baudrillard is not only interested in a turn to the image (we have always had images, and they have always defined the ontological reality of the world), but in synaesthetic reality such as the one McLuhan conceived: 'ours is a brand of allatonceness. "Time" has ceased, "space" has vanished. We now live in a *global* village . . . a simultaneous happening' (McLuhan and Fiore, 1967: 63). This is the world of the Gulf wars – where viewers from all round the world engage with image-driven simulation, but where the simulation goes deeper: all events within the simulated war are simulated, with only deaths at specific locations momentarily acquiring the sense of a less-simulated reality. From the 1990s on, Baudrillard's implicit claim for a global totality of simulation is moderated, notably in

The Gulf War Did Not Take Place (1995 [1991]) and *The Illusion of the End* (1994b [1992]), and he concedes that some areas of the world are less simulated than others – that is, they are in a system of earlier forms of simulatedness.

Nonetheless, the predominant drive is toward totalisation of every phenomenon in one bland and only apparently meaningful simulation. So, for example, he talks of the transpolitical (*TE*) – politics is everywhere, and in attaining that state, loses its meaning. The key moment in this is the ending of 'Communism' in Eastern Europe and Russia, and for Baudrillard, this is no 'end of history' where capitalist democracy triumphs – rather it is the end of the West having a mirror, and so its unreflective democracy spreads by contagion. The transeconomic (*TE*) is, similarly, the death knell for actual economics. The economic becomes viral – that is, it infiltrates everything, but is no longer a tool for either self-enhancement (as liberals would have it) or oppression (as Leftists would have it) – it creates its own structures of value and becomes increasingly arbitrary. Like fractal objects in what we think of as the real world, this type of economics creates clusters of wealth and poverty, but agency has disappeared, replaced by its illusion.

This possibility of not quite belonging to the fully simulated and increasingly total world can be used as a weapon, as it was in the attack on the World Trade Center of 2001. Baudrillard had long noted the centrality of this building in standing for the global economy (*SED, SA*), and in *The Spirit of Terrorism* (2003c [2002]) and *Power Inferno* (Baudrillard, 2002), it becomes a focal point for the possible reversibility of the hyper-real world: that is, briefly, the system glimpses its own death, the possibility of its not existing. Baudrillard had long been aware of the radical potential of Islamist rejection of western values (*TE*), which he equates with a resistance to the creeping simulation of democracy, technology and consensual reality (*RA*). In his book on the Gulf War (*GW*), he hints at agency in globalisation when speaking of the 'New World Order', which America would run, and the imposition of democracy, but this agency seems to be a product, not cause, of globalised simulation. Globalisation itself is also designated as the thing that has something like agency (he writes that the West did not win the war against Communism, globalisation did (*P*)), and so it is globalisation itself that meets resistance, not the imposition of economic models by corporations or the IMF, or democracy by American-led forces, and it effectively finds its other by making it, continually creating resistance as it spreads (*IEx, LP*).

Baudrillard's model of globalisation is complex and, for many, politically unsatisfying, but it offers a complete ontological critique of the phenomenon rather than what is often a superficial reading based on unquestioned agency on the part of powerful nations or companies. This is perhaps at its clearest when he deals with ecology. Globalisation is itself a form of total ecology, where our micro-climates are brought together into one overarching system. Critics of globalisation blame 'it' for the threat to the Earth's climate, arguing that the spread of technology, its overuse by certain countries, and the prevalence of capitalist economics have created the looming cataclysm. Baudrillard sees it differently – in fact the coming catastrophe is a driver of globalisation, a way of imagining all humans as part of one system. Further, it also gives us the perversely reassuring thought that global warming is our fault, which implies we are in charge of all that happens, and we can fix it: 'because it is unable to escape it, humanity will pretend to be the author of its destiny' (*IE*, 71). Global warming merely strengthens the alibi of a system that wishes to close down freedoms in the name of appropriate social behaviours. The West feasts on its own agency of destruction, consuming poverty, famine and hardship as visual and moral commodities (*IE*, 67).

Finally, globalisation is the death of even the good it seems to spread – 'the universal perishes in globalisation' (*SC*, 156). Baudrillard's take on 'the global' is very bleak – brought about by simulation and in turn feeding it, it can only destroy what remnants of meaning and value still exist. Its reach is limitless (we are all individually brought into 'the global' through IT screens). The only hope is slender, and not one we might like to cherish as hope: the prospect of viral attacks, terrorism and uncontrollable catastrophes. Just as it is not clear in Baudrillard who might be driving the 'system' of globalisation, neither is it clear who or what would be doing the hoping.

Passwords

Geopolitics
Gulf War
Hyper-reality
Postmodernism/Postmodernity
Reversibility
Simulation
Terrorism
Time + History
Transpolitical
Universality

GNOSTICISM

Jonathan Smith

In Baudrillard's deluge of thought, his distaste for the 'faecality' of signi-fied reality (*CS*, 30), his deliberate 'Evil Genius of matter' (*FF*, 95) and his desire 'Not to be there, but to see. Like God' (*PC*, 38) summarise a sensibility shaped by two Gnostic currents.

The ideas of Valentinus (AD 100–60) and Mani (AD 215–77) interested Baudrillard as steps into a philosophy which assumes the duality of reality, with Spirit (Good) enslaved in Matter (Evil), yet destined for liberation. Gnostics seek this destiny in gnosis: a divine knowledge, secret wisdom or meta-rational grace. This is anticipated as an ecstatic exchange with God (Jonas, 1963). Once God is so challenged, something like gnosis (*S*) can arise within, yet from beyond, our 'Hell of simulation' and its 'evil spirit of commutation' (*SS*, 18).

Baudrillard learnt about Gnosticism after Bataille (1985b) and Artaud (1958) and following the discoveries in Egypt in 1930 and 1945 of, among other scrolls, the *Manichean Psalm-book* (AD 350) and the Valentinian *Gospel of Philip* (AD 250). These ancient Coptic texts seem to have influenced the young Baudrillard after being translated. For example, Baudrillard's 'in the fields of dung winter has preceded us' (*UB*, 79) from *L'Ange de Stuc* (1978) appears to draw on the *Gospel of Philip*: 'the winter is the world . . . if any man reap in winter . . . his field is barren' (Isenberg, 1981: 132). Furthermore, 'this upright one . . . on this Persian stake' (*UB*, 78) seems to echo references in the *Manichean Psalm-book* to Mani on 'the upright Bema [seat] of the great judge' and to Mani's execution, plotted by 'the teachers of Persia' (Allberry, 1938: 8 and 16).

Thereafter, Gnostic thoughts marked Baudrillard's work for five decades, manifesting mostly as Manichean dualism yet sometimes as Valentinian monism (*F*; Dyakov, 2009). To appreciate the significance of these references, readers need to know about the dualist tradition Baudrillard inherited and the Gnostic distinctions he used. Monists, like Valentinus, assume everything (including dualism) arose when an origi-nal single principle divided in its desire to be creative (see Grant, 1996). Dualists, like Mani, assume the duality of Good and Evil was co-infinitely present from the very beginning and thus did not need to arise from any-thing prior to it (Jonas, 1963).

It was Manichean duality that animated the Albigensian (French Gnostic) tradition and then Baudrillard, via 'a prophetic moralism . . . inherited [. . .] from my ancestors, who were peasants' (Baudrillard, 1995b: unpaginated). Also called Cathars, these Gnostics were active

(991–1207) and actively persecuted (1208–1330), but left a legacy in French peasant life (Le Roy Ladurie, 1979). If *Cool Memories II* (1996b, [1990b]) is any guide, we may assume Baudrillard got Albigensian ideas like 'destiny' and 'the demonic' from his peasant grandparents in the Ardennes (*CM2*).

Duality as destiny eventually became 'the rule' guiding Baudrillard's quest for a 'secret' akin to gnosis (*FS*). Mani's duality of Good and Evil ushered Baudrillard towards this secret by being an antinomy (a pair of related, yet logically independent, contradictory concepts), not a Good/Evil binary opposition. The significance of this 'irreducible duality' was first announced in *Symbolic Exchange and Death* (1993a [1976]). The implications, for possible gnosis, were then fleshed out in several books (*S*, *FS*, *FF*, *TE*, *P*, *F*). Baudrillard summarised this potential: 'The totality constituted by Good and Evil together transcends us, but we should accept it totally. There can be no intelligence of things so long as this fundamental rule is ignored' (*TE*, 109). Here, the antinomy which enables an 'intelligence of things' is Manichean. As such, it cannot be contained within 'the tiny marginal sphere contributed by our rational model' (*TE*, 105) because it is, by definition, a co-infinite contradiction. Thus, like gnosis, the 'intelligence' must be gleaned from 'the symbolic level, which is the level of destiny' (*TE*, 105).

As philosophy, Baudrillard's use of antinomy for gnosis was saved from circularity only by falling into an infinite logical regress. However, he made a virtue of this problem by discerning 'the secret' in an infinite 'eternity of seduction', especially 'the seduction of appearances' (*EC*, 74). Gnosis-via-antinomy was, therefore, his penultimate exit from the 'faecality' of signified reality (*CS*). His final move was the paradoxical project of eluding ordinary life-and-death by cultivating 'disappearance' via 'pure appearance' (*FS*, *FF*). For this, Baudrillard interpreted the Gnostic assumption of metamorphosis as 'the law of appearances', wherein 'passing . . . from one form to another is a means of *disappearing, not of dying*' (*EC*, 47).

Here, 'to disappear is to disperse oneself in appearances [because] . . . dying doesn't do any good; one must still know how to disappear' (*EC*, 47). At this point, the Cathar practice of Endura (returning to God via sacred suicide) comes to mind (Runciman, 1947). Indeed, for Baudrillard, appearing and disappearing was, in fact 'suicidal, but in a good way . . . there is an art of disappearing, a way of modulating it and making it into a state of grace. This is what I'm trying to master in theory' (*FF*, 118).

The prospect of disappearing in pure appearance seems to have been the seed and the fruit of Baudrillard's Gnostic sensibility. 'From very high the white-tailed eagle destroys itself and returns to what it was', wrote the young Baudrillard (*UB*, 78–9). The older Baudrillard had similar thoughts, stressing 'the dizzying joys of disincarnation' as 'the deepest spiritual joy?' (*PC*, 38).

And yet, the dying Baudrillard evoked auto-da-fé (the ceremonial burning of heretics) before confessing that his 'major themes' were all shaped by his 'character traits, even character flaws': 'a disaffection with the physical world? . . . an unsuitability for the real . . . a denunciation of reality' (Baudrillard, 2007: unpaginated).

Passwords

Destiny
Disappearance
Duality
Manichaeism
Poetry

GRAFFITI – see 'city' and 'situationism'.

GULF WAR

Richard G. Smith

In 1981 Baudrillard argued that Francis Ford Coppola's film *Apocalypse Now* amounted to the extension and prolongation of the Vietnam War by means of media images, and that its success lay in the fact that it completed an incomplete war: 'the war in Vietnam "in itself" perhaps in fact never happened . . . [T]he war in Vietnam and this film are cut from the same cloth . . . [N]othing separates them . . . [T]his film is part of the war . . . *Apocalypse Now* is a global victory' (*SS*, 59 and 60). According to Baudrillard, *Apocalypse Now* demonstrated the fatal interdependence of war and cinema (*SS*), as the former has 'become cinematographic and televisual' (*ED*, 16), an argument that was to form the essence of the Gulf War thesis he advanced a decade later (*GW*). This thesis developed his long-standing theorisation of the mass media, hyper-reality and, more specifically, the precession of simulacra, to argue that the Gulf War was one where war itself had been exchanged for the signs of war, overexposed in an 'orgy of simulation' (*IE*, 62).

The Gulf War Did Not Take Place (1995 [1991]) was originally published as a series of three articles in the newspaper *Libération*: 'The Gulf War will not take place' (4 January 1991); 'The Gulf War: is it really taking place?' (6 February 1991); and 'The Gulf War did not take place' (29 March 1991). The title of the book was an allusion to Jean Giradoux's play *The Trojan War Will Not Take Place* (1983) – indeed Baudrillard noted 'many analogies between the Trojan and Gulf wars' (*IE*, 64) – and perhaps a reference to the Dadaist Johannes Baader's comments in 1920 on the media coverage of the Great War: 'The World War is a newspaper war. In reality it never existed' (cited in Green, 1993: 101; Merrin, 2005). However, despite such an obvious reference to Giradoux's play, Baudrillard's book (*GW*) became a *succès de scandale*, with many commentators (for example, Norris, 1992) rushing to accuse Baudrillard (caricatured as the postmodernist par excellence) of denying the 'reality' of war. Indeed, critics at the time failed to grasp that Baudrillard's critique of the Gulf War was based on the premise that it had no specific simulacrum – unlike the Trojan War which had the beauty of Helen as its simulacrum – but was rather the simulacrum of war itself. In other words, his critique of the Gulf War could not have been more grounded in 'reality' precisely because for him it was a 'pure war', a 'non-war', a slaughter of many thousands to further American power and a western desire for a New World Order.

The core argument of *The Gulf War Did Not Take Place* (1995 [1991]) is that the 1991 war in the Persian Gulf was a part of the logic of a New World Order based around the principle of self-deterrence: that the Gulf conflict dramatised a new kind of deterrence that emerged to replace the one that was lost after the end of the Cold War. In other words, with the Gulf War a new geopolitical logic of self-deterrence was confirmed, a deterrence whose function was to replace the balance of terror and calculated threat afforded by the orbital bomb and the always deferred nuclear shoot-out of the Cold War. Thus, for Baudrillard, the West is impotent, constrained by its own strength; it is incapable of waging war. This is why he hoped (his first newspaper article was published just eleven days before the deadline for Iraqi forces to withdraw from Kuwait expired) that fighting in the Gulf would not break out: 'paralysed by its own strength and incapable of assuming it in the form of relations of force. This is why the Gulf War will not take place' (*GW*, 24).

Against an Aristotelian logic where the actual follows the virtual (virtual catastrophe leads to real catastrophe), Baudrillard's perverse logic and 'stupid gamble' (*GW*, 28) was that arms proliferation and the overwhelming military superiority of the West had decreased the possibility of armed conflict: 'We are no longer in a logic of the passage from the virtual to actual but in a hyperrealist logic of the deterrence of the real by the virtual' (*GW*, 27). In other words, Baudrillard was beholden to Hölderlin's reasoning that 'where danger threatens, that which saves us from it also grows' (*GW*, 86–7).

Undeterred by the outbreak of fighting, Baudrillard continued to press his argument that a geopolitical model of 'self-deterrence' was not only operating but was also being confirmed daily – before our very eyes – through the war's media coverage. As a 'rotten simulation' (*GW*, 59), the Gulf War, he contends, is a 'non-war' (a reversal of Clausewitz's famous dictum that war is the continuation of politics by other means) because: 'It no longer proceeds from a political will to dominate or from a vital impulsion or an antagonistic violence, but from the will to impose a general consensus by deterrence' (*GW*, 83). In other words, the protagonists are fighting in the Gulf over nothing more than the 'corpse of war' (*GW*, 23). They are engaged in 'liquidating any confrontation likely to threaten the hence-forward unified system of control' (*GW*, 83–4). The end of war is necessary, contends Baudrillard, to 'impose a general consensus by deterrence' (*GW*, 83) on a global level, to ossify the New World Order as 'an immense democracy governed by a homogenous order which has as its emblem the UN and the Rights of Man' (*GW*, 83).

The target of Baudrillard's critique of the Gulf War is the West's wider geopolitical agenda, namely to establish a global consensus – a Hell of the Same or New World Order – through a violent eradication of the Other and the imposition of a logic of 'self-deterrence'. In other words, what the Gulf War was really about, says Baudrillard, is 'the consensual reduction of Islam to the global order' (*GW*, 85), a war to domesticate the 'symbolic challenge that Islam represents for the entire West' (*GW*, 85). In short, the Gulf War was 'a *simulacre* of a war' (*BL*, 207): a conflict between a western model of 'self-deterrence' and the singular and irreducible symbolic exchange of Islam. And it is a war that continues today – across western cities and the battlegrounds of Iraq, Afghanistan and Pakistan – as the West seeks to domesticate (not destroy) all radical alterity in the name of liberty, freedom, democracy, modernity and human rights.

Passwords

Geopolitics
Hyper-reality
Media
Model
Radical alterity
Simulacra + Simulacrum
Simulation
Symbolic exchange
Virtual

HYPER-REALITY

Mike Gane

Baudrillard's work involves a consistent effort to chart and theorise what happens to the idea of 'reality' in western cultures. For most readers this is paradoxical since it is assumed that 'reality' is universal and it might seem absurd to think there are societies which do not encounter the real world. For Baudrillard, however, the idea of the real and the real world is a cultural construction, certainly linked to the birth of the sciences and technology. When the real is born it engenders a profound modification from the primordial cultures which are symbolic to modern cultures that are organised around signs. The sign in the classic form theorised by Saussure is made up of the triad: signifier, signified and referent. The 'referent' here indicates the outside of thought – the real world (the 'signifier' refers to the word, the 'signified' refers to the concept). Evidently there is a perennial problem in this formulation – does the real refer to a representation (is it inside the sign) or is it merely that which is outside the sign? Clearly, as science passes through stages of development, even revolutions within science, earlier ideas of what constituted the real are abandoned and even treated as scientific illusions even if they once appeared impregnable. It is one of Baudrillard's most provocative ideas that in contemporary cultures from the middle of the twentieth century there is a return to a situation in which the reality principle is once more questioned and abandoned. But this does not lead to a situation in which there is no referent (as with the symbolic order), but to a state in which the sign conditioned by the mass media and the entertainment industry increasingly posits its own basis and non-reality. And this 'negation' is absorbed into the sign itself (*BL*, 142).

This identification of the hyper-real as a stage in the cultural development marked by the appearance of the mass media is framed by Baudrillard's general theory of the transition from the bourgeois culture of drama and the spectacle to that of a mass culture mediated by televisions and computers. Hyper-reality is a precursor of virtual reality. But Baudrillard also drew on other sources for the development of this term. In fact the concept of hyper-reality brings three of Baudrillard's thematics together. The first is the crisis of the sign already indicated: hyper-reality is born with third-order simulacra, that stage in which the real absorbs the image.

The second is the way in which modern cultures implode, in which they wipe out age-old boundaries or transgress boundaries (towards the 'transpolitical'). Here the hyper-real is that which moves towards the 'more real than real'. Indeed, as reality decamps into the image the image ironically absorbs the space of the real – and that, Baudrillard concludes, the hyper-real can 'no longer [be] the mirror of reality' (*AA*, 12). It is from this perspective that Baudrillard examines the modern art world – not just the phase of the image that is more real than real, but the disappearance of illusion in abstractionism and simulationism. It is important to note here that Baudrillard does not simply chart this as a negative development but distinguishes between artists who can genuinely explore this development (for example, early Warhol) and those whose work simply adds to disillusion and banalisation. This evidently has consequences that go far beyond the question of transaesthetics (see *TE*).

The third is the emergence of a popular culture which breaks down the difference between the real and the artifice. An example of the third is popular American culture and Disneyland, the 'perfect model of all the entangled orders of simulacra . . . the first great toxic excrement of a hyper-real civilization' (*SS*, 12 and13). Baudrillard thus here moves beyond an ideological analysis of Disneyland as alienated idealisation of American life, to his provocative analysis suggesting that it 'exists in order to hide that it is . . . "real" America that *is* Disneyland' (*SS*, 12). The reversal has taken place and the separation between the fun world and the 'real' world simply conceals the fact that 'the real is no longer real' (*SS*, 13). Baudrillard provides a long list of the institutions that reinvent and recycle lost dreams and illusions as a new hyper-real social 'function' (*SS*, 13).

Underlying this whole analysis of the emergence of the hyper-real is therefore an important continuation of the idea of alienation. Baudrillard locates classic Marxist theories of alienation in the phase of second-order simulacra when societies were marked by the threat of dialectical progression and social and political revolution. Marxist theories and practices belong to this epoch often referred to by Baudrillard ironically as 'the golden age of alienation'. Hyper-reality on the other hand belongs to third-order forms. Whereas alienation theories identified traumatic loss in a world that stood against the subject, Baudrillard sees the contemporary problem as belonging to a different order. Now, he suggests, the problem is the very lack of distance, the 'universe has swallowed its double, and it has lost its shadow' (*AA*, 13) – hyper-reality produces proximity, transparency, the absorption of the subject. In art it leads to hyper-realism in which the representation of the naked body is so realistic, says Baudrillard, that it is '*an image where there is nothing to see*', an 'obscenity of the real' (*EC*, 31). This movement towards a hyper-real culture invades all spheres but especially information. Baudrillard rejects the theory that this is driven simply by profit-making culture industries, and suggests that it is aligned with the fatal strategies of the silent majorities (*SSM*). A new sociality is produced, a hyper-real sociality which reflects not the alienation of the masses, held in check by repression as in the Marxist theories, but hyper-conformity and terrorism. The latter are conceived by Baudrillard as hyper-real forms that correspond to the hyper-real culture – indeed as vital responses to hyper-real culture.

Passwords

Art
Code
Image
Real
Sign
Simulacra + Simulacrum
Simulation
Transaesthetics
Transpolitical

HYPERTELIA – see 'hysteresis', 'pataphysics', 'the end' and 'time + history'.

HYSTERESIS

David B. Clarke

Although it is most frequently associated with physical systems, Baudrillard has characterised contemporary society in terms of hysteresis – 'the process whereby something continues to develop by inertia' (*A*, 115). Coined by Sir James Alfred Ewing (1855–1935) – from the Greek *hysteresis*, meaning shortcoming or deficiency, and *hysterein*, to be late, fall short, lag behind – the term refers to the property of any system whose state is not deterministically related to its inputs, which retains a 'memory' such that its present state is 'path-dependent'. Magnetised iron provides an example, since the effects caused by exposure to a magnetic field persist in the absence of the cause. It is in a similar sense that Baudrillard invokes the term: if modernity has already reached and, paradoxically, passed beyond its end, hysteresis is the appropriate term to capture its dogged persistence.

Despite modern efforts to impose a linear progression towards an end or finality, time has always possessed a secret curvature which modernity could only ever disavow and not destroy. This curvature puts an end to the end itself.

[W]e have to get used to the idea that *there is no end any longer, there will no longer be any end*, that history itself has become interminable. Thus, when we speak of the 'end of history', the 'end of the political', the 'end of the social', the 'end of ideologies', none of this is true. The worst of it all is . . . that there will be no end to anything, and all these things will continue to unfold slowly, tediously, recurrently, in that hysteresis of everything which, like nails and hair, continues to grow after death. (*IE*, 116)

Zygmunt Bauman similarly describes 'postmodernity' as modernity's posthumous form, while Giorgio Agamben speaks of the persistence of the *means* developed by modernity long after the abandonment of the *ends*. Hysteresis thus describes the zombified state of the body politic, while outbreaks of 'hysteresia' engulf the *socius*:

those who continue to vote although there are no more candidates . . . The phantom limb which goes on hurting even after it is amputated . . . The man who is made redundant but goes regularly to his former place of work every morning. (*CM3*, 129)

Although etymological connections between 'hysteresis' and 'hysteria' are eschewed by lexicographers, symptomatological resonances abound. In Ancient Greek nosology, hysteria – deriving from *hystera*, womb – was regarded as a set of symptoms caused by the 'wandering womb'. For Freud, such symptoms relate to an imaginary anatomy, having no present physical cause. For Lacan, hysteria is a neurosis articulated by a particular question that being poses for a subject. Insofar as this is a question the subject cannot answer, it is apt that a similar question is finally posed for history, a process without a subject. The consequent interminable simulation of the social is best captured in Baudrillard's appeal to the comic vision of 'the cyclist in Jarry's *Supermale*, who has died of exhaustion on the incredible trip across Siberia, but who carries on pedalling and propelling the Great Machine, his rigor mortis transformed into motive power' (*A*, 115).

Passwords

Modernity
Pataphysics
The end
Time + History

I

IDEOLOGY – see 'ambivalence' and 'political economy of the sign'.

ILLUSION

William Pawlett

Illusion and its cognates – appearance, image, double, mirror, simulation, shadow – are terms woven throughout Baudrillard's writings, from his earliest studies of consumption to his last provocations on evil and the 'dual form'. In his early studies Baudrillard understands the consumer society as presenting the illusion of freedom, and he suggests that Marxist and psychoanalytic theory produce only the illusion of critique. Yet illusion is often used in a positive sense, for example in Baudrillard's argument that symbolic ritual is the illusion that conjures away the opposition of life and death, and concerning seduction he insists '*to seduce is to die as reality and reconstitute oneself as illusion*' (*S*, 69). Baudrillard defines the simulacrum as the illusion 'that hides the truth's non-existence' (*S*, 35), and his final works suggest a stage beyond the orders of simulacra, that of 'integral reality'. Integral reality or 'virtuality' is, for Baudrillard, the 'final solution' that seeks to dispel illusion forever; however, the dual form is 'indestructible', he argues, and even virtual technologies preserve something of the 'original illusion' (*LP*, 85).

It is useful, heuristically, to distinguish three senses of illusion in Baudrillard's work. However, these are always in tension, spiralling together and cannot be isolated; this is more than a polite caveat as Baudrillard insists on 'the interconnection of appearances' (*FS*, 210). First, there is radical or original illusion. Second are the 'degraded' forms of illusion including representation and simulation which is 'the lowest degree of illusion' (*P*, 3). Between these are the symbolic forms, ritual, seduction, play, the *trompe l'œil*, destiny: the cycles of appearance and disappearance. On radical illusion Baudrillard states:

One can imagine the world even before the appearance of human beings and thought, when there's nothing there to give it meaning, when it is, strictly speaking, without truth or reality – hence in a state of radical illusoriness . . . that's what I mean by 'radical illusion'. (*ExD*, 44)

Rational thought, for Baudrillard, attempts to exert control over the world by reducing its power of illusion. Yet the world will not be controlled or ordered by human thought, indeed thought is plunged 'beyond objective reality, which is an unstable form, into integral reality . . . into a total elimination of illusion and of the dual situation' (*ExD*, 46). And it is illusion itself 'profound' and 'indestructible' that 'takes its revenge by plunging the real into simulation, then into the virtual and integral reality' (*ExD*, 46).

Radical illusion should not be confused with the symbolic order or symbolic exchange, yet symbolic ritual does enable the play and metamorphosis of appearance and disappearance. In elaborating this sense of illusion, Baudrillard stresses the etymology of the term '*Il-ludere* is to put into play, to put oneself into play. And for that you have to create the rules of the illusion' (*ExD*, 44). To engage in the play of illusion is to be 'initiated' within a set of rules, a convention 'in which something other than the real is at stake' (*FS*, 211). Illusion works against the real and truth, it is their enemy. In the play of illusion the sign becomes 'pure', charged with a uniqueness or singularity, 'art, theatre, language have worked for centuries to save illusion . . . to maintain the tiny distance that makes the real play with its own reality, that plays with the disappearance of the real while exalting its appearance . . . they have kept something of ceremony and ritual in the violence they do to the real' (*FS*, 211). Whether in poetic language, in the gestures of seduction, in ritual or gaming, symbolic forms are 'vectors of a vital illusion' (*VI*, 29).

With the progressive loss of banal, transcendent or degraded illusion in the contemporary age we face the prospect of 'unhappy uncertainty', yet Baudrillard raises the alternative of a 'happy uncertainty', the embracing of the world as pure form, as immanence, as 'poetic illusion'. Here the world is accepted as 'wholly enigmatic' (*IEx*, 9): 'illusion, being *par excellence* the art of appearing, of emerging out of nothing, protects us from *being*. As the art of disappearance, it protects us from death. The world is protected from its end by its diabolical indeterminacy' (*IEx*, 10). For Baudrillard illusion is enchanting as well as protective, it 'creates a kind of absolute gain by removing causes, or by distorting effects and causes' (*IEx*, 11). In this way it opens up the play of destiny, 'the passion of illusion and appearance', the encounter with 'that which comes from elsewhere, from others, from their face, their language, their gestures . . . outside of you, *without you* . . . without your having anything to do with it' (*FS*, 172–3). By contrast objectivity and subjectivity, the prerequisites of rational thought, are for Baudrillard twin illusions of equal banality. Though they might seem self-evident, the situation is never certain. We experience great pleasure, Baudrillard asserts, in denying or suspending reality, and the world and human consciousness live in a state of complicity, reciprocity and 'entangling' which prevents a final resolution. Influenced by Nietzsche, Baudrillard states 'representation, this superstition of an objective reality . . . is itself a part of the general illusion of the world, of which we are a part at the same time as we are its mirror' (*LP*, 40). Thus knowledge itself is part of the illusion of the world. An acceptance and embracing of this complicity constitutes, for Baudrillard, the 'lucidity pact' (*LP*).

The world in its immanence is an appearance, an illusion, a play of forms. We can only attempt to capture the illusion through techniques of representation, or alternatively attempt the replacement of illusion through the modelling techniques of simulation and virtualisation. In either case we cannot move beyond the play of appearances to the absolute, to truth or reality, and this, for Baudrillard, is itself a positive outcome as we remain free from the unbearable burdens of reality and absolute truth. And further, Baudrillard insists ritual, ceremony, seduction, the play of illusion and metamorphosis are 'in no sense an illusory mastery, but a mastery of illusion' (*IEx*, 88).

Passwords

Consumption + Affluent society
Double
Evil
Image
Mirror
Simulacra + Simulacrum

IMAGE

John Lechte

The key to understanding the image in Baudrillard's work is that it is not representational. In other words, it does not re-present reality or the real.

Semiotically speaking, the existence of the referent is problematic. All of the texts written in the 1970s and early 1980s had presaged this position which is given one of its strongest articulations in the publication of a lecture Baudrillard gave in 1984 entitled, *The Evil Demon of Images* (1987 [1987a]). Images, this text tells us, are diabolical because they seem to conform to reality: 'It is precisely when it appears most truthful, most faithful and most in conformity to reality that the image is most diabolical' (*ED*, 13). Because, in Baudrillard's view, there is still (in the early 1980s) a naive belief in the image's realism and fidelity to reality, the demonic aspect becomes more pronounced.

Taking a cue from his earlier essay, 'The Precession of Simulacra' (Baudrillard, 1978), Baudrillard proceeds to analyse films such as Woody Allen's *Zelig* and Francis Ford Coppola's *Apocalypse Now* in order to demonstrate that reality, if there is one, is the production and presentation of the film itself – or at least films such as these show how the simulacrum precedes reality and constitutes it. Coppola's film, for example, is an instance of how war itself has 'become cinematographic and televisual' (*ED*, 16). The image, then, 'begins to contaminate reality and to model it' (*ED*, 16). *The China Syndrome*, subject of an earlier analysis, shows, for its part, that reality is anticipated by images, so that upon release of this movie about a nuclear catastrophe, a 'real' incident occurred at Harrisburg (*ED*, 19).

Baudrillard's purpose in invoking the image, then, is to argue vigorously for the primacy of the image in its own right (= simulacrum) over any putative reality. In his mind, there is still much naivety about when it comes to grasping the truly non-representational nature of the image. In putting this case, Baudrillard, along with Deleuze, albeit in a different way and with a different purpose, is opposing Plato's condemnation of the simulacrum. In Plato, it is a question of the relation between *eidos* (real, or truth), *íkon* (image) and *eidôlon* (simulacrum). The issue here has always been about the relation between the true model – and the model as truth – and the attempt to capture this model in a representation (*íkon*). There is general agreement that Plato is not against a good representation which, by definition, cannot be the same as, or identical to, the truth; a good copy (*íkon*) is acceptable. What is unacceptable for Plato is the *eidôlon*, or simulacrum, that which, because it has no relation to the model, escapes the strictures of Platonic mimesis altogether. Baudrillard, against Plato, promotes the image that has no essential connection to reality – the image as autonomous, engendering effects in its own right.

In passing it is to be noted that Baudrillard does not include television in his list of media concerned with the image. Cinema, he says, still has an authentic image status because it is able to tap into and be animated by 'an intense imaginary' (*ED*, 25), whereas television is ultimately a screen that fascinates without allowing the image as such to appear.

Images also participate in what Baudrillard calls a 'fatal strategy', which he compares with a 'banal strategy'. The latter refers to the possibility that images can reveal, or be exchanged for, a true reality or meaning. The image thus becomes a means to an end, not a transcendent end in itself. A fatal strategy, by contrast, is one of immanence, where there is no transcendent destiny (= meaning) – no finality – of images. Images, in short, come to refer to other images – ad infinitum. Jean-Luc Godard's quip that 'there are no just images, just images' captures the spirit of Baudrillard's approach.

In the end, though, Baudrillard personalises his notion of the image. For him, it is a question of the pure enjoyment of images for their own sake independent of any transcendence or ultimate meaning. As he puts it: 'There is a kind of . . . anthropological joy in images, a kind of brute fascination unencumbered by aesthetic, moral, social or political judgements' (*ED*, 28). There can be no doubt that Baudrillard's is the most trenchant version, illustrated via the image, of a more general scepticism, if not nihilism, circulating in postmodern society. The question is: is such a thorough-going 'fatal strategy' sustainable? Or does it, on the contrary, ignore key aspects of the history of the image which point to something fundamental in the human relation to transcendence?

Passwords

Fatal
Film + Cinema
Gulf War
Image
Model
Simulacra + Simulacrum

IMAGINARY

John Lechte

In Lacanian psychoanalysis, the Imaginary is one of three relatively permanent orders constitutive of human subjectivity, the others being the Symbolic (which includes language, signs and symbols of all kinds) and the Real. The Imaginary, the order of the ego, relates to the world through what the ego experiences as an entirely transparent Symbolic order. With the example of language, the Imaginary always seeks what it takes to be meaning and truth; it never consciously experiences language in itself. Put more sharply: the Imaginary accepts the Symbolic as a window on reality, a notion which Baudrillard would say is ideological.

Baudrillard is clearly aware of this psychoanalytic take on the Imaginary (*SED*), but he effectively argues against it in favour of a full-blooded acceptance of the Symbolic, right to the moment where the key to understanding social life is to grasp the nature of the simulacrum which has no link whatever with any reality. Baudrillard's use of the term imaginary thus has an everyday sense not found in psychoanalysis. Baudrillard's imaginary is what psychoanalysis would call imagination. Take death: we can never know death; we can only imagine it: 'death is our imaginary' (*SED*, 133). Thus the radically unknowable, such as the real event of death, becomes imaginary. This is the case on a broader plane with regard to a European experience of the Third World and vice versa, as it is also the case for every term that connotes otherness (for example, nature in the human–nature opposition, or high-brow culture as the imaginary for popular culture).

The imaginary as imagination is illustrated in Baudrillard's analysis of Disneyland. Here, the general public are understood to believe that Disneyland is a fantasy world: a world of pure make-believe which contrasts sharply with external reality. The true nature of reality is hidden precisely by this distinction between Disneyland as fantasy and the world outside as the real world. But, in fact, Disneyland is the truth of the real world, which is itself based in fantasy. Baudrillard goes further and claims that the power of capitalism itself is 'based in the imaginary' (*SED*, 129). Just as religion gave, and continues to give, rise to all sorts of imaginary beings, so capitalism becomes its 'fantastic secularisation' (*SED*, 129). All reality, then, is implicated in an imaginary realm whose only limit is the limit to human imagination. To think the opposite – to subscribe to an objective world independent of imagination – is to become mired in a metaphysics and ideology of the ultimate reality, or origin. But there is no ultimate reality or foundation Baudrillard never tires of reiterating. Little changes in the later works, where the 'world' becomes a 'radical illusion' (*PC*, 1) and '"reality" is an imposture' (*IEx*, 3). So, what we have is an imaginary governed by the entirely autonomous simulacrum (a sign or an image without a referent or a real object, a sign that cannot be exchanged for reality). Paradoxically, to say that the simulacrum is a kind of truth implies the transcendence of the imaginary–reality divide, insofar as if everything is imaginary a non-imaginary realm becomes irrelevant. Or rather, we are left with what Baudrillard calls 'hyper-reality'. An elaboration is given in an interview as follows: 'now we are dealing with a sign that posits the principle of non-reality, the principle of the absolute absence of reality' (*BL*, 143).

Another domain in which the imaginary is in play is in what Baudrillard called, following the radical French playwright Alfred Jarry, 'pataphysics', the science of imaginary solutions. Pataphysics is a response to the dominance of the code in society. The code makes everything equivalent and tautologous. It gives rise to what Baudrillard calls a 'banal strategy', even as it pretends to be the ultimate real, and even though it has no finality, so that every concrete effort made to oppose the existing state of affairs is recuperated by the code – that is, is turned into a quasi-legitimate part of the capitalist system. Left-wing thought in particular has been appropriated by the code and turned into an entity that, far from being a threat to the system, becomes an integral part of it (the opposition needed to affirm the power of capital). Politically, therefore, it is necessary, Baudrillard estimated, to challenge the putative real, to move things to the extremes in order to avoid recuperation. These extremes, however, are precisely products of the imaginary. Whether or not he was successful in this enterprise remains a constant source of debate with regard to Baudrillard's intellectual legacy.

Passwords

Code
Death
Hyper-reality
Orientalism
Other + Otherness
Psychoanalysis
Simulacra + Simulacrum

IMPLOSION – see 'Beaubourg', 'excess', 'hyper-reality', 'masses', 'media', 'model', 'pataphysics' and 'postmodernism/postmodernity'.

IMPOSSIBLE EXCHANGE

Rex Butler

In his mid-to-late-career *Impossible Exchange* (2001a [1999b]), Baudrillard theorises the term 'impossible exchange' (*IEx*). Although it is privileged for the first time there, the term originally occurs in the books *Fatal Strategies* (2008a [1983]) and *Cool Memories II* (1996b [1990b]), and it later becomes one of Baudrillard's 'passwords' (*PW*). Indeed, although the term takes on a specific meaning and serves a particular purpose in Baudrillard's later work, we can trace a genealogy of it in Baudrillard's earlier writings. In its most general sense, it arises as a variation of symbolic exchange, a concept that, as Baudrillard has admitted and as numerous commentators have pointed out, comes out of a reading of the anthropologists Marcel Mauss and Emile Durkheim and their elaboration of a form of sumptuary, non-economic exchange that occurs in tribal societies. In symbolic exchange, objects are exchanged for each other beyond any use value or even exchange value and without any ulterior end in mind. As Baudrillard explains in *Symbolic Exchange and Death* (1993a [1976]), his most detailed attempt to articulate the notion, it is a 'circulation of gifts and counter-gifts as intense as the circulation of precious goods and women' (*SED*, 131). It is an exchange that is not 'reciprocal' in terms of any foreseeable quid pro quo, or even 'symbolic' in the sense of implying some legal or cultural indebtedness. Rather, Baudrillard's symbolic exchange is a freely given exchange of something for nothing that begins and ends without leaving traces, but for all that creates a more profound connection between the two parties than ordinary economic relationship.

We can see examples of this 'symbolic exchange' throughout Baudrillard's work. Indeed, Baudrillard's point is that symbolic exchange is everywhere, insofar as economic exchange itself would not be possible without it. Even though it is not named or theorised as such, we see it in such moments as the exchange between the unique object and the rest of the collection in *The System of Objects* (1996a [1968]) or the relationship between 'free' and labour time in *The Consumer Society* (1998a [1970]). But, after this, symbolic exchange is visible and specifically elaborated in Baudrillard's work. We might just give here two examples that are relevant to the notion of 'impossible exchange' that Baudrillard subsequently develops. In *For a Critique of the Political Economy of the Sign* (1981 [1972]), Baudrillard speaks of the way that in an art auction there is no relationship between the work of art and the money that is paid for it. The work of art does not have a use value or even properly an exchange value, and the money that is paid for it is understood to be lost or consumed in advance. As Baudrillard writes: 'There is no longer an equivalence, but an aristocratic *parity* established between money, which has become a sumptuary material through the loss of its economic exchange value, and the canvas, which has become a sign of prestige' (*CPS*, 117). In *Fatal Strategies* (2008a [1983]), Baudrillard makes a similar point with regard to the relationship between the hostage and the terrorist. When a hostage is taken by a terrorist out of the general circulation of a society, they do not somehow become representative of the sins and faults of that society. Rather, they become a radical exception that bears no relationship to society and that cannot easily be returned to it. In this sense, there can be no possible rational calculation to the terrorists' actions; their political demands cannot be exchanged for anything. But it is exactly in this way that the terrorist act mirrors the radical inexchangeabilty of society, in which every contingency is taken into account and at once everyone and no one is responsible for everything. Without actually making the hostage equivalent to anything, an impossible exchange nevertheless takes place between the hostage and the fact that all of us are in a way taken hostage by society. Again, as Baudrillard writes: 'One must conceive of terrorism as . . . experimentally staging an impossible exchange, and thereby verifying at its limit a banal situation, our own, that of the historical loss of the scene of exchange, the rule(s) of exchange, and the social contract' (*FS*, 72–3).

Impossible Exchange (2001a [1999a]) in fact begins with a description of a certain radical inexchangeability that characterises our current situation. What Baudrillard means by this is that our contemporary, self-referential systems of simulation have no external point of reference and can be judged only in their own terms. Or, more precisely, because these systems have no external point of reference they can no longer be judged at all. They can continue to expand, increase in size or become more efficient, but only in their own terms. And Baudrillard's point is that everything is like this today; all systems attempt to account for all of reality: 'The other spheres [apart from economics] – politics, law and aesthetics – are characterised by this same non-equivalence . . . and cannot be exchanged for anything' (*IEx*, 4). And it is not a matter of somehow calling a halt to this process of extrapolation or exponentialisation, of seeking to impose some outside standard of judgement. There is nothing that can be held against these systems of simulation that is not revealed to be already part of them, indeed possible from the beginning only because of them. And yet, as Baudrillard emphasises, it is just when all uncertainty disappears that it also reappears, because it is at the very moment when domination is total that, because there is nothing outside of it, it cannot be realised, has no objective effect (*IEx*). It is at this point that stakes re-enter the game, that a kind of exchange – at the same time impossible – is shown to be necessary. There is, in Baudrillard's complex terminology, a 'Nothing' (*IEx*, 7) that the system must exchange itself with, insofar as it does not exist unless there is something outside of it, some place from where it can be named or thought. This interrelationship between something and the nothing from where it is remarked must be understood in the light of Baudrillard's comments about the beginning of the world as a certain splitting of 'nothing' from itself (*PC*), and perhaps even Hegel's understanding of the relationship between Being and Nothing in Book I of his *Logic*. This impossible but necessary exchange can be seen, according to Baudrillard, in the 'poetic transfer' between something and nothing that occurs in photography, living money, the event and thought itself (*IEx*).

Passwords

Art
Gift
Photography
Symbolic exchange
Terrorism

INTEGRAL REALITY

William Pawlett

The notion of integral reality appeared relatively late in Baudrillard's career, becoming important thematically in *The Perfect Crime* (1996c [1995a]) and discussed in detail in his final major work *The Intelligence of Evil or The Lucidity Pact* (2005a [2004]) and in contemporaneous interviews. To grasp the meaning of this important term it is necessary first to clarify Baudrillard's understanding of the real, the sign and simulation and their 'murder' which paves the way for integral reality.

Baudrillard is consistently clear that 'the real' is a 'particular case' of simulation (*PC*, 10) and warns: 'let's never forget that the real is merely a simulation' (*P*, 69). Reality and simulation then are not binary opposites; 'reality' is simulated through the breaking of symbolic exchange relations and the positing of the discrete and 'disenchanted' universe of the sign. The sign produces the effect of reference or representation, as the signifier produces the effect of the signified (*CPS*). The effect of the real consists in pairs of binary relations, such as true/false, nature/culture, male/female, built on the foundation of the sign; 'the *effect of the real* is only ever therefore the structural effect of the disjunction between two terms' (*SED*, 133). Further, Baudrillard insists that this real-ity is a relatively short-lived affair; born with the Renaissance 'reality has barely had time to exist and already it is disappearing . . .' (*LP*, 17). Baudrillard clarifies his position as follows:

when we say reality has disappeared, the point is not th.
physically, but that it has disappeared metaphysically. Realit
it is its principle that is dead . . . objective reality – reality relat
representation – gives way to 'Integral Reality', a reality withou
everything is realised and technically materialised without referei
ciple or final purpose [*destination*] whatever. (*LP*, 18)

Reality without limits or direction, without anything 'not re.. against which it could be contrasted, is, for Baudrillard 'obscene', 'unbearable': 'integral reality is the perpetrating on the world of an unlimited operational project whereby everything becomes real, everything becomes visible and transparent, everything is "liberated"' (*LP*, 17).

   Though there is clearly an overlap or commonality in the terms Baudrillard employs to evoke simulation and integral reality, the two can be distinguished. Integral reality is distinct from simulation because the mechanism of the disenchanted sign, on which simulation depended, is eliminated by the virtual, by information, by the flow of zeros and ones that characterise integral reality. If simulation hyper-realises the real by generating its effect from abstract models and codes (fashion, consumerism, sexuality), integral reality comes about through the elimination of the sign and its capacity for both representation and simulation. The murder of the sign is far more serious than the murder of reality because without the sign the symbolic, poetic, illusionary, anagrammatic and aphoristic dimensions of language are lost: 'without the arbitrary nature of the sign, there is no differential function, no language, no symbolic dimension' (*LP*, 67–8). The murder of the sign is also the 'murder of illusion' (*F*, 46) and creates a 'totally deciphered' world where 'everything that exists only as idea, dream, fantasy, utopia will be eradicated, because it will immediately be realised, operationalised . . . real events, will not even have time to take place. Everything will be preceded by its virtual realisation' (*VI*, 66–7). Without the sign there can be nothing but a virtual copy of the world, what Baudrillard calls 'radical fetishism . . . the sign's becoming pure object once again' (*LP*, 72). However, the 'pure object' of integral reality is distinct from the object in symbolic exchange or seduction where the object is alive and charged with destiny. In contrast integral reality eclipses the sign's transcendence in the immanence of technology and data flow; meanings are 'de-vitalised' by the expulsion of 'otherness, alterity or negativity' (*LP*, 67), and 'things are no longer anything but what they are, and, as they are, they are unbearable' (*LP*, 26).

   Baudrillard develops a number of examples of the 'integral drive': digital technology, the notion of 'real time' and the 'integrist' thrust of neo–liberal globalisation. Music, he argues, is reduced to digital code by computer technology such that all 'impurities', such as feedback and distortion, are moved. These can be reintroduced digitally, at a later date, for greater 'authenticity', but this reduces 'authenticity' to a special effect: 'is this still music?' (*LP*, 28). The 'quality' of music is, increasingly, measured by its degree of technical fidelity rather than existing in the measureless realm of the imagination; digital coding purges music of negativity as digital image processing purges the image of its negative. Schematically, if linear time replaced the cyclical time of symbolic exchange, it in turn is replaced by so-called 'real time' which is not 'real' at all but virtual because the flow of past, present and future are 'contracted to a single focal point, to a fractal form of time. The differential of time having disappeared, it is the integral function that wins out: the immediate total presence of a thing to itself. All that is absent from itself, all that differs from itself, is not truly real' (*LP*, 31).

But, Baudrillard asserts, fortunately the perfect crime of the complete imposition of integral reality is impossible. The world in its radical illusion, along with everything and everyone, is non-identical, enigmatic and radically Other. Destiny and its symbolic or dual forms are 'indestructible' (*LP*, 21) and it is with globalisation that the backlash against the integral drive can be most clearly felt in 'dissent working away at it from the inside. It is the global violence immanent in the world-system itself which, from within, sets the purest symbolic form of the challenge against it' (*LP*, 22). There is no way of resolving the antagonism between the 'integral drive' and the 'dual drive' and we have, Baudrillard declares, all already taken sides; we are either for integral reality or against it.

Passwords

Anagram
Code
Globalisation
Hyper-reality
Music
Perfect crime
Real
Sign
Simulation
Symbolic exchange
Time + History
Virtual

IRAQ – see 'Gulf War'.

JARRY, ALFRED (1873–1907) – see 'hysteresis', 'imaginary', 'modernity', 'pataphysics' and 'time + history'.

LACAN, JACQUES (1901–81) see 'clones + cloning', 'cool memories', 'imaginary', 'language', 'psychoanalysis', 'other + otherness', 'sign' and 'utopia'.

LANGUAGE

Gerry Coulter

For Baudrillard language is always aimed at the social (*SED*) and is understood as an artifical system (*TE*). While discourse tends to produce meaning he says that language (and writing) always create illusion (*PC*). Fortunately, for Baudrillard, we can use language to play with this illusion (*P*). Only fragments survive the catastrophe which is the destruction of language and meaning (*F*) and the dispersion of language is only a disaster from the point of view of communication and meaning (*PC*). Communication, for Baudrillard, is to language what reproduction is to sexuality – merely one possible outcome (*CM2*). Language, according to this view, is merely the involuntary accomplice of communication (*PC*). Following Lacan, he says that language does not convey meaning, rather it stands in place of it (*CM*).

All languages are beautiful for Baudrillard precisely because they are foreign to one another (*TE*). Baudrillard prefers to see language as a kind of inhabitable void (*F*). He disliked political and ideologically laden languages which he said are 'spongy'. They absorb 'the fluid secretions of thought the way a Tampax absorbs menstrual blood' (*CM3*, 120).

He was wary of language as propaganda (which does not fully occur, he says, until the October 1917 Revolution in Russia and after 1929 in the

West). 'Mass languages' (which for him includes advertising), when aimed at a 'total public', become totalitarian (*UB*) and all languages become absorbed in advertising's depthlessness (*SS*). Here, Baudrillard says, languages are reduced to mere neo-languages which are beyond truth and falsity, thriving on codes and models rather than reference or veracity (*UB*).

He is likewise suspicious of linguistics which attempt, he says, 'to reduce the poetic to a meaning' (*SED*, 205). The poetic, for its part, is an 'insurrection of language against its own laws' (*SED*, 198). A good example of this in his writing occurs when he says that Americans live in the most developed state of simulation without a language to describe it (*A*).

Among the problems we face with the capitalist system is that it tries to rationalise language (*MP*). Today the pressure is on to reduce all languages to computer language and for Baudrillard the day we speak this machine language we will truly be beaten by technology (*SC*). He believed that when everything is encoded digitally, language becomes as useless as the sex function of a clone (*VI, IEx*). From here he moves to undermine our faith in cyberspace 'where the ultra-simplification of digital languages prevails over the figural complexity of natural languages' (*VI*, 69). For him the symbolic dimension of language cannot survive 'binary coding and decoding' (*VI*, 69). Digital languages are the 'Perfect Crime against language' (*VI*, 69).

Language 'speaks us', he said (*IEx*, 89), and 'prevents everything from signifying at every moment' (*PC*, 53). In short, 'language thinks' (*PW*, xiii). When writing he said he sought to get 'to the end of the sentence, before language has had time to feel pain' (*CM*, 101). He added elsewhere: 'you have to surprise it and let it surprise you' (*P*, 32). Language, when it plays in illusion, can be joyful for Baudrillard but he felt that meaning, for its part, is always unhappy (*PC*).

Passwords

Advertising
Clones + Cloning
Communication + Non-communication
Fragments
Illusion
Poetic resolution
Writing

LEFEBVRE, HENRI (1901–91) see 'literature', 'May 1968', '*Traverses*' and '*Utopie*'.

LÉVI-STRAUSS, CLAUDE (1908–2009) – see 'cool memories' and 'gift'.

LITERATURE

Richard G. Smith

In the early 1960s, Baudrillard wrote literary reviews of fiction from Italo Calvino, Uwe Johnson and William Styron for Jean-Paul Sartre's periodical *Les Temps Modernes*. The reviews were Baudrillard's first publications (1962a, 1962b, 1962c), written before he took up employment as an academic sociologist, and represent the most explicit examples of literary criticism in his *oeuvre*. However, these reviews are not in themselves important for appreciating the role that literature came to play in Baudrillard's theoretical writings. From the 1970s onwards, literature by authors such as J. G. Ballard, Jorge Luis Borges, Elias Canetti, Arthur C. Clarke and Philip K. Dick became an important resource for Baudrillard as he drew on their novels and short stories to both shape and illustrate his theoretical writings.

Science fiction is the literary genre on which Baudrillard draws most often as a resource for his writings. In *Simulacra and Simulation* (1994a [1981]) Baudrillard published two essays on science fiction: an essay entitled 'Simulacra and Science Fiction', where he conflated the themes of technology and utopia in discussing both science fiction and, more generally, the fate of theory; and the essay 'Crash', which considered J. G. Ballard's novel of the same title (*SS*). Baudrillard is interested in *Crash* because of the world it portrays: it both presents and supports his view that 'technology is the deadly deconstruction of the body', which is in stark contrast to the view that had been pertinent from Marx to McLuhan that 'technology is an extension of the body' (*SS*, 111) – see Baudrillard's (*UB*) critiques of McLuhan and Lefebvre. For Baudrillard *Crash* is indicative of the possibility of violence and violation that technology provides – not to the body, anatomy or physiology but in creating a 'semiurgy of contusions, scars, mutilations, wounds that are so many new sexual organs opened on the body' (*SS*, 112). A non-referential sexuality is presented by the (auto)accident as the body is given over to 'symbolic wounds'. The body is sign. Echoing the concerns of *Seduction* (1990a [1979]), Baudrillard insists that here 'death and sex are read on the same level as the body, without phantasms, without metaphor, without sentences' (*SS*, 113); sexual desire is simply the opportunity for sign-exchange at the locus of the body, so that rather than an imagined future,

Baudrillard contends that Ballard's novel is a superficial abyss, a portrayal of the world that confirms his own vision of the contemporary: a world dominated by simulacra and simulation. Thus Baudrillard is drawn to *Crash* because it mirrors his own terminology and theory. The story of *Crash* is neither reality nor fiction, but is instead an account of the hyper-real: '*Crash* is the first great novel of the universe of simulation, the one with which we will all now be concerned – a symbolic universe, but one which, through a sort of reversal of the mass-mediated substance (neon, concrete, car, erotic machinery), appears as if traversed by an intense force of initiation' (*SS*, 119).

In *Symbolic Exchange and Death* (1993a [1976]) Baudrillard draws on Arthur C. Clarke's SF story 'The Nine Billion Names of God', where a brotherhood of Tibetan monks employ computer experts to speed up their recitation of the many names of God, to demonstrate how the model of symbolic exchange operates within the field of language. While the monks believe that, upon completion of their task, the world will end, the computer programmers don't believe the prophecy, but as the computer completes the recitation the stars of the night sky begin to disappear. As with Ballard, Baudrillard interprets Clarke's fable for his own purpose, so 'the nine billion names of God' becomes 'the extermination of the name of God' and consequently the liquidation of the signified, an example of how poetic language is the deconstruction of the sign and representation: 'a site of the extermination of value and the law' (*SED*, 195). Likewise, in *Seduction* (1990a [1979]) Baudrillard presents a not very faithful reading of Borges' story 'The Lottery in Babylon' (Borges, 1970) to further his own theory (see Gane, 1991b). Borges is the most frequently cited literary author in Baudrillard's *oeuvre*, and undoubtedly Baudrillard's most well-known usage of a Borges story is that of the map that exactly covers its territory so that the two become indistinguishable, which he uses to introduce his discussion of the precession of simulacra (*SS*; Smith, 2003).

Finally, it is worth noting that Baudrillard's writings themselves have had a profound influence on the novels of many writers of contemporary fiction. This influence has been either indirect, providing the context of 'hyper-reality' for the novels of, for example, J. G. Ballard, Douglas Coupland, Don DeLillo and Thomas Pynchon, or direct, with authors such as Michel Houellenbecq and Maurice G. Dantec openly acknowledging the importance of his ideas for their works. The Native American writer Gerald Vizenor even features Baudrillard as a character in his novel *Hotline Healers* (1997) which makes widespread reference to his work on simulation to critique the popular culture of contemporary America for its misrepresentation of Native American 'reality'.

Passwords

Anagrams
Hyper-reality
Poetic resolution
Science fiction
Seduction
Simulacra + Simulacrum

LYOTARD, JEAN-FRANÇOIS (1924–98) – see 'cool memories' and 'postmodernism/postmodernity'.

MANICHAEISM

Jonathan Smith

The ideas of Mani (AD 215–77), a Persian philosopher of good and evil, helped Baudrillard locate his thinking within the dual form, thereby enabling his production of concepts like symbolic exchange, seduction and the perfect crime. Mani's ideas were revived following translations into French, German and English of Manichean scrolls discovered in Chinese Turkestan (1908) and Egypt (1930). This material seems to have influenced the young Baudrillard. For example, Baudrillard's passage 'this upright one . . . on this Persian stake' (*UB*, 78) apparently echoes references in the *Manichean Psalm-book* (Coptic, AD 350) to Mani's execution and to Mani on 'the upright Bema [seat] of the great judge' (Allberry, 1938: 8). In the same passage, Baudrillard also refers to 'the Taillades', once a Cathar village in southern France. Furthermore, the life-forming duality of good and evil in *The Novels of Italo Calvino* (*UB*) appears well-informed by the intermingled and creative Demonic and Divine in Chinese Manichean Text # three (AD 731; Greenlees, 1956). Thereafter, Baudrillard would regularly refer to Manichean ideas. To appreciate these references, readers need to know about Mani's 'Two Roots, Three Epochs' doctrine.

'Mani's developed doctrine . . . undertook to expound "beginning, middle and end" of the total drama of being,' explains Jonas (1963: 209).

Referring to Light (Good) and Darkness (Evil), Jonas notes: 'The foundation of Mani's teaching is the infinity of the primal principles; the middle
part concerns their intermingling; and the end, the separation of the Light
from the Darkness'. Here, creation happens in the second epoch, when
Light (God) lets Darkness trap some of it in matter (Jonas, 1963). This is
done, Mani reckoned, to seduce Evil into the third epoch, where God will
be unmixed from matter, reality reversed and the world destroyed; leaving
Good once again separate from Evil (Jonas, 1963). These ideas animated
the Albigensian (French Cathar) tradition and then Baudrillard via 'a
prophetic moralism . . . inherited from my ancestors, who were peasants'
(Baudrillard, 1995b: unpaginated). Riding with his peasant grandparents
on an oxcart attacked by Nazi dive-bombers while fleeing the Ardennes in
1940, Baudrillard the boy may have thought that the world was created by
'the Evil Genius of matter' (*FF*, 95).

Given these sources and circumstances, readers could expect to find
Manichean ideas in Baudrillard's early major work. Indeed, some distaste for the signified material world is apparent in his first four books
(*SO, CS, CPS, MP*). There is, for example, his emphasis on the 'faecality' of reality (*CS*, 30). However, it was six years later that Baudrillard
first announced his preference for Manichean dualism (*SED*, 149).
Writing in light of Freud's duality of Eros (life) and Thanatos (death),
he noted Mani's 'very powerful vision' to emphasise 'the irreducible
duality' of good and evil and thereby critique a persecuting church
seeking to make evil 'dialectically subordinate' within a Good/Evil
binary opposition.

Baudrillard deepened his Manichean critique of binaries in *Seduction*
(1990a [1979]) by showing how twin terms like 'good and evil' need not
be conceived as 'diacritical oppositions', but can be thought of 'within
the framework of an enigmatic duel and an inexorable reversibility?' (*S*,
103). Here, Mani's roots and epochs are brought to mind, but Baudrillard
waited until *Fatal Strategies* (2008a [1983]) to be explicit: 'Imagine a good
resplendent with all the power of Evil: this is God, a perverse god creating the world on a dare and calling on it to destroy itself . . .' (*FS*, 29).
Furthermore, he boldly drew on Mani to intensify Hume's critique of
causation (*FS*). During this period, Baudrillard also used Manichaeism
and Scepticism to inform *Simulacra and Simulation* (1994a [1981]) and
lectured in Australia, telling interviewers: 'For me the reality of the world
has been *seduced*, and this is really what is so fundamentally Manichean
in my work' (*ED*, 46). By the time he published work done for a doctoral
degree at the Sorbonne, Baudrillard was writing openly as a Manichean
metaphysician (*EC*).

An epiphany of Good and Evil during his Tautavel Gorges accident

(*CM3*) drew Baudrillard further into Manichaeism in the 1990s (*TE*, *PC*, *IEx*). At this time, he even dared to anticipate Mani's third epoch (*PC*) before carrying his Manichean torch into the new century (*PW*, *F*, *ST*). This move led him to interpret 9/11 via Manichean *illusion* (*PC*) and intermingled good and evil (*ST*). Elsewhere he noted the Cathars, confessing 'my transcendental Manicheism' (*F*, 81) and echoing Voltaire's Manichean Martin (*F*). 'Oh yes, I love the world of the Cathars because I am Manichean', he later told *Der Speigel* (Baudrillard, 2004b: unpaginated).

Even so, as death beckoned, Baudrillard began to critique his Manichean career. In *The Intelligence of Evil or The Lucidity Pact* (2005a [2004]), he declared: 'The idea of evil as a malign force, a maleficent agency, a deliberate perversion of the order of the world, is a deep-rooted superstition' (*LP*, 160). And yet, in the same book, he upholds 'the *agon*' as a key symbolic form (*LP*, 161). This suggests that Baudrillard's mature Manichaeism involved moving away from Mani's metaphysical story towards the form of duality itself.

Passwords

Duality
Evil
Metaphysics
Perfect crime
Seduction
Symbolic exchange

MARX, KARL (1818–83) – see 'advertising', 'anagrams', 'double', 'evil', 'hyper-reality', 'illusion', 'literature', 'masses', 'mirror', 'modernity', 'nature + animals', 'nihilism', 'object', 'political economy of the sign', 'post-Marxism', 'production', 'sign', 'symbolic exchange', 'translations' and 'value + structural law of value'.

MASSES

Patricia Cormack

The issue of the masses was central to the intellectual scene in postwar Europe, especially for Marxists who looked to the proletarian masses to become self-conscious agents of revolutionary change. The apparent effectiveness of Nazi Germany in turning its population into a receptive audience (with organised rallies, radio speeches, propaganda films) made many intellectuals wonder if the masses were easily seduced by spectacle. While some held on to the hope that communication technologies would demystify the cultural and social world for the proletarian, others (especially those who emigrated to the US during the war and experienced American mass culture first hand) concluded that the homogenisation of culture in mass media would continue to degrade the taste and critical capacities of mass populations. For Baudrillard, both of these positions mistakenly understood the masses in terms of the extreme poles of complete passivity or organised agency, and ignored the interrelationship of the masses, communication systems and spectacle in contemporary life.

Baudrillard took up this question of the masses by inspecting both the postwar social landscape (characterised, he argued, by the frenzied proliferation of mass-produced signs and images) and the conventional academic understandings of the mass audience (*SSM*). Specifically, he questioned the metaphysic that both assumes a simple relation between sign and signified (images and reality) and projects an essence (desire, will, identity) onto the audience. From these mistaken assumptions mass media are studied as the misrepresentation or distortion of reality and the manipulation of the desires. Academics have fallen into the trap of thinking of the mass audience the way administrators, politicians and advertisers think of it – as having desires that can be studied, measured, tapped and directed. He also reminded his readers that the masses are not someone else, but are all of us in that we all live within this circulation of signs and measurement of desire and are thus constantly socially organised and invoked as a mass.

Media systems do not circulate or manipulate opinion or desires. They are a unidirectional mode of address and machines for the generation of spectacle. As an audience, our very fascination with spectacle creates an unconscious subversion of the media code or system (and its grounding in traditional notions of reality and persuasion). This position is foreshadowed by Baudrillard's earlier critique of Marx's theory of the commodity, which depended on the dichotomy of 'use values' and 'exchange values', and assumed both essential human needs and the alienation of these needs by the capitalist market (*MP*). Baudrillard inserted into Marxian theory the semiotic and anthropological notions of 'symbolic exchange' by which new meaning can cohere to objects that originate in the commodity system. He explained, for example, that while a ring is usually a part of the capitalist fashion system (and interchangeable with all other rings in the incessant circulation of signs), a wedding band (once ritualistically given) becomes a unique and irreplaceable symbol of a particular relationship and no longer a part of market logic (*CPS*). Contra Marx, therefore, the logic of the commodity form can be negated in its consumption. Here Baudrillard began to formulate a version of agency that does not dismantle the market system, but undermines it in its very use. Like his consumer, the mass audience will frustrate the logic of the system that calls it into existence.

The masses are not then an empirical referent (a social class, category, group), but a shadowy figure of communication practices (a 'silent majority') and an ideological justification for political projects (*SSM*). Since these communication practices are premised upon simplistic notions of representation and influence, they can be absorbed or dispersed in their consumption. The constant measurement, reporting and circulation of mass responses cover over that the only thing left is the incessant movement of responses itself. These responses are not indications of cultivated thought, debate, political values or reflection on the part of the audience (as we consume as entertainment our own solicited responses). As a mass, we do not deflect back the messages projected on to us, nor do we take up the projects of History (progress, enlightenment) or the Social (rationally organised lives) handed to us, but instead enthusiastically take on the formless object position claimed for us. This passivity allows for the absorption of messages and suspension of meaning. When asked to exercise a serious and considered political will, we offer instead an endless delight in popular spectacles. When asked to express consumer preferences, we vacillate capriciously. When asked to be objects of social policy, we refuse to provide or comprehend practical information. Since this system of communication requires that we, as a mass, are at once subjects (with real wants, desires, opinion, wills) and objects (to be addressed, measured, polled, surveyed and inspected by pre-structured 'yes'/'no' interrogation), the production of confusion, hyper-conformity, circular talk, contradiction and infinite hesitation works to parody and neutralise the logic of the media system.

In academic circles, Baudrillard's work helped initiate an approach to media studies that put aside elitist assumptions of a duped mass in need of media literacy. Media studies now include the inspection of semiotic play, audience subversion, multiple and contradictory interpretations, and general media environments. His understanding of the media–mass relation is indebted to Marshall McLuhan who argued that particular media messages are irrelevant to understanding a medium's radical effects on the organisation of social life. In fact, issues of media content act as convenient political 'problems', distracting us from the fact that media are themselves technologies of administration. The so-called problems of the masses also exist an as alibi or simulation for the projects of reason, history, culture, education and social administration. The continued insistence that the masses suffer from misled tastes, opinion and desires covers over the ideological poverty of these projects. The constant measurement of the mass covers over that it is a simulation of opinion, desire and political will. Moreover, media systems depend upon the notion of the mass audience and are undermined by the very notion they invoke.

Passwords

Communication + Non-communication
Fashion
Media
Symbolic exchange
Value + Structural law of value

MATRIX TRILOGY – see 'film + cinema', 'real', 'science fiction' and 'singularity'.

MAUSS, MARCEL (1872–1950) – see 'disappearance', 'gift', 'impossible exchange', 'modernity', 'object' and 'symbolic exchange'.

MAY 1968

Richard G. Smith

In the spring of 1968 Baudrillard was engaged in his university career, teaching sociology at Nanterre (Université de Nanterre Paris X) as a *Maître Assistant*. Thus Baudrillard was based at Nanterre when, on 22 March, radicalised students occupied one of the university's administration buildings. That incident subsequently initiated months of conflict at the university between students and senior management, finally leading to the shutdown of the university on 2 May. The discontent spread from Nanterre across Paris and to elsewhere in France, the social upheaval eventually resulting in a general strike that paralysed the French economy. The events forced the de Gaulle government to the edge of collapse before its successful restoration of political and economic stability – with the help of the French Communist Party (*Parti Communiste Français*, PCF).

Despite being at the epicentre of the May 1968 revolts, Baudrillard was never a nostalgic 'sixty-eighter', one of those soixante-huitards who dreamed of placing 1968 in a revolutionary series with 1848 (The European Revolutions), 1871 (Paris Commune), 1905 and 1917 (Russian Revolutions):

Nanterre . . . the sociology department . . . Cohn-Bendit . . . the 22nd of March . . . We were at the center of the 'events'. We participated . . . we went to the barricades . . . The 'spirit of May' circulated for several years at Nanterre. We still had a certain power. The students were behind us. We defended the department of sociology above all. The situation lasted until 1973–4. I stayed on a few more years, through inertia. During the work of mourning, for me, there was no longer any activity. I had passed to the side of theory. Leftism, or what it had become, closed militarism, was no longer an option. (*UD*, 16)

For Baudrillard the events of 1968 were 'the forerunner of nothing' (*FF*, 115), an indecipherable event that was 'impossible to rationalize or exploit, from which nothing has been concluded' (*FF*, 114–15). Nevertheless, while not a disappointed '68er' veteran, it is evident that the failure of May 1968 was an important watershed for Baudrillard, throwing into question the role of the intellectual. In an interview Baudrillard states that after 1968 it was 'extremely difficult . . . to take up, once again, the position of the intellectual who is conscious of himself', to be able to speak in someone else's name: 'I don't think an intellectual can speak for anything or anyone' (*BL*, 79).

Passwords

Consumption + Affluent society
Politics
Post-Marxism
Utopie
Writing

McLUHAN, MARSHALL (1911–80) – see 'communication + non-communication', 'cool memories', 'globalisation', 'literature' and 'masses'.

MEDIA

David J. Gunkel

Baudrillard provides a characterisation of media that contests and inverts conventional wisdom. Typically media are understood and defined as mechanisms of communication – more or less transparent conduits through which messages of various types and configurations pass from a sender to a receiver. However, for Baudrillard, media have nothing to do with communication, but rather 'fabricate non-communication' (*CPS*, 169).

Communication, as Baudrillard understands it, is primarily concerned with the reciprocity of symbolic exchange, a social relation that – influenced by the idea of the gift from Bataille, Durkheim and Mauss – understands communication as a 'reciprocal space of a speech and a response' (*CPS*, 169). The media, and the mass media in particular, do not facilitate this kind of reciprocity but foreclose it, imposing an irreversible asymmetrical relationship, or what Baudrillard calls 'speech without response' (*CPS*, 169). Media, therefore, are essentially irresponsible and constitute one of the objects by which communication through symbolic exchange is reduced and replaced by the non-communication of semiotic circulation.

This characterisation not only describes broadcast media, with its central transmission tower emitting signals to dispersed receivers who remain fundamentally passive and receptive, but also explains recent innovations in interactive technology. Although new media, from early experiments with interactive television and hypertext to MMORPGs (massively multiplayer online role-playing games) and Web 2.0 applications, are often celebrated for incorporating various modes of user involvement and responsiveness, they only simulate response. That is, they provide 'forms of response *simulation*, themselves integrated in the transmission process, thus leaving the unilateral nature of the communication intact' (*CPS*, 170). And Baudrillard's later works provide numerous illustrations of the way 'new media', from mobile phones (*CM4*) to virtual reality (*IEx*), actually provide for nothing that is new in this respect.

In this way, Baudrillard, like Marshall McLuhan with whom he is often associated, formulates an understanding of media that is more interested in formal aspects as opposed to content. But unlike McLuhan, who understood media as technological extensions of the human subject, Baudrillard is concerned with 'the sign-object' of the media (*CPS*), the structural components of its system and the social relationships that it makes (im)possible. Additionally, because media are not involved in communication, the typical concern, whether they provide a more or less accurate portrayal of world events, is no longer operative. In fact, media implode the very distinction between an immediate real and its mediated reproduction, an occurrence that Baudrillard marks with the word 'simulation' (*SS*). Baudrillard, therefore, advances a radical interpretation of McLuhan's most famous statement about media:

there is not only the implosion of the message in the medium; in the same movement there is the implosion of the medium itself in the real, *the implosion of the
medium and the real* in a sort of nebulous hyperreality where even the definition
and the distinct action of the medium are no longer distinguishable. (*SSM*, 103)

This implosion has at least two important consequences. On the one hand,
it renders media increasingly difficult to identify, distinguish and define.
It is, as McLuhan famously once quipped, like trying to describe water to
a fish. Baudrillard identifies and confronts this particular problem in the
first sentence of 'Requiem for the Media', the often-quoted and deliberately provocative 'there is no theory of the media' (*CPS*, 164). Media,
then, are characterised by a fundamental self-effacement and disappearance. This disappearance, however, is not the result of transparency – the
assumption that media comprise virtually noiseless channels for com-
municating information about the world. Media disappear because they
are functionally indistinguishable and opaque. On the other hand, this
implosion also means that 'the real is abolished' (*SSM*, 101). 'I have',
Baudrillard writes, 'already said that, as I see it, to bring a real world into
being is in itself to produce that world, and the real has only ever been a
form of simulation. We may, admittedly, cause a reality-effect, a truth-
effect or an objectivity-effect to exist, but, in itself, the real does not exist'
(*PW*, 39). This not only destabilises the traditional understanding of
media content as derived reproductions and representations of a prior real
event but also leads Baudrillard to conclude that 'real events' do not take
place as such but are themselves fabrications of an absolutely self-involved
media system (*IE*, *SC*, *GW*).

All these aspects appear in stark contrast to the optimism that is so
often associated with media in the later part of the twentieth century.
And Baudrillard directly and unapologetically opposes its 'two major
tonalities': McLuhan's technological optimism, where media inaugurate
a general planetary communication culminating in the global village; and
Hans Magnus Enzensberger's ideological optimism, whereby media open
up new democratic possibilities for mass participation and critical resistance (*SSM*). Although Baudrillard shares important affinities with both
thinkers, his conceptualisation of media is, by comparison, 'pessimistic'.
But this pessimism, despite the opinion of critics, is not one of defeat,
nostalgia or resignation. It is a critical pessimism, one that is crucial for
analysing and contesting current modes of thinking.

Pessimism is not Baudrillard's final word, however, and beginning
in the late 1970s he reformulates the 'absence of response' as a critical
'counter-strategy' (*SSM*, 106). 'About the media', Baudrillard concludes
that 'you can sustain two opposing hypotheses: they are the strategy

of power, which finds in them the means of mystifying the masses and imposing its own truth. Or else they are the strategic territory of the ruse of the masses, who exercise in them their concrete power of the refusal of truth, of the denial of reality' (Baudrillard, 1985: 587). For Baudrillard, this opposition is not something that can or even should be resolved. 'No one can control this process: the media are the vehicle for the simulation which belongs to the system and for the simulation which destroys the system' (Baudrillard, 1985: 587). Consequently the two hypotheses behave according to the 'circular logic of the Möbius strip' where there is no resolution just a 'logical *exacerbation*' (*SSM*, 106) and 'speculation to the death' (*SED*, 5).

Passwords

Communication + Non-communication
Gift
Gulf War
Hyper-reality
Symbolic exchange

METAPHYSICS

Matthias Benzer

Metaphysics is commonly understood as the philosophical discipline that inquires into the fundamental truth or absolute principles (transcendence) which govern the objective reality apprehended by subjects (immanence). Exemplary metaphysical concerns include the essence of the world and the meaning of being. The statements of metaphysics are based on theoretical speculation and are not open to empirical testing. Positivist philosophy and much scientific thought dismiss metaphysics as meaningless. Baudrillard's self-description – 'Metaphysician? Perhaps' (*BL*, 43) – echoes the complexity of his relationship with this discipline.

Baudrillard often uses the term 'metaphysics' pejoratively to denounce the '*metaphysics of realism*' (*CS*, 150) buttressing all simulations of reality. For example, he castigates the 'metaphysics of the code' which allegedly underpins biology's conception of a genetically determined life. This conception, Baudrillard holds, does not simply reflect empirical facts. It hinges on speculation: on the 'phantasm' of a referable nature specifically, and on the formalisation of the world as a fixed reality more generally (*SED*). From this perspective, genetics inadvertently grants DNA the status of a 'molecular transcendence' and ennobles the genetic code as the absolute principle regulating existence (*UD*).

In other writings, Baudrillard discloses a more delicate connection between his thinking and metaphysics. He even seems to advance metaphysical hypotheses himself, notably when he speaks of the world's 'absolute illusion' (*PC*, 61) and the 'principle of Evil' (*FS*, 220). Yet these hypotheses intend neither a fundamental truth nor an objective reality. Hypermodernity, which exposes everything to transparency, no longer knows any transcendence secretly governing reality (*EC*) or indeed any reality that could be represented (*LP*). Instead, Baudrillard experiments with metaphysical speculation to trace the logic of reality's disappearance and the emergence of extreme phenomena destabilising its system.

According to Baudrillard, it is the hypermodern system's excess – not its lack – of reality and sophistication that conditions the end of reality and the appearance of catastrophic phenomena (*VI*). This is the problem of 'fatality' (*FS*, *PW*). Since the universal extension of reality already prepares its collapse, since the same 'logic that informs' the 'system's expansion' ultimately 'proceeds to devastate it' (*TE*, 40), the breakdown of the reality order is inevitable. Metaphysical hypotheses of the world's fundamental resistance to reality (illusion) and recalcitrance to reconciliation (evil) allow Baudrillard to think the impossibility of maintaining a perfect reality system purified from negativity. However, the disappearance of reality and the fracturing of the system are necessitated by the expansion of the reality order itself: 'it is from the inside, by overreaching themselves, that systems . . . fall into ruins' (*IEx*, 6). Consequently, even though 'a somewhat metaphysical . . . curiosity' (*BL*, 133) is conducive to capturing the unavoidability of reality's collapse and the inevitability of extreme phenomena, it is 'a question of a metaphysic come from a redoubling' (*BL*, 53) of hypermodernity's own immanent logic.

In short, Baudrillard plays on metaphysics without renouncing his distance from it. 'You can only know that things . . . are not real' (*AA*, 49) because the extension of the reality order necessarily undermines its own universality. But this is not the same as deciding that the world obeys fundamental principles, which, irreconcilable with reality's system, inevitably divert things from reality. 'You can't know' illusion (*AA*, 49) any more than whether evil is 'original or not' (*F*, 38).

Speculations which track the internal logic of the self-defeating reality system while simultaneously alluding to transcendental principles combine the 'empirical refutation' of the system with 'pure fiction' (*IEx*, 150). Yet given the dissolution of truth and reality, the theory of hypermodernity is free to radicalise its hypotheses, even render them 'a little metaphysical' (*F*, 74). To the vanishing of objective reality into 'integral reality' corresponds an 'Integral Metaphysics' linked to 'pataphysics', the 'science of imaginary solutions' (*LP*, 45). This radicalisation, Baudrillard emphasises, enables theory to move beyond conveying hypermodernity's immanent dilemma, towards accelerating the logic of the system of the real, pushing its catastrophic condition to extremes and precipitating its downfall (*EC*, *BL*, *IEx*).

For Baudrillard, 'speaking evil' and 'illusion' is 'criminal' (*P*, 116). Hypotheses which express the impossibility of a perfect reality system, anticipate its ruin and, in the same movement, transgress its imperative to adhere to the truth and real referents expedite the 'radical disillusioning of the real' (*PC*, 104). Here Baudrillard's metaphysical allusions reveal their strategic impetus. They turn thought itself into an extreme phenomenon and make it a participant in his theoretical challenge to the reality order.

Passwords

Evil
Excess
Fatal
Illusion
Integral reality
Pataphysics

METASTASIS – see 'clones + cloning', 'double', 'fatal', 'obscene', 'pataphysics', 'simulation', 'singularity' and 'transsexuality'.

MIRROR

David B. Clarke

Many of Baudrillard's concepts appear in the recurrent motif of the mirror. The mirror seems to capture perfectly a world forged in the image of the reality principle: a world dedicated to the eradication of *deceptive* appearances in the name of dependable reality. For mirrors are 'condemned to the servile fate of resemblance' (*PC*, 149), to slavishly giving back a *faithful* reflection of reality. They yoke appearances to the burden of re-presentation, bearing witness 'to the world with a . . . touching fidelity' (*ED*, 14). They are 'the watchdogs of appearance' (*S*, 105). The mirror accords to the principle of production in the original sense of that term, which 'is not . . . that of material manufacture; rather, it means to render visible, to cause to . . . appear: *pro-ducere*' (*FF*, 37). Invoking the 1926 film, *The Student of Prague*, however, Baudrillard considers what happens when the image escapes its model, when the representation is detached from the original.

The film concerns a pact with the Devil, the hapless party to which, Balduin, witnesses the Devil peeling his 'image from the mirror as though it were an etching' (*CS*, 187). His image is subsequently made flesh and proceeds to stalk Balduin, with ultimately fatal consequences.

As the good image it is, it remains attached to its model; but, as the bad image it has become, it now accompanies him not only when he chances to pass by mirrors, but in life itself, wherever he goes. (*CS*, 187)

Like all doppelgängers, 'From having been an assurance of immortality, it becomes the uncanny harbinger of death' (Freud, *SE XVII*: 235). In the film's denouement, a violent confrontation sees Balduin fire a pistol-shot at his double in front of the very mirror from which his image became detached.

Naturally, the mirror is smashed and the double, become again the phantasm it once was, vanishes into thin air. But . . . it is *he* who is dying . . . In his death throes . . . he grasps at one of the fragments of the mirror scattered about the floor and realizes that *he can see himself again*. (*CS*, 188)

Insofar as it is governed by the logic of commodity exchange – the Faustian bargain earns Balduin a fabulous sum of gold – '*The Student of Prague* is a remarkable illustration of the processes of alienation' (*CS*, 190). It drama-tises the fact that 'There is a part of us which gets away from us in this process, but we do not get away from it' (*CS*, 189). Such is the *méconnais-sance* of the subject – for the appearance of the image in the mirror does not leave being intact. It is in the mirror of production that 'the human species comes to consciousness [*la prise de conscience*] *in the imaginary*' (*MP*, 19). The imaginary, 'through which an objective world emerges and through which man recognizes himself objectively', is overcoded by 'this scheme of production, which is assigned to him as the ultimate dimension of value and meaning' (*MP*, 19). Such are the terms of 'the identity that man dons with his own eyes' when he gazes into the mirror aligning the 'discourse of production and the discourse of representation' (*MP*, 20).

By invoking *The Student of Prague*, Baudrillard contends that the clas-sical phase of alienation – likewise played out in Marx's *Capital* (1954) – is over, having lost itself in reversal: 'there is no longer any soul, no shadow, no double, and no image in the specular sense. There is no longer any contradiction within being, or any problematic of being and appearance' (*CS*, 191). Modernity's vain attempt to abolish appearances in the name of reality succumbs to that 'fatal reversibility' to which all such efforts fall prey: 'the more they go towards universality, towards their total limits, there is a kind of reversal which they themselves produce, and which destroys their own objective' (*BL*, 91). This short-circuits the distinction between being and appearance, real and imaginary, culminating in their ex-termination: their abolition as terms. It 'definitively shatter[s] the specularity of the sign' (*EC*, 58).

Despite the realism of signs and images, despite our naive confidence in their ability to conform to the real, their destiny lies elsewhere. Unbeholden to the reality principle, the sign regales in its clandestine capacity 'to oppose another scene to the real one, to pass to the other side of the mirror' (*AA*, 12). It is 'precisely when it appears most truthful, most faithful and most in conformity to reality that the image is most diabolical' (*ED*, 13).

One should distrust the humility of mirrors. The humble servants of appearances, they can reflect only the objects that face them, without being able to conceal themselves . . . But their faithfulness is specious, for they are waiting for someone to catch himself in their reflection. One does not easily forget their sidelong gaze. They recognize you, and when they surprise you when you least expect it, your time has come. (*S*, 105)

Such is the strategy of seduction – from '*se-ducere*: to take aside, to divert from one's path' (*S*, 22). "'*I'll be your mirror*" does not signify "I'll be your reflection" but "I'll be your deception"' (*S*, 69). Increasingly, however, the image 'can no longer transcend reality, transfigure it, nor dream it, because it has become its own virtual reality' (*AA*, 12). In its mediatised, high-definition resolution, the image comes too close to reality, effecting its disappearance qua image: 'In this space, where everything is meant to be seen . . . we realise that there is nothing left to see. It becomes a mirror of flatness, of nothingness, that reflects the disappearance of the other' (Baudrillard, 2003: 13). The implosion of the real and the imaginary ensures the disillusion of the image: 'the extermination of the real by its double' (*AA*, 9). Yet, although the power of the image wanes where 'images have passed over into things' (*AA*, 12), the image's power to challenge the world to exist, to connect with the radical illusion of the world, is not so easily vanquished: '*Objects in this mirror may be closer than they appear!*' (*A*, 1) – and they are poised to take their revenge.

Passwords

Illusion
Imaginary
Modernity
Production
Reversibility
Seduction

MODEL

Gary Genosko

Baudrillard's thinking about models had two distinct phases. The first belonged to the period of *The System of Objects* (1996a [1968]) in which he worked through the difference between models and series; the second emerged in his critical writing on communication theory in *For a Critique of the Political Economy of the Sign* (1981 [1972]).

Baudrillard introduced the models/series distinction to characterise the modern object of industrial production. Pre-industrial artisanal production of period furniture generated models whose status was imbued with the transcendent social reality of those who owned them. Class separated models from series that did not yet properly exist. With serial production, models lose their exalted status and social specificity and enter into the everyday universe of accessible (through credit) functional objects. Models are diffused through series, and series internalise models and cling to them. Some objects apparently have no models – like small household appliances – while others like certain dresses and automobiles manage to retain luxury and exclusivity.

The more specific an object's function, the less likely the models/series distinction will apply. The more personalised (accessorised) an object is, by selecting cultural markers of distinction like colour or detailing, the more serial objects paradoxically claim something of the status of models. Modelisation proves to be only a variant of serialisation as marginal differences support personalisation: 'every object is a model, yet at the same time there are no more models' (*SO*, 142). Nonetheless, cultural consumption moves from series to models as the latter are conductive ideas of absolute difference ('originals'). The model's singularity is signified by the user's strategies of personalisation by means of serialisations in a system-bound, internal transcendence.

One of the key markers of serial objects, claimed Baudrillard, is their shoddiness, a result of inessential qualities, and they are found in cluttered interiors, while models allegedly last longer, are nuanced and sit well; similarly, series are mainly pastiche and models have an open-ended syntax. In our world of objects, regression in time unites models and antiques, whereas serial objects belong to the flea market and are hard to date. Ultimately, series will not rejoin models for 'the only progression possible here is up the ladder of objects, but this is a ladder that leads nowhere' (*SO*, 154).

Mass media 'fabricate non-communication' (*CPS*, 169). This modelling process precludes a genuine space of reciprocal exchange governed by mutual, personal responsibility. Baudrillard rejects outright transmission models of communication that make genuine exchange impossible; thus, the type of reciprocal communication Baudrillard has in mind is ruled out in the mass media. Mediatic non-communication is unilateral, excludes response and monopolises speech, reserving a controlled space for feedback. Restoration of the symbolic responses is still possible, yet media without response and consumption that takes without giving are hard to break. Social isolation, indifference and pseudo-competition are persistent barriers.

The dreams of May 1968 and the Yippies in the US have operated under a 'strategic illusion'. Media spread news of the actions of student revolutionaries, but this is not subversive:

By broadcasting the events in the *abstract universality* of public opinion, they imposed a sudden and inordinate development on the movement of events; and through this forced and anticipated extension, they deprived the original movement of its own rhythm and of its meaning. In a word: they short-circuited it. (*CPS*, 173)

Baudrillard favoured artisanal production, graffiti, homemade signage, to-and-fro banter and discussion, new modes of collective activity and expression: symbolic reciprocity destroys media (as intermediary, as technical structure, as social form).

Baudrillard's truncated version of Roman Jakobson's (1960) poetic model of communication is:

| TRANSMITTER | – | MESSAGE | – | RECEIVER |
| (ENCODER) | – | MESSAGE | – | (DECODER) |

Baudrillard telescoped Jakobson's concepts into a fatal formula: the 'vectorization' of a communication process into a single message issued unidirectionally from either encoder to decoder or decoder to encoder.

Thus communication claims objectivity and scientificity yet is built on 'ideological categories that express a certain type of social relation, namely, . . . one speaks and the other doesn't . . . one has the choice of the code . . . the other only liberty to acquiesce or abstain' (*CPS*, 178–9). Much of this analysis exposed the ideological imbalances lurking in what appeared to be structural correspondences. The kind of communication that Jakobson's model suggests is presented by Baudrillard in terms of a mutually exclusive polarity of encoder and decoder artificially held apart and simulacrally reunited by an 'inter-medium' of the coded message: The social relation in question excludes reciprocity. The code/message terrorises communication by positioning the encoder and decoder in an 'abstract separateness', while privileging the sender (strategic value). Jakobson's phatic function (contact that checks whether the channel is working) in his model of communication, for instance, is evidence for Baudrillard of the distance between the poles and an alibi for the communication that the model promises but actually simulates. Baudrillard claims that it is the code that speaks since it dictates the unidirectional passage of information and guarantees the legibility, univocality (or multivocality, as it hardly matters for Baudrillard who dismisses ambiguity and polysemy) and 'autonomous value' of the message, conceived as information.

Generally, the term model helped Baudrillard pose and explore the problem of simulation as belonging to an order beyond the truth or falsehood of representation and characterised by unidentifiable determinations, unlocatable distinctions, incessant circulation, undecidable and profligate interpretability. Disneyland is a model of all the orders of simulation (*SS*), yet simulation itself is defined as the precession of models because 'models come first' (*SS*, 16) – like language in relation to speech and codes in relation to messages – and they are the sites from which all facts and interpretations are derived. Models have generative force, just as the interdependency of signifiers produce meaning effects (signifieds), or needs are effects of the system of objects in a society of consumption. Precession is Baudrillard's keyword for the confusion between real and model, watcher and watched, active and passive, in which 'it becomes impossible to locate one instance of the model' (*SS*, 29). Precession precipitates implosion and implosion entails indifferentiation. Such is the predicament of simulation and the sad destiny of communication.

Passwords

City
Communication + Non-communication
May 1968

Media
Object
Simulation

MODERNITY

Ryan Bishop

Although Baudrillard is often associated with postmodernity, his writings, just as postmodernity itself, have been forged in the intellectual, political and aesthetic fire of Modernity. Modernity remains operative within a postmodern world, but has undergone enough permutations, extensions and contractions as to make the 'post-' in postmodern useful for indicating both an intellectual and temporal relation to 'the modern'. A tricky and elusive term, Modernity denotes a few larger trends useful for considering Baudrillard's writing: these include the economic shifts from feudalism to mercantilism to capitalism, the emergence of the subject and the human as central political and historical tropes, the increasingly secular nature of society in the West, the shift in science from merely describing nature to turning it to human advantage (including the prominence of technology), the increase of urbanisation and industrial production, consumer culture, the emergence of different kinds of media, a glorification of innovation and progress, and wholesale changes in social stratification and political systems. Revolutions mark the historical epoch of Modernity, and revolutions of thought, representation, signs, images and objects mark the work of Baudrillard.

However, the boons of Modernity have always been mixed, and Modernity contains within itself the spirit of self-reflexivity and critique. In other words, any heralded revolution can be just as static and stultifying as that which it replaced: that the first act of revolution is to ensure the cessation of any further revolutionary ideas or possibilities. Modernity as the symbol of revolutionary spirit ironically seeks to impose its unitary vision on the world and make it a mirror of itself. 'Modernity is neither a sociological concept, nor a political concept, nor exactly a historical concept,' Baudrillard writes. 'It is a characteristic mode of a civilization, which opposes itself to tradition' (Baudrillard, 1987: 63). For Baudrillard, though, the idea of revolution and the posture of opposing tradition are worth celebrating but should never be confused with actual change or progress in social justice.

Lyotard (1986) has argued that an incredulity toward metanarratives constitutes postmodernity: that is a suspicion of the 'grand stories' that constitute the hermetic explanatory encapsulations of thought that characterise knowledge production in Modernity. Examples of metanarratives can be found in the works of Darwin, Marx, Freud and Einstein, in which all organisms, all of economics/history, all of the mind and all of the universe, respectively, are explained. If metanarratives are indicative of Modernity, then Modernity enters Baudrillard's writings through the work of those writers who had the most difficulty being contained and domesticated by metanaratives. In other words, Baudrillard accesses Modernity by the alternatives and excesses Modernity seeks to contain but ultimately cannot. These thinkers include Artaud, Nietzsche, Hölderlin, Jarry, Bataille, Mauss, Borges, Licthenberg, Ciroan and Heidegger among others. Nonetheless, Baudrillard is a Modernist thinker through and through, reading deeply from the major Modernist avant-garde traditions, so Modernity with the varied opportunities and crises it wrought formed the subtext and pretext of his writings.

His rhetorical mobilisation of binarisms and Manichean thinking, however, reveals an earlier and particular anti-modern aspect of his thought because it does away with dialectic and its attempts to ameliorate oppositional forces. Dialectic resolves oppositions in a singularity that becomes for Baudrillard the basis of what he calls 'integral reality' (*LP*), or the global triumph of the Real. Thus he writes about Modernity that the '*dialectic of rupture*' becomes instead '*the dynamic of amalgamation*' (Baudrillard, 1987: 70). Difference is absorbed, revolution domesticated. Modernity repeats Tradition, with both sporting capital letters befitting static proper nouns.

Baudrillard's own encyclopaedia entry on 'Modernity' helps us to understand his unique reading and critique of the conceptualisations of Modernity, but only in a limited fashion. The entry proves most useful when it explicitly connects the immaterial and material domains, to argue that the 'technical, scientific and political upheavals' (Baudrillard, 1987: 65) begun in the sixteenth century were translated into structural and symbolic changes within the social and noetic domains. That is, Modernity conceived of itself as Modern, and thus understood the ways in which this very conceptualisation could change relationships in the world, that the map could change the territory, or even replace it altogether. In so doing, Modernity paved the way for postmodernity and the third order of the simulacrum.

As an extended example of the epochal shift out of Modernity, we can look with some detail at Baudrillard's *The Ecstasy of Communication* (1988c [1987b]) and examine his analysis of the ways in which broadcast media have changed the status of the object, therefore reconstituting the subject–object relationship that characterises one of the major divisions of Modernity: the subject and the object. Baudrillard argues that the traditional subject–object relationship still existed in the 1970s, at the time of composition, but that it was rapidly disappearing, giving way to one predicated on the screen and the network. The traditional subject–object relationship inherited from at least the Enlightenment constitutes the object as a mirror for the subject, in which the subject comes to understand the self as a self similar to but different from others. The subject also realises that s/he functions as an object in a similar fashion for others in their consciousness as subjects. From this relationship follows a range of attributes for modern existence: similarity and difference, connection and alienation, exteriority and interiority, public and private. This relationship constitutes a 'common-sense' notion of the subject and becomes the basis for agency and action in the world.

The subject–object relationship plays itself out in what Baudrillard calls 'the scene', which is divided into the private scene (time for the self, the domestic sphere, the cultivation of interiority) and the public scene (engagement with object-others, the site of historical and political action). The scene is theatrical (or performed) as well as natural; that is 'the way things are', the way society is arranged, our existential condition. The theatricality of the scene allows us to understand, critically, the historical conditions of and the ideology operative in the construction of the natural.

Baudrillard argues that the subject–object opposition and the private–public opposition began to disappear in the early 1970s under the onslaught of numerous telecommunications and broadcast technologies, the most influential and pernicious of which being television. The mirror, he argues, has yielded to the screen and the network enacted in a nonspace called 'the obscene'. The scene, too, is disappearing and is being replaced by the obscene, a term he uses in an unusual manner while also maintaining elements of its common usage in that the obscene is the space where all difference is obliterated and everything is viewable.

These transitions from subject–object to screen–network and from scene to obscene are indicative of others: from the second stages of simulation to the third, from the virtual to the Real, knowledge to information, secrecy to visibility, violence to terror, material to immaterial, and so on. Each also indicates a shift from Modernity to postmodernity for Baudrillard. However, he does not argue that the shift is complete or without traces of the previous stage in the present. Modernity remains omnipresent though perhaps occluded by its most recent avatar, postmodernity.

Passwords

Integral reality
Manichaeism

Object
Obscene
Postmodernism/Postmodernity
Real
Simulacra + Simulacrum
Simulation

MUSIC

Richard G. Smith

The drive towards the technical perfection of music, the 'stereo effect' of quadrophonics, high fidelity and hyperstereo, has drawn comment from Baudrillard on a number of occasions (*S, IE, CM, F, LP*). In *Seduction* (1990a [1979]) he describes the invention of quadraphonic musical reproduction, with its addition of a fourth dimension to give perfect sound reproduction, as obscene: 'The technical delirium of the perfect restitution of music (Bach, Monteverdi, Mozart!) *that has never existed*, that no one has ever heard, and that was not meant to be heard like this' (*S*, 30). It is not that Baudrillard laments the loss of 'authentic' or 'real' music, but rather that he considers 'perfect music' as charmless, fascinating but not seductive:

At the heart of hi-fi, music threatens to disappear. At the heart of experimentation, the object of science threatens to disappear. At the heart of pornography, sexuality threatens to disappear. Everywhere we find the same stereophonic effect, the same effect of absolute proximity to the real, the same effect of simulation. (*IE*, 6)

Music approaches its vanishing point as its production becomes a realm of activity that is governed by a drive for flawless technical execution: 'a false destiny for music' (*CM*, 83). Baudrillard describes his experience of quadraphonic rooms, on a visit to Japan in the 1970s, as that of the simulation of a total environment where one has the experience of 'a sort of musical perfect crime' (*F*, 66). In other words, the perfection of the reproduction (also evident in CDs and the 'composing' of music on computers), the addition of new dimensions ('triphony, then quadriphony, then multiphony' (*F*, 66)), is predicated upon the elimination of a 'specifically musical illusion' (*F*, 66), such as that which is afforded by the 'live experience' of the concert hall or opera house where music is heard at a certain distance. More recently, Baudrillard has equated the perfect reproduction of music with 'the Virtual' ('the more perfect the reproduction, the more it becomes virtual' (*F*, 66)) and 'integral reality' ('integral music' (*LP*, 27)) implying that music has merged into its own model: 'The sounds of such music are no longer the play of a form, but the actualization of a programme. It is a music reduced to a pure wavelength, the final reception of which, the tangible effect on the listener, is exactly programmed too, as in a closed circuit' (*LP*, 28).

The news that vinyl records are now back in demand would perhaps meet with Baudrillard's approval. The once seemingly extinct format, whose heyday was in the 1960s and 1970s, is once again the height of 'music cool' because of – among other things – the 'imperfection' of its audio reproduction: the noise and static that makes it more 'musical'. Indeed, the song entitled *Jean Baudrillard* by the English band Maxïmo Park is available on 7-inch white vinyl; perhaps this is so that we can enjoy its imperfection, its distance from the vanishing point, its musicality.

Passwords

Disappearance
Integral reality
Model
Obscene
Perfect crime
Simulation
Virtual

NATURE + ANIMALS

Laurence Simmons

Baudrillard's views on nature (and by consequence the animals that inhabit it) are shaped by his account of the precession of simulacra, the practice of 'substituting the signs of the real for the real' (*SS*, 2). Traditionally that which is constructed by organic processes without the help of human devices is considered to be natural as opposed to that which is constructed by humans, which is a simulation or simulacrum. But for Baudrillard, 'nature' *is* a simulacrum: it exists because it is completely artificial. Both in the sense of a 'reality' shaped over many thousands of years by human activity, and as an empty signifier whose referent is constituted by its relationship to other free-floating signs. There is no 'original' nature, it is not an 'other' to culture, and, as Baudrillard declares elsewhere, 'You cannot trust nature' (*PC*, 119). So our ecological awareness that nature is good is just that, an illusion. Nature is malevolent and contains Evil (*IE*). Nature may take its revenge: cows with BSE take their retribution for 'being turned into butcher's meat' (*SC*, 172). Indeed, Baudrillard believes that the ecology movement fundamentally misunderstands our relation to nature.

Furthermore, we have lost touch with any sense of the natural world. Even natural spaces (national parks and wilderness regions) are now understood as 'protected', which is to say that they are defined in contradistinction to an urban 'reality', often with signs to point out just how 'real' they are. Baudrillard would argue this constructed and thoroughly mediated artifice nevertheless constitutes our experience of nature, and that experience is no less 'authentic' in and of itself. We can elaborate this concept of nature as simulacrum using four examples from Baudrillard.

In an early attack on classical Marxism (*MP*) Baudrillard argued that the model of production inherited and enforced by Enlightenment thought depends on the belief in a constant Nature (with a capital N), which, in turn, imposes unceasing restraints. Marx hoped to overcome the restraints by 'denaturalising' (understanding to be socially determined and mutable) certain ideological concepts and thereby unchaining the productive power of labour. But, suggests Baudrillard, Marx's desire for a totalising model, which would protect use value from critique, simply reinvoked Nature and made Marx complicit with the very natural order he wished to deconstruct. Secondly, in *For a Critique of the Political Economy of the Sign* (1981 [1972]) Baudrillard asserts the displacement of nature by 'environment' which belongs to the sphere of design. As a real referent nature is dead and is survived by the environment: a designed semio–aesthetic form for the circulation of signifiers disconnected from their referents. 'Man no longer even confronts his environment: he himself is virtually part of the environment to be protected' (*CPS*, 203). Here it is clear that nature ceased to exist from the moment of its naming with the contradictory move that designates a cultural idea (nature) as natural. Thirdly, for Baudrillard the traveller, who finds himself in the midst of 'natural' landscapes, among the most seductive parts of America are its natural deserts. Indeed, he asserts, America 'is' the desert (*A*). But his references to the deserts of the American west are, he notes wryly, always mediated by cinematic experiences. For Baudrillard, the desert assumes the status of a primal scene in

America and even the large cities have, he says, the desert at their hearts and have become places of the 'extermination of man' (*BL*, 162). Lastly, in his discussion of cloning (*SS*) Baudrillard understands the equivalence of cloned animals that share exactly the same genes as a biological expression of the idea of the loss of the original, the simulacrum. When Dolly the cloned sheep shares the exact same genetic code with another sheep, it is impossible to say that one is real and one a copy, or even that one was 'created' after the other. 'The clones are already there; the virtual beings are already there. We are all replicants!' (*SC*, 199).

Interestingly, Baudrillard's short discussion of the animal in *Simulacra and Simulation* (1994a [1981]) prefigures some of the concerns expressed by Jacques Derrida and Giorgio Agamben in the early twenty-first century. Baudrillard notes the parallels between the laboratory experimentation and industrial harvesting of animals and 'men on an assembly line' or incarcerated in prisons and concentration camps (*SS*, 131). 'All the aspects of the modern treatment of animals retrace the vicissitudes of the manipulation of humans' (*SS*, 130). The fundamental fact about animals, the fact that finally accounts for our boundless cruelty towards them, is the fact that they do not speak. Through the disappearance and speechlessness of the animal in the context of consumer capitalism, animals become our beasts of burden, demand, consumption and somatisation (*SS*). Baudrillard's crucial insight is that the silence of animals dooms them paradoxically to a vociferous fate; since they do not/will not speak they are ceaselessly spoken (for), sentimentalised, anthropomorphised, endlessly troped and cast into a variety of discursive registers. But Baudrillard also cautions that our 'sentimentality toward animals is a sure sign of the disdain in which we hold them' (*SS*, 134).

Passwords

America
Clones + Cloning
Disappearance
Evil
Production
Simulacra + Simulacrum

NIETZSCHE, FRIEDRICH (1844–1900) – see 'destiny', 'evil', 'fatal', 'illusion', 'modernity', 'nihilism', 'perfect crime', 'real', 'simulation' and 'value + structural law of value'.

NIHILISM

Rex Butler

Nietzsche is one of Baudrillard's defining influences. He is one of the few thinkers whose presumptions are not turned against them – as Baudrillard was to do with Marx in *The Mirror of Production* (1975 [1973]) and Saussure in *Symbolic Exchange and Death* (1993a [1976]). Indeed, as Baudrillard admits in interviews, Nietzsche barely features in his work because he is so deeply embedded in it. He is in a sense the absence around which Baudrillard's work is built. And Nietzsche brings with him the problem of nihilism. Generalising broadly, we might say that nihilism takes either one of two forms in Nietzsche. The first is when the world is devalued in the name of some supposedly higher, transcendent value, as in Platonism or Christianity. Life is judged as wanting in relation to something outside of it, as though it has meaning or value only because of some quality that is always missing. The second form of nihilism is when these higher values are themselves devalued, as in the project of critique of the Enlightenment. Here there is no meaning or value in life, as all values fall prey to doubt and scepticism. And, for Nietzsche, the great test of any philosophy is how it deals with these two pitfalls, which are not definitively to be overcome but are inherent to thought. Nietzsche's well-known solution was his doctrine of the Eternal Return, which was at once to accept things as they are, insofar as they will return forever, and a principle of selection, in that not all things will come back.

Baudrillard inherits – like every other French intellectual of his generation – this Nietzschean problematic. His most extensive commentary on the subject is the essay 'On Nihilism', which was published as part of the collection *Simulacra and Simulation* (1994a [1981]). In 'On Nihilism', Baudrillard in slightly different terms follows Nietzsche's original argument in discerning two historically distinctive forms of nihilism: the first that of Romanticism, which corresponds to the 'destruction of the order of appearances' (*SS*, 159); and the second that of surrealism, dada, the absurd and the political, which corresponds to the 'destruction of the order of meaning' (*SS*, 160). But Baudrillard then goes on to argue that we have passed beyond the terms of Nietzsche's analysis, in that we are now in a nihilism of 'transparency' (*SS*, 160). Here it is not a matter of the violent destruction of appearances or meaning, but of their 'neutralisation' (*SS*, 160), which takes place as a slow and gradual 'disappearance' (*SS*, 160). What Baudrillard can be understood to mean by this is that it is no longer a matter either of devaluing the world by pursuing higher values or devaluing these values by subjecting them to the evidence of the world. Rather, if we can put it this way, the auto-referentiality of our contemporary systems of simulation is the effect of them posing their own higher values. In our contemporary systems of simulation, that is, both the world and higher values coexist, which is to say both are equally devalued. In Baudrillard's exact formulation, ends or higher values are done away with not through critique or denegation but through a kind of 'hyperfinality' (*SS*, 161). It is for this reason that Baudrillard emphasises that it is no longer a matter of diagnosing the collapse of critical values and then beginning the process of revaluing them from there. Not only is self-criticism part of the system, but even the Nietzschean gesture of speaking of the collapse of critical values is already part of our systems of simulation. As Baudrillard writes: 'When God died, there was still Nietzsche to say so . . . [but today] (God is not dead, he has become hyperreal), there is no longer a theoretical or critical God to recognise his own' (*SS*, 159).

It is for this reason that Baudrillard is able to say that he is a 'nihilist' (*SS*, 160). Of course, in saying this, Baudrillard seems to be going against the whole Nietzschean problematic of somehow going beyond nihilism while nevertheless recognising it. Is Baudrillard, in claiming to be a nihilist in 'On Nihilism', rejecting or breaking with Nietzsche? Things are not quite so straightforward as they might at first appear. Later in his essay, Baudrillard introduces an ambiguity into nihilism, in a manner akin to Nietzsche's own distinction between its 'active' and 'passive' forms. After claiming to be a nihilist, he goes on to speak of a nihilism that carries, 'to the unbearable limit of hegemonic systems, this radical trait of derision and of violence' (*SS*, 163). What does Baudrillard mean by this, which resorts to the very language of violence and terrorism he has argued is no longer possible? Here again, there is a surprise: in the final words of his essay, Baudrillard conjures up the notion of 'appearance', which he previously said had been 'neutralised' by our systems of simulation. As he writes, in a translation that is undoubtedly awkward (although, in fact, the original French is not much clearer): 'But that on which [meaning] has imposed its ephemeral reign, what it hoped to liquidate in order to impose the reign of the Enlightenment, that is, appearances, they, are immortal, invulnerable to the nihilism of meaning or of non-meaning' (*SS*, 164). Perhaps what Baudrillard is trying to think here is that moment 'before' that nihilism in which meaning and non-meaning exchange themselves for each other, and in which the system is no longer able to be criticised because it already proposes values opposed to itself. He is attempting to capture a brief and fugitive 'appearance' that would be neither the world nor something beyond it but a split or division within the world, which means it can never be equal to itself and is never entirely able to be realised. It is a 'nihilism' that Baudrillard conjures up later in *The Perfect*

Crime (1996c [1995a]) when he asks: 'Why is there nothing rather than something?' (*PC*, 2), and in his most recent book (*WD*). Baudrillard is indeed a nihilist in the sense that he wants to think that 'nothing' with which the world began and – if cosmology is to be believed – to which it will one day return.

Passwords

Disappearance
Film + Cinema
Hyper-reality
Simulation

OBJECT

William Pawlett

The object is possibly the most important notion in Baudrillard's *oeuvre* (*RC*). He writes of 'an obsession with the object . . . the magic of the object' (*F*, 3). His *Passwords* (2003b [2000c]) begins with 'The Object': '[I] wanted to break with the problematic of the subject. The question of the object represented the alternative . . . and it has remained the horizon of my thinking' (*PW*, 3). Thinking the object links Baudrillard's early studies of consumer goods, his thought on the object in symbolic exchange, his theme of the revenge of the object and the object's seduction, and his later provocations concerning 'impossible exchange'.

Baudrillard's early work explored the system of objects that comprised the postwar consumer societies of Western Europe and North America. He emphasised the proliferation of consumer objects whose meaning or purpose extended far beyond their use value. As consumer objects demand the investment of time, money and desire, enabling consumers to 'personalise' their lifestyles by signifying distinctive status positions, the system of consumer objects operates on the symbolic as well as economic/ semiotic level, forming a system of moral constraint and obligation. The advertising industry presents new objects and gadgets as 'gifts' to the con- sumer, indebting them to the system by conferring a myriad of choices. The consumer system is likened to a 'festival' – a celebratory ritual of buying and selling where consumer objects become tokens of (simulatory) salvation and 'enforced happiness'.

During the early 1970s Baudrillard developed the contrast between semiotic or simulational orders of object-signs ('dead' objects) and the object within symbolic exchange ('living' objects). Drawing on the anthropology of Mauss (1966), Baudrillard refuses to reduce symbolically exchanged objects to the signification of social power or position. Where Marxist and structuralist thinkers understand gift exchange as a cultural process which obfuscates the underlying economic reality of power, Baudrillard explores spiritual and symbolic dimensions of symbolically exchanged objects (objects given, received and passed on cyclically (*SED*)). Such objects are ambivalent and volatile; they may fuse the sentiments of giver and receiver in ways neither can anticipate, explain or control, in ways which cannot be inferred from established belief systems. The object in symbolic exchange has 'a life of its own' (*PW*, 3); it is able to pass through the binary conceptual oppositions that, since the Renaissance, have structured 'reality'. Taking the life/death opposition as an example, the 'pact' forged between parties in the symbolic exchange of objects is not halted by (biological) death. Indeed the death of the giver tends to increase the symbolic potency of the given object, provoking a metamorphosis in, rather than the termination of, symbolic relations.

Baudrillard examines (*CPS*, *SED*) the object abstracted from the cycles of symbolic exchange; the object becomes residual and 'real', it becomes sign or signifier to be traded in accordance with the terms and values set by the code. This applies both to linguistic object-signs (words and concepts) and to material objects or things. The code assigns value to all object-signs in terms of 'sign exchange value', that is as signs of fashion or prestige, underwritten by the illusory opposition between sign exchange value and (fictive) use value. However, Baudrillard (*S*, *FS*) depicts the object as escaping, eluding and defying the code's logics of value. Objects proliferate 'indefinitely, increasing their potential, outbidding themselves in an ascension to the limit' (*FS*, 25), such that 'there is no longer a system of objects' (*EC*, 11). Indeed for Baudrillard a definitive limit or point of no return is crossed. Objects become 'ecstatic', viral and reversible without the assistance of the subject as agent of symbolic exchange: '*the object itself takes the initiative of reversibility, taking the initiative to seduce and lead astray*' (*EC*, 80). This is the revenge of the object, the object has a destiny beyond the code, beyond the meanings and definitions imposed on it by economics, politics or science: 'the destiny of signs is to be torn from their destination, deviated, displaced, diverted, recuperated, seduced' (*EC*, 80). Objects elude the regimes of control erected by subjects, becoming 'pure' or 'fatal'. Language itself becomes a fatal object; its materiality or literalness prevents or suddenly shatters the development of coded, referential meanings which dissolve in wit, poetry, slips of the tongue, nonsense and aphorism.

Baudrillard does not claim that the subject is dead, or that it has been eliminated from his analysis: 'When I speak of the object and its fatal strategies, I'm speaking also of people and their inhuman strategies' (*FS*, 222). The 'subject' for Baudrillard has had the banal illusion of identity, agency, *subjectivity* thrust upon it, and the object, he warns, should not be seen as 'supersubject' (*VI*, 79). Rather there is a duel or dual relation at work, a (hyper-)reality of subject positions using, buying and selling objects, and another game, register or symbolic dimension: 'above all the subject has *the passion to be object*, to become object' (*EC*, 93). The masses or 'mass object' (defined as 'us, you, everybody' (*SSM*, 65)) are Baudrillard's major example of the 'subject' of modern knowledge taking revenge, becoming refractory, impenetrable, 'crystalline' object. Unintelligible to sociological and political analysis, the masses disappear into silence, hyper-conformity or 'voluntary servitude', the better to obscure their fundamental 'absence' from the system of control.

With Baudrillard's putative 'fourth order', that of virtuality and integral reality, there are further transformations in his theorisation of the object. Virtuality is not an order of simulacra as such, but the 'final solution' to the problem of the simulacra. Baudrillard writes, 'initially, the real object becomes sign: this is the stage of simulation. But in a subsequent stage the sign becomes an object again, but not now a real object: an object much further removed from the real than the sign itself . . . a fetish . . . a double abstraction' (*IEx*, 129). With 'radical fetishism' reality becomes total; everything is 'real' and visible – dreams, fantasies, desires, illusions – such that 'reality' even as myth loses its meaning and distinctiveness. This is the 'becoming-object of the sign' (*LP*, 71), reality becomes integral, crushingly banal, 'nondescript' and 'unexchangeable': the worthless self-evidence of 'reality' TV, Internet pornography, real-time news footage of 'non-events'. Yet, Baudrillard insists, there is always the potential for a 'blow-back' or revenge of symbolic forms from within the virtual sphere; these gravitate around 'singular objects' and take place through catastrophic chain reactions, major examples being Chernobyl, the Berlin Wall and the twin towers of the World Trade Center.

Passwords

Ambivalence
Code
Consumption + Affluent society
Gift

Impossible exchange
Integral reality
Masses
Seduction
Symbolic exchange
Virtual

OBSCENE

Paul A. Taylor

'I think like a girl takes off her dress. At the extreme, thought is impudence, obscenity even' (Bataille, in Surya, 1987: 8). The totalitarian semiotic order Baudrillard's theory so resolutely opposes creates a qualitatively different form of obscenity to Bataille's simile. Rather than thought occurring like a girl provocatively disrobing it becomes more akin to the gyrations of a lap dancer seeking a tip. The obscene results from media society's insatiable need to create as much explicit content as possible and its corresponding inability to deal with the seductive and the ambiguous. Pornography is thus reinterpreted by Baudrillard as a trope for a wider social condition and purpose: 'This is sex as it exists in pornography, but more generally, this is the enterprise of our entire culture, whose natural condition is obscene: a culture of monstration, of demonstration, of productive monstrosity' (*S*, 35).

The obscene denotes much more than a simple moralistic condemnation. The prefix *ob* refers to the idea of hindering or being against. The ob-scene therefore expresses the collapse of distance in our social experience and the deleterious effect this has on our ability to experience reality in a non-mediated state. The scene traditionally viewed upon a stage necessitates a gap between the viewer and the actor (for example, the theatre's proscenium arch), but now that distance has imploded and there is no longer the necessary separation from the scene or stage of action that allows us to witness or reflect upon events properly.

Paradoxically, we are now so close to the action we fail to see it: '*We no longer partake of the drama of alienation, but are in the ecstasy of communication. And this ecstasy is obscene. Obscene is that which eliminates the gaze, the image and every representation*' (*EC*, 22). Obscenity can thus be understood as a qualitative description of the lived in experience of the society of the spectacle. For Baudrillard, the mediascape's promotion of fascination represents a social sphere emptied out of the more enchanted and seductive properties present in a symbol-rich pre-mediated society. Obscene culture is an etiolated, pervasively commodified realm of signs rather than events.

In the essay 'Dust Breeding' (*CA*) Baudrillard discusses *Loft Story*, a French version of the *Big Brother* programme, and Catherine Millet, the author of a best-selling autobiographical account of a large number of compulsively anonymous sexual encounters – *The Sexual Life of Catherine M*. Both, he says, represent the simulation of real experience. Reality TV seeks to 'screen' society thereby manifesting the situationist notion of the spectacle as society's universal concept, while Millet's couplings reduce seduction to a mechanical act. Each example rests upon the privileging of the synthetic over the original, a tele-genetically modified culture becomes the corollary of bio-genetically orientated science. Notwithstanding the media's status as a purportedly key element of democratic society, the obscene serves to eliminate the meaningfully political and replaces it with a transpolitical culture:

The transpolitical is the transparency and obscenity of all structures in a destructured universe . . . in a dehistoricized universe . . . in a universe emptied of event, the transparency and obscenity of space in the promiscuity of networks, transparency and obscenity of the social in the masses, of the political in terror, of the body in obesity and genetic cloning . . . (*FS*, 45)

Meaning in a society of the obscene is decontextualised from its grounding in history and grounded symbolism, marks a 'passage from growth to excrescence, from finality to hypertely, from organic equilibria to cancerous metastases. This is the site of a catastrophe . . .' (*FS*, 46). In such a catastrophic culture, Millet becomes the literal embodiment of the culture industry's inability to grasp the paradox that the true nature of social reality is to be found in its shrouding, not in its blatant exposure.

'Think like a woman taking off her dress,' said Bataille. Yes, but the naiveté of all the Catherine Millets is to think that they are taking of their dress to get undressed, to be naked and therefore reach the naked truth, the truth of sex or of the world. (*CA*, 186)

The paradoxical truth of Baudrillard's notion of obscenity reduces the communicants of the new global media networks to the mythical fate of Tantalus – the more one seeks to reveal society in an excessively explicit and systematic fashion, the further away we push it.

Passwords

Music
Sex/Gender
Transpolitical

ORIENTALISM

Rex Butler

Like many of Baudrillard's key terms, 'otherness' [*altérité*] is divided in its meaning: it is both what is lost in today's society and what Baudrillard opposes to society. It is this that complicates tremendously any analysis of Baudrillard's 'Orientalism'. He can be accused of it, but also has a discourse about it. He is critical of it, but argues as well for it (or something like it). Thus it can be asked, even of such lengthy analyses as Almond's (2007), whether they truly grasp the ambiguity or even 'reversibility' of the 'other' in Baudrillard's work. That is, for all of Almond's acknowledgement that Islam plays the role of ironic, hyperconforming object in Baudrillard's text, Almond still condemns him for not allowing Arabs to speak; and, in terms of the Orientalist clichés in Baudrillard's text, Almond does not ask whether for Baudrillard Orientalism (at least of a certain kind) is necessarily a bad thing. It is, indeed, perhaps in its silencing that the 'other' exerts its revenge. And it is a silencing that would continue exactly through Almond's demand that it speak. It is these ambivalences that are the ultimate fate of all those who 'criticise' Baudrillard.

Baudrillard undoubtedly comes equipped with the typical cultural imaginary of his time and place. There exists, of course, a whole line of early-to-mid-century 'Orientalism' that was the result of French colonisation throughout northern Africa, Asia and the Pacific that Baudrillard inherits. Baudrillard at several points expresses his admiration for the French explorer and ethnographer Victor Segalen, who coined or at least popularised the term 'exotic', which Baudrillard adopts in his work (*TE*, 146–55). Baudrillard also follows figures like Bertolt Brecht and Roland Barthes in his appreciation of the artificiality of the Peking Opera, which he sees as creating an 'empty space' (*FS*, 214) between bodies that can never be crossed. And Baudrillard follows Alexandre Kojève too in privileging Japan as embodying a certain end to western history in its ability to move directly to the global without passing through the universal (*SC*). In all of these ways, Baudrillard is diagnosable as coming from a particular European-speaking position. His examples are precisely reflexive or projective and not the result of any real anthropological insight or research. And this is an accusation that Baudrillard's critics have not failed to make.

But what these critics fail to realise is that any analogies we might make between Baudrillard's examples and those of any other thinker remain only approximate. If both Kojève and Baudrillard appear to speak of Japan in similar terms, the comparison is not exact. Each thinker's system is distinctive; the role the same term plays within it is different. All of this is to say that Baudrillard's system of thought is not 'realist' and cannot entirely be explained socially or historically. The cultures and places Baudrillard refers to are also rhetorical or technical terms that take on meaning only within the context of Baudrillard's own work, operate as much as shorthand for extended chains of argument as for any cultural or geographical reality. Of course, in this sense, Baudrillard's arguments are still 'Orientalist' in Edward Said's (1979) definition of an expression that does not simply misrepresent some Oriental essence but is intended for western ends. But, if we can say this, Baudrillard puts his Orientalism to absolutely non-western purposes. What Baudrillard admires about such cultures as the Japanese and Islamic is that they will '*never* become Western' (*TE*, 140). Or they are 'other' and not merely 'different' from the West, not part of that dialectical trick by which Europe extends its self by positing its alternative (*TE*). There is thus inaugurated the complex game in which Orientalist terms are used to speak about the unassimilability of the other. It is a strategy Baudrillard sums up by means of a typically caustic double negative: '[The envy and resentment of the West by non-Western countries] would lead me to detest the Southern – and the Islamic – peoples for their feeble-mindedness, their suicidal rhetorics, if I did not already detest even more the little hardline Whites, who are so sure they will always have the upper hand' (*CM*, 71).

Passwords

Geopolitics
Globalisation
Other + Otherness
Reversibility
Universality

OTHER + OTHERNESS

Ashley Woodward

The Other and otherness are themes which derive in large part from the philosophy of Hegel, which was popularised in France by Alexandre Kojève's 1933–9 lectures, and from phenomenology, introduced into France by Emmanuel Levinas, Jean-Paul Sartre and others. These themes subsequently became well-established in French thought. Like many of his contemporaries, Baudrillard inherited these themes from earlier

German and French intellectual traditions and developed them in his own unique way.

Baudrillard's concern with otherness is double. On the one hand, he is concerned with the erasure of otherness and its subordination to the Same in contemporary western thought and culture: 'Our society is entirely dedicated to neutralising otherness, to destroying the other as a natural point of reference in a vast flood of aseptic communication and interaction, of illusory exchange and contact' (*TE*, 121). On the other hand, he is concerned to demonstrate the ultimate intractability of otherness: despite the threat to it from this apparent erasure, Baudrillard insists that otherness cannot be exterminated and will have its revenge. Thus otherness is another theme through which Baudrillard develops the Möbian 'double spiral' of his thought. One side of this spiral enacts a radical critique of Enlightenment rationalism and liberal humanism by charting the destruction of otherness. The other side of the spiral defends a radical form of otherness which is posited as a fundamental dynamic of the world.

Otherness is threatened by the attempt to understand, represent and model all that which is designated Other and in this sense reduce it to the Same through universal comprehension. The erasure of otherness thus accompanies the same process which leads to simulation, hyper-reality and integral reality: '*With the Virtual, we enter not only upon the era of the liquidation of the Real and the Referential, but that of the extermination of the Other*' (*PC*, 109). Moreover, otherness is not just threatened by an overt logic of the Same, it is also threatened in a more subtle way by a logic of difference, which on face value appears to recognise and value otherness. For Baudrillard otherness is not difference; difference is in fact what destroys otherness. Difference is the simulation of otherness, produced in our (post)modern culture because there is so little genuine otherness left.

According to Baudrillard, 'differences mean regulated exchange' (*TE*, 128). With difference, exchange is regulated by a principle of equivalence through which differences and their values can be compared. Otherness reduced to difference is exchangeable, substitutable, negotiable, comprehensible, tolerable, reconcilable and useful. Baudrillard contrasts difference with radical otherness, which is irreducibly singular, irrecuperable, irreconcilable, incomprehensible, unexchangeable, incomparable and intolerable. In Baudrillard's characterisation of contemporary culture as a vast orgy in which everything is exchangeable for everything else (*TE*), otherness is being erased by virtue of this very exchangeability. Communication, which saturates our media culture, is also destructive of otherness, insofar as it establishes a medium of exchange between the poles of communication. Furthermore, Baudrillard criticises those social movements which attempt to recognise and legitimise differences – such as women's liberation, racial tolerance, respect for cultural difference and so on – as destructive of radical otherness. The darker side of these movements is revealed in the fact that, according to Baudrillard, racism functions according to the same logic as liberal tolerance: the Other only appears as a threat when they seem similar to us, and it is only then that we seek to exclude them.

Baudrillard sees the erasure of otherness as a deeply destructive process. One way in which he tries to show this is with reference to major figures in continental philosophy – such as Hegel, Sartre and Lacan. In this tradition, the Other (with a capital 'O') designates something which plays a constitutive role in its very opposition to the self. For example, in his theory of the 'mirror phase', Lacan suggests that our sense of self is constituted by an identification with the Other, which splits the subject and alienates us from ourselves, but which is nevertheless necessary for our identity. Because otherness is a constitutive condition for our identity, our very attempt to erase otherness and constitute pure identity ends up being self-destructive. Baudrillard ingeniously identifies recent developments in science and culture, from cloning to devitalised substances such as sugar without calories, as denials of otherness which will have destructive effects on identity. Because they bypass constitutive otherness, Baudrillard sees these ideals of full positivity as a kind of hell in which we lose what it means to be subjects or selves. He paraphrases Sartre: 'No longer the hell of other people, but the hell of the Same' (*TE*, 122).

Although he sometimes alludes to Hegel, Lacan, Sartre and so on strategically to make his point, there is an important sense in which the otherness Baudrillard defends is not simply the otherness of these thinkers, which is typically another consciousness, a human Other. Baudrillard's insistence on the irreducible singularity and incomparability of genuine otherness is arguably more extreme than any of his predecessors or contemporaries. For Baudrillard, that which is radically Other is of a completely different order and cannot be brought into a relation of opposition. An instructive example of this is his discussion of the otherness of microbes to the human race: 'the absolute Other is indeed the microbe in its radical non-humanness – a being of which we know nothing, and which cannot even be deemed *different* from us' (*TE*, 163).

Despite pervasive attempts to eradicate it, Baudrillard insists that otherness cannot be destroyed; it persists in the contemporary world and will have its revenge. This is, first, because identity without otherness is impossible and any attempt to establish this will be self-destructive. Moreover, the otherness expelled from the contemporary system will become monstrous and destructive because the system can neither eradicate it nor incorporate it into itself. Baudrillard argues that radical otherness is a necessary rule or principle which governs the world at a fundamental level. In this sense, radical otherness has strong affinities with other concepts which play this role in Baudrillard's thought, such as seduction, impossible exchange and so on.

Passwords

Clones + Cloning
Communication + Non-communication
Double spiral
Impossible exchange
Radical alterity
Seduction
Singularity

P

PATAPHYSICS

Gary Genosko

Baudrillard discovered pataphysics through the influence of his school-teacher. The 'neo-science of imaginary solutions' was created by French playwright Alfred Jarry (1873–1907) and expounded by his characters Père Ubu and Doctor Faustroll. Attracted by the intellectual game playing, the mockery of the *Collège de Pataphysique*'s organigram of power and the acid wit, monstrous proportions and excess of Ubu, Baudrillard first distinguished his position from that of Antonin Artaud's *Theatre of Cruelty*. At around twenty years of age Baudrillard rejected the 'raw cruelty' of Artaud for the more terrible self-defeating rules of pataphysics and the gaseousness of its predicament: 'The humour of this story is crueler than Artaud's cruelty, since Artaud was only an idealist' (*CA*, 215). Baudrillard rejects the revalorisation of creation for bloodless parody and the pursuit of the void. From pataphysics Baudrillard learned to mock science, write cryptically and allusively and seek politically inutility. Baudrillard did not attempt to preserve pataphysics through his writing; his referencing was not a mission to prove its value for critique.

Yet pataphysics appears throughout Baudrillard's writings. *La gidouille d'Ubu* has served him well as a symbol of hopeless self-cancelling circularity and pseudocyesis. Ubu is the central character in the 'Ubu cycle' of three plays. Baudrillard rhetorically employed rhetorical ploys developed by Jarry. Ubu's great gut is marked by a spiral; his excremental humour is legendary; his stupidity and obesity make him an ideal transmodern figure of ecstasy and obscenity. Ubu is an ecstatic form who potentialised himself by producing more and more of himself. Transmodernity thought Baudrillard is Ubuesque due to its hyperplastic spiral into what is realer than real. Obese systems are rhetorically and pathologically metastatic in pursuing their own delirious ends in a culture turned viral. Ubu is the symbol of transmodernity's destiny: hypertelic growth towards uselessness. Ubu is misshapen like the social, for which Baudrillard teaches his readers to experience horror and disgust. For Ubu absorbs everything, swelling, farting, belching and shining in the void of his own making.

In both *America* (1988b [1986]) and *The Transparency of Evil* (1993b [1990a]) Baudrillard uses Jarry's image of a Perpetual-Motion-Food-Bicycle Race across Siberia between a team of cyclists (the best performer is dead) and a train to express how extreme phenomena possess a cadaver-like mobility and a chaotic declination of energy that feeds on itself. This is Baudrillard's vision of New York.

Baudrillard's attitude to science is also contained in his use of pataphysics. Ubu and Faustroll's imaginary science possesses the features it describes: hyperplastic exaggeration of physics by metaphysics, and beyond. Just as Jarry sourced many figures from the work of Charles-Vernon Boys, William Crookes and Sir William Thomson (Lord Kelvin), Baudrillard dabbles in the writings of Benoit Mandelbrot and Jacques Monod. From Boys' work on soap bubbles Jarry derived the musical jet of urine sounding in a porcelain bowl. Baudrillard extracted his crystal of revenge from Jarry's pilfering of the crystal from Lord Kelvin. The idea of the wily and active object that takes revenge on the subject is a pure and enigmatic crystal that functions in Baudrillard's thought as a Jarryesque principle: the magical 'physics-stick' explicated by Faustroll and whose spinning flips back and forth from plus to minus, revealing the equality of opposites, infecting all registers with undecidability and randomness.

Ubu's great gut bears a symbol of implosion. Implosion is the figure Baudrillard attributes to the masses engaged in the process of hyper-conformity: paradoxical participation that does not justify but destroys. Ubu and the masses are the end waste products of the social whose destiny is to serve as avatars of a new kind of violence. Baudrillard's essay 'The Beaubourg-Effect' explains the implosive force of amassing people in the building itself: 'Make Beaubourg bend!' (*SS*, 69) by going there en masse in order to realise power's saturation point in an expansive violence running in reverse.

Referring to the masses as an 'imaginary referent' (*SSM*, 48) beyond representation, Baudrillard develops this strategy further in *In the Shadow of the Silent Majorities* (2007b [1978]). The mass is waiting to seek its revenge on the social and it is figured in an Ubuesque glory of absorption and distortion: 'The masses and their involuntary humour would introduce us to a pataphysics of the social which ultimately would relieve us of all that cumbersome metaphysics of the social' (*SSM*, 57). Excess, brutality, rejection of objective inducements to meaning, politics, health and welfare, the Baudrillardian masses operate in pataphysical mode by pursuing a hyper-logic of reversion without exception. This is neither sociology nor philosophy; instead, it is an imaginary textual strategy of 'ubesity' (Merrin, 2009: 64), a theory that proffers virulent imaginary solutions: an imaginary pata-science of simulation.

Stylistically, pataphysics helped underwrite Baudrillard's penchant for caustic wit and acidic self-annulling paradoxes. The association of Ubu with a resplendid void is a tendency that Baudrillard works out in his conception of radical thought that tends eccentrically towards the empty periphery and deploys tools of unintelligibility against positivity, proof and philosophical reason – whose promoters wait in line before Ubu's de--braining machine.

Passwords

Beaubourg
City
Excess
Masses
Metaphysics
Obscene
Reversibility

PERFECT CRIME

Jonathan Smith

The dual misfit between the world and its appearances, and between our thoughts and the world, cast truth into doubt for Baudrillard, persuading him that the world's reality is like a perfect or unsolvable crime – a dreadful enigma offering few clues about its fate, its meaning or why it came into being (*PC*, *IEx*). The world may even be a crime from the very beginning – an 'original crime' marked by illusion or 'the world in the play of seduction and appearances' (*PC*, 2). Here, '[t]he perfection of the crime lies in the fact that it has always-already been accomplished . . . A misappropriation of the world as it is, before it even shows itself' (*PC*, 1).

Because we cannot know the world as it is or exchange our thoughts for its appearances (*PC*), there is a sense of 'impossible exchange' between the world and us (*IEx*). It is this epistemic misfit which suggests the world may be a metaphysical crime. Baudrillard calls this misfit 'the material illusion of the world', 'the sacred illusion' or the 'vital illusion' (*PC*). It may also be called reality-illusion: 'here, the "illusion" is not simply irreality or non-reality' (*ED*, 45), explains Baudrillard; 'rather, it is in the literal sense of the word (*il-ludere* in Latin) a *play* upon "reality" or a *mise en jeu* [putting into play] of the real' (*ED*, 45–6). The roots of the perfect crime can be traced to Baudrillard's early reading of Nietzsche (*F*), particularly the truth/illusion critique (*PC*). *Symbolic Exchange and Death* (1993a [1976]) contains another root: the 'irreducible duality' and 'Manichean' vision that Baudrillard gleaned from Freud's duality of Eros (life) and Thanatos (death).

'This is the key to the whole position', said Baudrillard (*ED*, 45) about the reality-illusion implied by Freud's duality: 'the idea is that of a most fundamental and radical antagonism, of no possibility existing at all of reconciling the "illusion" of the world with the "reality" of the world.' This grave misfit became 'the perfect crime' in the 1990s when Baudrillard engaged with the nothing/something duality of Argentine metaphysician Macedonio Fernandez (*PC*, *IEx*, *F*). Nietzsche, Freud and Fernandez helped Baudrillard conceive of reality-illusion without making illusion into non-reality within a binary opposition of Reality and illusion.

On this point, Fernandez's duality was particularly helpful to Baudrillard (*IEx*) insofar as it is an antinomy (a pair of related, yet logically independent, concepts), not a binary. This dual figure suggested to Baudrillard that 'illusion' can be both nothing and something. Fernandez's influence is especially apparent in Baudrillard's end-of-the-century books where the misfit effect, reality-illusion and the world as a perfect crime are essayed in detail. For example, in *The Perfect Crime* (1996c [1995a]), Baudrillard reckons: 'The great philosophical question used to be "Why is there something rather than nothing?" Today, the real question is: "Why is there nothing rather than something?"' (*PC*, 2). An answer is approached in *Impossible Exchange* (2001a [1999a]) where Baudrillard suggests 'the Nothing' is part of the perfect crime insofar as it is 'the product of the dramatic illusion of appearances . . . the divine incoherence of the world' (*IEx*, 12).

Here, the something of the world is thought to be accompanied, incognito, by 'the continuity of the evil, the continuation of the nothing' (*PC*,

2) which, in a Manichean manner, renders the world vulnerable to an 'enigmatic machination' by 'the Nothing', with such thinking being 'the perpetuation of this crime' (*PC*, *F*).

Given his interest in the duality of reality, it is unsurprising that Baudrillard entertained a Manichean metaphysics of the perfect crime via Fernandez's antinomy. Earlier, in work prepared for a doctoral degree at the Sorbonne (*EC*), Baudrillard argued that the world seems marked by diabolical simulation and thus might have come into being via evil's 'original seduction' of it, within a cosmic duality of good/evil (*EC*, *ED*).

Manichean or not, Baudrillard regarded the perfect crime's reality-illusion as a vital sacred mystery – a secret shining with 'pure appearance' (*PC*, 2). We dread this, he argued, and want it reduced to a pure reality without any misfit effect – a simulated reality that immediately corresponds to our models and images of it (*PC*). This, he argues in *Passwords* (2003b [2000c]), is an attempt to 'eliminate duality . . . to reduce everything to a kind of single principle' (*PW*, 62).

Paradoxically, this dread-driven pursuit of pure reality was regarded by Baudrillard as a contemporary form of the perfect crime, even 'the accomplishment of this crime' (*PC*, 2). Here, we attempt the disillusionment of reality (*PC*) by simulating it as hyper-reality (reality produced via models) or rendering it as 'integral reality', a hyper-realised form of simulation wherein the world and our representations of it suffer an 'immersion in the visual' that is 'diabolical' (*F*, 47). Baudrillard resolved the problem of how this anti-duality can possibly be complicit in the reality-illusion of the perfect crime by arguing that reality production is always already a form of illusion (*PC*). 'Under these circumstances' of simulation saturation, 'only few things and at rare moments attain pure appearance, and only these are seductive' (*EC*, 62), argues Baudrillard. Nevertheless, 'there is something secret in appearances, precisely because they do not readily lend themselves to interpretation. They remain insoluble, indecipherable' (*EC*, 63).

The capacity of appearances to confound any interpretation persuaded Baudrillard that the perfect crime (original and contemporary) is, in effect, less than perfect. It is, after all, also a simulation model, albeit one that presupposes dualism. And yet, by developing his philosophy of reality-illusion via Fernandez's nothing/something antinomy, Baudrillard (*PC*) was able to argue that the world's appearances thwart both our simulations of pure reality and the world as a perfect 'Perfect Crime'.

Passwords

Duality
Hyper-reality

PHOTOGRAPHY

Alan Cholodenko

Baudrillard comes to photography in two ways: as theorist of photography as image, object and medium in its own right; and as photographer whose photographs offer him a singular means with which to demonstrate and perform his theory of photography, indeed with which to theorise photography. Baudrillard's fatal theory conceptualises photography, not as of the order of production, reproduction, representation, resemblance, meaning, truth, reality, the subject, identity, psychology, the good, all of which constitutes second-order 'reality' and the reality principle, but as seduction, as seducer of all that constitutes second-order 'reality' and its principle. Baudrillard aligns photography with his sovereign forms and processes of seduction, illusion, evil, fatality, destiny, irreconcilability, radical exoticism, the Object, the radical Other, with the illusioning of the world as radical, irreducible apparition.

   Baudrillard gives attention to photography from the 1960s (Baudrillard, 1963). However, it is his essay 'Please Follow Me' (*SV*) – where he comments on Sophie Calle's *Suite vénitienne*, theorising her seductive game of photography as an art of disappearance, of shadowing and being shadowed, of reciprocal absence, of vanished presence, of the trace – that seems to be the animating moment that leads him to the development of his theory of photography. Thereafter, photography will occupy an increasingly significant theoretical focus for him – one seemingly commensurate with his activity of taking and exhibiting his own photographs, a reply on his part to photography's seductive call of 'please follow me'. That activity of taking and exhibiting his own photographs started in 1983 when his partner, Marité Bonnal, gave Baudrillard a camera with which to take images of their trip to the United States that year (one of a number of trips that would result in *America* (1988b [1986])). These images afforded Baudrillard his first 'exhibition', in two venues: in Bonnal's book *Passage* (1986) and at the launch of that book in Paris. Over the following decades Baudrillard would have a number of exhibitions of his photographs, the most significant being perhaps the 1999 show at the

Neue Galerie in Graz, Austria (*PH*). Nevertheless, despite this success he rejected the label of 'professional photographer' and being 'a part of photographic culture' (*AA*, 35), even on occasion refusing the tag of 'photographer' period, seeing himself as just a maker of images (Baudrillard, 2004c).

Initially, Baudrillard sees his photographing as something unrelated to his theoretical practice, rather a kind of avocation; but his position soon reverses. It becomes for him a second mode of fatal theorising, with images rather than words, taking the form of the fragment – 'a snapshot' (*F*, 98) – in both cases. As a form of seduction, photography is for Baudrillard a mode of disappearance. In seducing reality, the photograph makes reality, the subject and so on vanish into it. He writes that 'everything pivots upon the art of disappearance. But nevertheless, this process of disappearing has to leave some kind of trace, be this the site at which the [O]ther, the world or the object appears' (*AA*, 28). In short, 'Every photographed object is simply the trace left behind by the disappearance of everything else' (*AA*, 28).

For Baudrillard, the disappearance of the subject is 'in a sense, an invocation . . . to the Other, the object – to emerge . . . to exist in order to make me exist' (*LA*, unpaginated). In this leave-taking, the Other (the radical Other, not the other in a system of the same and the different), the world or the object (the object 'as such', what he calls the pure Object) do not simply appear. The photograph shows not the Other, the world or the object 'as such' but rather what remains of them as traces in its image and of its image itself as trace, trace of what at once appears in its disappearing and disappears in its appearing, even as the photograph is the trace of not only the object photographed but the subject, too, including the photographer as subject.

The photograph shows not simply what takes leave but what takes leave of taking leave, showing what returns and remains of the Other, as apparition, as illusion. Insofar as Baudrillard declares the model exclusion, the model of all Others, that of 'the dead and of death' (*SED*, 126), the photograph shows what returns from the dead and death, in so doing 'to exhume its [the world's] otherness buried beneath its alleged reality' (*PH*, 132).

But the photograph does not show the dead and death directly. Nothing could. It shows 'what remains of the Other when s/he isn't there' (*PH*, 147). For Baudrillard 'Photography is always . . . the veiled message from death in the Samarkand story' (*LP*, 103), offering the subject a penultimate encounter with death, with death as Seduction, as Illusion.

In this regard, Baudrillard concurs with Roland Barthes, who in *Camera Lucida* (1982) makes death the *eidos* (that is, appearance, constitutive nature, form) of the photograph, designating Barthes' punctum as 'that figure of nothingness, absence and unreality . . . at the heart of the image which lends it its magic and its power' (*PH*, 139). For Baudrillard the photograph brings the subject 'to the heart of the illusion of reality' (*P*, 91), singularly literalising the reality of the illusion in the form of its (the photograph's) fiction (*IEx*, 142).

Asserting 'photography's affinity with everything that is savage and primitive, and with that most essential of exoticisms, the exoticism of the Object, of the Other' (*TE*, 151), Baudrillard proclaims: 'Photography is our exorcism' (*TE*, 153). Not only is the photograph for Baudrillard 'the purest of images' (*TE*, 154), it brings us 'closest to a universe without images, or in other words to pure appearance' (*PH*, 132). Insofar as, for Baudrillard, the photograph is analogical and aligned with and 'retains the moment of the negative' (*AA*, 30), in the unconditional sense, that of 'the sovereignty of illusion' (*BL*, 62), the hyper-realist ('real-time', virtual, digital, computer-animated, technologised) photograph is for him no photograph at all.

Passwords

Death
Disappearance
Fatal
Following
Image
Other + Otherness
Seduction

PLATO (428/427–348/347 BC) – see 'image' and 'real'.

POETIC RESOLUTION

Gerry Coulter

Baudrillard possessed a radical temperament which held more in common with poetry than other forms of thought and writing (*TE*). Poetry and the poetic appear numerous times in his writing but the most important concept concerning both for his overall *oeuvre* involves poetic resolution. Baudrillard accepts that Truth with a capital 'T' no longer affords a solution as truth, the real and meaning are multiple and appear only locally as partial objects (*SS*). Because of this circumstance, he says, 'perhaps we can aim at a poetic resolution of the world' (*VI*, 68). Poetic resolution is an important part of his attempt to think without making a contribution to any system. It stands against the empirical resolution of the world of the social sciences. In a time of an epistemological break, when so called 'scientific' thinking has swept all other forms of thought into some prehistory of knowledge (*MP*), Baudrillard aims his thought at a more poetic destination. He hints that he borrowed the concept from Saussure (*PC*).

The key to poetic resolution for Baudrillard is that it allows thought and writing their greatest liberty. The 'task of philosophical thought' for Baudrillard is to 'go to the limit of hypotheses and processes, even if they are catastrophic'. 'The only justification for thinking', he says, 'is that it accelerates these terminal processes'. Poetic resolution then is about going 'beyond the discourse of truth . . . for, facing a world that is unintelligible and enigmatic, our task is clear: we must make that world even more unintelligible, even more enigmatic' (*VI*, 83). Baudrillard's challenge to philosophy runs against its tendency to transform the enigmas of the world into philosophical questions. He would rather that the enigma remain total (*CM2*). This rests at the core of his concern to turn philosophy, which has long sought to understand that there is something rather than nothing, on its head, by seeking to understand why there is nothing rather than something (*CM*).

The poetic plays a significant part in Baudrillard's strategy to bring resolution, through thought and writing, to the unsatisfactory times in which he finds himself. Along with fables, countless literary and artistic references, the poetic is Baudrillard's great inspiration in his struggle against the forces of integral reality (*F*). In his thought Baudrillard felt a radical opposition between a poetic, singular configuration, linked to the metamorphosis of forms, as against the kind of virtual reality that is prevalent today. In a poetic approach it is the forms which become – language as the passage of forms – a kind of inhabited void (*F*). Poetic resolution (and nothing is more poetic for Baudrillard than reversibility) was a way out of the restrictions of the social sciences and political commitments to 'improving' our world until it becomes a technoscientific nightmare.

Beyond discourses of Truth, Baudrillard did find his own way to make the world, which came to him as enigmatic and unintelligible, even more so. Rather than pointing to Truth he pointed to its absence in a way which goes beyond traditional forms of inquiry. We must keep in mind that system failure was a lesser concern to Baudrillard than the possibility that our system might succeed into a modelled and computerised nightmare. Thought was not to be aimed at contributing to this system but to enigma and uncertainty. This enabled Baudrillard to think and write in a very independent manner without debt to cultural or philosophical systems, or to politics. What allowed him to open up to this approach was that he understood that theory precedes the world. 'Things appear to us only through the meaning we have given them' (*F*, 91). Thinking is what brings the world into existence for each of us. Radical thought was the kind in which words and concepts refer to each other and can, as in Baudrillard's writing, create a pure event, without the need to form practical instructions or empirical knowledges (*CA*).

An example of Baudrillardian poetic resolution is his story of the soldier who meets Death in the marketplace. The soldier, frightened because he thought he saw Death make a menacing gesture in his direction, flees to Samarkand on a fast horse. Death, when called into account by the king, says he too was surprised to see the soldier – as his rendezvous with the soldier was not until tomorrow, in Samarkand (*S*). This is a very poetic way of making the point that we can run towards our fate by trying to avoid it – something Baudrillard felt happened at the individual level and that of systems. Another of many poetic passages in his writing involves his resolution of simulacra drawing on Borges' fable of the map and the territory. Our case is reversed from that described by Borges, says Baudrillard, because for us we only have a few fragments of the real remaining to float and drift on the map (*VI*).

Passwords

Anagrams
Death
Destiny
Integral reality
Poetry
Reversibility
Writing

POETRY

Richard G. Smith

Baudrillard's poems were published in 1978 as *L'Ange du Stuc* (*The Stucco Angel*) – an unpaginated book with no preface or afterword – and were not fully translated into English until 2001 (*UB*). Baudrillard wrote the sequence of seventeen poems in the 1950s when he was interested in the works of German poets such as Goethe, Hölderlin and Rainer Maria Rilke.

Baudrillard's passion for poetry in his twenties – like his interests in German and pataphysics – was to touch the theoretical writings he wrote some decades later (especially *Symbolic Exchange and Death* (1993a [1976]) and *Seduction* (1990a [1979])). Indeed, several lines from Baudrillard's poems are scattered as fragments in his theoretical writings. For example, the tenth poem begins with 'A clock without hands imposes time but leaves the hour to be divined . . . soft to the touch like a natural death' (*UB*, 84–5) and appears in *Seduction* (*S*, 61–2). And the epigraph to the poems, 'And they saw a stucco angel whose extremities were joined along one curve' (*UB*, 78) also appears in *Symbolic Exchange and Death* (*SED*, 53) and *Forget Foucault* (*FF*, 58) as Baudrillard draws on this image to illustrate his idea of the simulacrum as a single substance in a closed space.

Gane (1991b) examined whether Baudrillard's interest in the 1970s in Saussure's notebooks on anagrams as a form of symbolic exchange in language (*SED*) is evidenced in the structure of the poems he wrote as a young man. After a close (and imaginative) analysis Gane's conclusion is that any claim of an anagrammatic structure underlying Baudrillard's poetry from the 1950s, which would link through to his interest in anagrams as a subversion of orthodox linguistics and Saussure's own structural linguistics of the sign a few decades later, is no more than a 'fanciful suggestion'. However, what Gane does suggest is that the appearance, themes and sometimes content of some lines of Baudrillard's poetry (*AS*) in *Seduction* (1990a [1979]), where Baudrillard is concerned with *trompe-l'œil* and the changing experience of space in the Renaissance, is indicative of how, for Baudrillard, the poetic is a non-accumulative process where meaning and value are annulled. Thus Baudrillard's poetry – and his interest in poets (such as Kenneth White (*BL*)), poetry and the poetic more broadly – can be better understood if one locates it within the horizon of symbolic exchange.

Passwords

Anagrams
Fragments
Poetic resolution
Reversibility
Symbolic exchange

POLITICAL ECONOMY OF THE SIGN

Richard G. Smith

A collection of eleven thematically related essays, *For a Critique of the Political Economy of the Sign* (1981 [1972]) is Baudrillard's third book (the second to be fully translated from French to English). The collection represents both a clarification and extension of the argument from his first two books – theorising the dominance of the 'code' in consumption-oriented western societies – (*SO*, *SC*), and a precursor to the specific arguments of his next two books, namely a radical critique of use value (*MP*) and a theory of symbolic exchange (*SED*). In addition, the book is also an explicit theoretical explanation (as are *MP* and *SED*) of the 'double spiral', a metaphor Baudrillard was to employ in 1987 (*EC*) to highlight his struggle against signification in the name of symbolic exchange: 'signs must burn' (*CPS*, 163).

When Baudrillard's first (*SO*) and second (*SC*) books are read in conjunction with his third book (*CPS*), it is evident that, taken together, they constitute a critical fusion of Marx's theory of value and Saussure's description of the linguistic sign to detail the transition to the 'political economy of the sign' (that is, the 'code'). What is more, it is Baudrillard's theoretical demonstration of the homologous relation of the commodity-sign form that serves as the foundation and rationale for not only his analysis of the sign form and description of the political economy of the sign (the field of general political economy), but also for his parallel development of a theory of symbolic exchange (*CPS*, *MP*, *SED*), a form of exchange outside of the field of value, as its critique.

For a Critique of the Political Economy of the Sign (1981 [1972]) contains a critique of Louis Althusser's conceptualisation of ideology as an infra-superstructural relation, 'as a sort of cultural surf frothing on the beachhead of the economy' (*CPS*, 144). That is because with an understanding of the sign form comes a realisation that ideology is '*that very form* that traverses both the production of signs and material production' (*CPS*, 144). Thus structural Marxism (or any thought that is predicated on an 'artificial distinction between the economic and the ideological' (*CPS*, 144)) does not unravel ideology as form, only as content. In other words, after the dominance of Althusser's approach in France in the 1960s, Baudrillard placed the articulation of culture and economy from the roots of the commodity-sign form on the theoretical agenda. In short, Baudrillard inaugurates a new type of analysis:

Today consumption . . . defines precisely *the stage where the commodity is immediately produced as a sign, as sign value, and where signs (culture) are produced as commodities.* But this whole area of study is still occupied, 'critically' or otherwise, by specialists of production (economy, infrastructure), or ideology specialists (signs, culture), or even by a kind of seamless dialectician of the totality. The partitioning of the object domain obscures even the simplest realities. If any progress is to be made at this point, 'research' – especially Marxist research – must come to terms with the fact that nothing produced or exchanged today (objects, services, bodies, sex, culture, knowledge, etc.) can be decoded exclusively as a sign, nor solely measured as a commodity. (*CPS*, 147–8)

In short, Marxists such as David Harvey (1989: 287) with their faith in, and need for, the reality of 'use value' are quite incorrect when they reference *For a Critique of the Political Economy of the Sign* (1981 [1972]) to assert that Baudrillard's position is no more than a simple inversion of signs over commodities, 'that Marx's analysis of commodity production is outdated because capitalism is now predominantly concerned with the production of signs, images, and sign systems rather than with commodities themselves'. Indeed, it is clear that Baudrillard's argument is quite different: '*the logic of the commodity and of political economy is at the very heart of the sign*' and '*the structure of the sign is at the very heart of the commodity form*' (*CPS*, 146). In other words, in late capitalism the commodity has fused with sign (commodity-sign), a manoeuvre that has the consequence of liquidating all kinds of Marxist 'truths' from use value to alienation (*MP*).

For Baudrillard, 'we have to be more logical than Marx himself' (*CPS*, 131) to understand that ideology is present in the internal logic of the political economy of the sign – in the relations between use and exchange value and between signified and signifier – with use value and the signified serving as the capitalist system's ideological guarantee. In other words, to realise that use value is nothing but the horizon of exchange value in the commodity-form, and the signified is only the satellite or 'alibi' of the signifier in the sign-form. Thus it is not the case that use value and the signified are guarantors of reality, they are simulacra:

If the system of use value is produced by the system of exchange value as its own ideology – if use value has no autonomy, if it is only the satellite and alibi of exchange value, though systematically combining with it in the framework of political economy – then it is no longer possible to posit use value as an alternative to exchange value. Nor, therefore, is it possible to posit the 'restitution' of use value, at the end of political economy, under the sign of the 'liberation of needs' and the 'administration of things' as a revolutionary perspective. (*CPS*, 139)

Thus it is by reading Marx through Saussure that Baudrillard understands use value and signified as nothing but 'mirages' and this consequently leads him – drawing on authors such as Bataille and Mauss – to posit symbolic exchange as a critique of the political economy of the sign – precisely because such exchange stands outside of the field of value and the commodity-sign. In other words, through a theoretical understanding of the sign-form as 'beyond use value' (*CPS*, 130) and the signified, Baudrillard concludes that 'To break the circuit of exchange value, it is necessary to restore exchange itself – not value (not even use value)' (*CPS*, 212), which logically means that it is the framework of 'political economy which is opposed, as a whole, to symbolic exchange' (*CPS*, 125).

Passwords

Accursed share
Code
Consumption + Affluent society
Death
Double spiral
Gift
Sign
Symbolic exchange
Value + Structural law of value

POLITICS

Diane Rubenstein

One of the most common misconceptions concerning Baudrillard is that he has little to offer political theory, that he is an 'irresponsible' or even a reactionary voice when it comes to issues of multiculturalism, feminism or identity politics in general. This is the case even when some of his positions are not all that different, for example, from those of Žižek on multiculturalism. Or he is associated with some of his more polemical and punctual interventions such as *The Gulf War Did Not Take Place* (1995 [1991]) or *The Spirit of Terrorism* (2003c [2002]). However, when one considers both the sheer number of political topics addressed in his writings – everything from the terrorism of the Baader Meinhof and Red Brigade groups (*SSM*, *FS*), the Watts riots (*CS*), disenfranchisement (*A*), both Gulf Wars (*GW*), racial hatred and the *Front National* (*SC*), human rights and Doctors Without Borders (*IE*, *SC*), to name just a few examples – as well as the way that these subjects are inextricably linked to his central concepts (simulation, impossible exchange, integral reality) it is difficult to maintain such a facile assessment.

Baudrillard's writings on simulation are often associated with his discussion of Disneyland (figured as a deterrence machine to dissuade citizens that the rest of America is real). But the crucial sections of 'The Precession of Simulacra' essay (the section on 'The Strategy of the Real') foregrounds simulation as a *political* problem (*SS*, 19). This section follows an analysis of Watergate (as another scandal deterrence machine): 'Watergate. The same scenario as in Disneyland (effect of the imaginary concealing that reality no more exists outside than inside the limits of the artificial perimeter): here the scandal effect hiding that there is no difference between the facts and their denunciation' (*SS*, 14). It is the staged presidential assassination of Ford that is the frame for Watergate as it is also for Baudrillard's remarks on leaders in general, whether Mao, Franco (*SS*) or Mitterand and Chirac (*SC*). 'These staged presidential assassinations are revealing because they signal the status of all negativity in the West: political opposition . . . a simulacral contrast through which power attempts to break the vicious circle of its nonexistence, of its fundamental irresponsibility, of its "suspension"' (*SS*, 24). Watergate was a ritual putting to death of Nixon and (American) power; post-Watergate presidents (Ford, Carter, Reagan) are simulacra of this already dead power, immunised by their impotence (*SS*). Baudrillard's *America* (1988b [1986]) has a meditative penultimate chapter on Reagan (and obliquely Thatcher): 'The End of U.S. Power?'(*A*, 107).

Baudrillard's idea of deterrence is an unconventional one and is similarly derived from his semiotic critique of reality. The nuclear – including both weaponry and '*peaceful* nuclear power stations' (*SS*, 33) – is the 'apotheosis of simulation' (*SS*, 32). There is thus no strategy, no adversary, nor subject of deterrence: only a 'pretext' for 'installing a universal security system' (*SS*, 33) whose deterrent effect is aimed not at a nuclear event but rather *any* real event that would upset the balance of forces. Deterrence circulates as 'international capital in the orbital zone of monetary speculation' (*SS*, 33). Now only the 'simulacra' of conflicts remain. Baudrillard's examples are of the Vietnam (and Algerian) Wars. Why were there so little internal repercussions (politically) from what the Americans experienced as a resounding defeat? Baudrillard reads the war as a confirmation of his theories that the Vietnam War was not one (a war), but was a crucial episode in the 'peaceful coexistence' (*SS*, 36) of China. The normalisation of Peking–Washington was the true stake of the Vietnam War, and once this occurred the war could end '"spontaneously"' (*SS*, 36). What Baudrillard's inventive analyses demonstrate is that behind the well articulated rationale for war, 'the murderous antagonism of the adversaries

. . . behind this simulacrum of fighting to the death and of ruthless global stakes, the two adversaries are fundamentally in solidarity against something else, unnamed, never spoken' (*SS*, 37).

Baudrillard similarly presents singular interpretations of the dissolution of the Eastern bloc countries in *The Illusion of the End* (1994b [1992]). One example is that Chernobyl was the 'real starting point in this involuntary, but brilliant strategic inversion . . . It was the Eastern bloc that exploded that bomb in its own heart and it was that bomb which, in the form of the first atomic cloud, crossed the Wall . . .' (*IE*, 45). The events in Romania – both the Timişoara massacre and the trial of the Ceauşescus – as well as the Gulf War – represent a radicalisation of Baudrillard's theories from deterrence to '"*desimulation*"' (*IE*, 54). These are highly mediatised televisual (CNN) events, and raise serious questions about what happens to the political import of an event that passes through a virtual medium (unlike cinema and photography) that lacks a negative. Romanians are dispossessed of their televised 'revolution' or placed 'under house arrest' watching it on the home TV screens (*IE*, 56).

Baudrillard's enabling critical distinction between the orbital and the nuclear in the simulation essays return in the later period of *Screened Out* (2002 [2000a]) as an equally pertinent opposition between the 'global and the universal'. Universality pertains to values and the global to the realm of exchange. The 'singularity of forms' provides the third part of this model including 'languages, cultures, individuals and characters, but also chance, accident, etc. – all that the universal, in keeping with its law, impugns as an exception or anomaly' (*SC*, 158) The global/universal opposition frames his essays on European integration as well as his later editorial (Baudrillard, 2005) concerning the 'No' vote on the European Constitution. His writings during the Serbian/Kosovo war were similarly prescient (*SC*) and reveal him to be an astute reader of Islamic fundamentalism (especially when compared with Foucault's writings on the Iranian Revolution). Writing on Serbia in 1995 and foreshadowing his essay after 9/11 (*ST*) Baudrillard presents an alternative imperialism of values and asserts that a 'transpolitical fault line . . . today passes mainly through Islam' (*SC*, 65).

Baudrillard's last writings detail a further development of simulation called integral reality that has implications for the extreme objects of war and terrorism. As integral reality is characterised by immersion and an umbilical relation, not a scene and a gaze, it will be the 'embedded' and not the hostage that is the figure of this new world of 'immersion, immanence and immediacy' (*LP*, 31). Integral reality comes about at a terrible cost of exclusion and exile for those who found themselves 'on the wrong side of the universal' (*P*, 101). We live in the shadow of the imminent revenge of this 'anti-matter' that haunts, constitutes and limits our material world. It put an end to the strike of events on September 11, 2001 and it is in this context that Baudrillard's more provocative statements in *The Spirit of Terrorism* (2003c [2002]) should be read.

Passwords

America
Feminism/Feminine
Globalisation
Gulf War
Integral reality
Terrorism
Universality

POMPIDOU CENTRE – see 'architecture', 'art', 'Beaubourg', 'masses' and '*Traverses*'.

PORNOGRAPHY – see 'body' and 'obscene'.

POST-MARXISM

Stuart Sim

Post-Marxism can be interpreted in two main ways: either as a rejection of Marxism as a body of thought, or as a continuation of that tradition in terms of its spirit rather than its letter. Ernesto Laclau and Chantal Mouffe are the most influential figures in the latter category, as expressed most forcefully in their book *Hegemony and Socialist Strategy* (1985), whereas Baudrillard, along with such contemporaries as Jean-François Lyotard and Michel Foucault, fits into the former. In Laclau and Mouffe's (1985) reading, it was to be construed as the difference between being '*post*-Marxist' and 'post-*Marxist*'. Laclau and Mouffe argued that Marxist thought had attempted to cover up the failure of its predictions, most importantly that capitalism would ultimately collapse under the weight of its internal contradictions, by the use of the concept of hegemony. Consistent recourse to that concept constituted a denial of Marxism's theoretical deficiencies for Laclau and Mouffe, and led them to press for a less dogmatic interpretation of Marx's work. For French thinkers of Baudrillard's generation, however, the critical event in their development of a post-Marxist outlook was 1968 and the *événements* in Paris. A generation of intellectuals who had been very sympathetic to Marxism, which had a high profile in French public life, were to turn against it in the aftermath of the *événements*, angered at what they took to be an act of betrayal by the French Communist Party in siding with the government against the combined forces of the strikers and students. Thereafter we are to note a definite drift away from official Marxism by intellectuals on the Left.

Baudrillard launches a sustained attack on Marxism in *The Mirror of Production* (1975 [1973]), criticising in particular its obsession with exerting control over Nature, as well as with production: 'A specter haunts the revolutionary imagination: the phantom of production' (*MP*, 17). Marxism is held to be locked into the ideals of modernity, viewing Nature purely as a resource to be drawn into the production process, on the grounds that increased production will enable communism to outstrip capitalism. Baudrillard dismisses that assumption, complaining that 'the concept of production is never questioned' by Marxist theorists, and arguing that 'it will never radically overcome the influence of political economy . . . Can the quantitative development of productive forces lead to a revolution of social relations? Revolutionary hope is based "objectively" and hopelessly on this claim' (*MP*, 59–60). Production has become an end in itself, subordinating humankind to its dictates, and it cannot be seen as an agent of liberation. It is an argument against the totalising thrust of Marxist thought, exemplified by the communist system then in operation in the Soviet bloc and China, and Baudrillard's critique reflects a more general unease on this issue among the French Left post-1968 – Deleuze and Guattari and Lyotard are making very similar noises in *Anti-Oedipus* (1983) and *Libidinal Economy* (1993) respectively. It might be fairer to call such thinkers anti- rather than post-Marxist, and that was a criticism that did come to be made of the post-Marxist movement in general by classical Marxists.

Baudrillard regards Marxism as being in thrall to political economy, leading to a false interpretation of history: 'Marxism is the projection of the class struggle and the mode of production onto all previous history; it is the vision of a future "freedom" based on the conscious domination of nature. These are extrapolations of the economic' (*MP*, 67). Like all totalising belief systems Marxism is trying to erase difference, and Baudrillard's postmodern orientation comes through strongly at this point, the cultivation of difference being an abiding concern of the burgeoning postmodernist-poststructuralist movement of the time. Baudrillard may have rejected the label of postmodernist, but his defence of difference and critique of totalising thought in general aligns him with that movement in its broad sense.

Marxism is rejected as a revolutionary force by Baudrillard, for whom it is a mirror image of capitalism rather than the ideological opposite it purports to be. Baudrillard is also critical of Marx's concept of value, arguing that the distinction he makes between use value and exchange value is largely illusory (*SED*, *CPS*). In the uncompromising quality of his critique of Marx Baudrillard reveals himself to be, in Laclau and Mouffe's terms of reference, very much a *post*-Marxist, who believes the theory is now irrelevant to our lives.

Passwords

Consumption + Affluent society
May 1968
Mirror
Nature + Animals
Political economy of the sign
Postmodernism/Postmodernity
Production
Value + Structural law of value

POSTMODERNISM/POSTMODERNITY

Ashley Woodward

Baudrillard briefly used the term 'postmodern' in the early-to-mid 1980s before expressing deep dissatisfaction with it and seeking to disassociate himself from it. In response to a request to explain postmodernism, he once quipped:

I cannot explain and I will not explain. Post modernism for me is nothing. I do not worry about this term. I am very exhausted with this post modernism. All that I will say is that the post modern is maybe postmodern. (Baudrillard, cited in Sim, 2004: 43)

Nevertheless, Baudrillard was labelled and hailed as one of the key theorists of the postmodern, and any adequate understanding of postmodernism must take his work into account. Moreover, Baudrillard's thought displays key themes in common with other postmodern thinkers. As Zurbrugg (1994: 227) asserts, 'Baudrillard's disclaimer "I have nothing to do with postmodernism" is rich with irony. Considered in terms of his general arguments and assertions, Baudrillard has *everything* to do with postmodernism.' Despite his disclaimers, Baudrillard's work can readily be interpreted as providing a theory of postmodernity, replete with insightful characterisations of many aspects of postmodern culture, and can itself be understood as a postmodern form of theory.

Fredric Jameson (1991) understands postmodernism as 'the cultural logic of late capitalism', and Baudrillard can be seen as a theorist of postmodernity insofar as he develops theories of both the nature of late capitalism and the cultural logic which accompanies it. From his early writings on consumer culture to his later, more metaphysical works, Baudrillard asserts a recent, radical change in the nature of capitalism and its cultural logic. He theorises this change as a move from production to consumption as the primary mode of the capitalist system (CS), and as a shift from the commodity law of value to the structural law of value (SED). With these changes in capitalism, cultural logic also changes, as emphasis shifts from the use value and exchange value of objects to their sign value. Baudrillard develops and extends his analysis of this cultural logic in his later works through ideas such as simulation, hyper-reality and the radiant stage of value.

Like other theorists of postmodernity such as Jameson, Lyotard and Vattimo, Baudrillard sees a 'derealisation' of reality as characteristic of postmodern culture. This derealisation is paradoxically produced by the attempt to capture reality and represent it in systems of signs. For Baudrillard, this produces a hyper-reality in which signs and images float free of any reference in the real. This superficiality of signs implies a certain flatness or lack of depth, another characteristic of postmodern culture identified by theorists such as Jameson. Another key feature of postmodernity Baudrillard identifies is a loss of social cohesion and stratification in contemporary society. He describes this as an implosion of the social into 'the masses', where the social indicates the modernist understanding of society as comprehensible through categories such as class and improvable through advances in education, social welfare and so on. 'The masses', on the other hand, indicates an undifferentiated society resistant to categories and distinctions: 'no analysis would know how to contain this diffuse, de-centered, Brownian, molecular reality' (SSM, 55).

At the broadest level of analysis, Baudrillard can be seen as a theorist of postmodernity because he theorises the end of modernity. Like Lyotard and others, he believes that the values of modernity, bound up with the Enlightenment dream of the progressive emancipation of humanity through the development and application of reason, have become bankrupt. This has not been because of a failure of the modernist project, but because its very success has undermined its own values: the triumph of reason has led to a superficial culture in which all values are confused. This means that the prospect of understanding human history as progressive emancipation is no longer possible. Baudrillard thus posits the end of history, another central postmodern theme. Summarising his vision of postmodernity, he writes:

Postmodernity is neither optimistic nor pessimistic. It is a game with the vestiges of what has been destroyed. This is why we are 'post-': history has stopped, one is in a kind of post-history which is without meaning. One would not be able to find any meaning in it. So, we must move in it, as though it were a kind of circular gravity. We can no longer be said to progress. So it is a 'moving' situation . . . postmodernity is the attempt – perhaps it's desperate, I don't know – to reach a point where one can live with what is left. It is more a survival among the remnants than anything else. (Laughter.) (*BL*, 95)

Baudrillard's work may be understood as postmodern both because of the theoretical positions it explores and the style(s) in which it is written. Postmodern theory is popularly associated with the rejection of reality and truth, the embrace of an ironic standpoint and the adoption of a rhetorical style. Baudrillard's work has important connections with all these themes, but has too often been read as endorsing a whimsical disregard for truth and reality. A more precise way of understanding Baudrillard's thought as postmodern is to see it as a critical reaction to a specifically modern image of thought originating with René Descartes and dominating the contemporary world. Richard Rorty (1979) has analysed modern thought as viewing the mind as a mirror of nature. In this model, the task of thought is to represent the world of objects as accurately as possible in the mind of the subject. Through his many critical themes, such as the political economy of the sign (*CPS*), simulation (*SS*), transparency (*TE*) and so on, Baudrillard argues that the project of modern thought is internally contradictory and destined to failure. This critical stance leads him to reject the traditional modes of theoretical discourse to which modern thought gave rise, and to explore ironic and rhetorical modes in an attempt to find ways of thinking and writing about the world which are something other than simply representations.

Passwords

Hyper-reality
Masses
Modernity
Simulation
The end
Time + History

PRODUCTION

Marcus A. Doel

While many concepts employed by Baudrillard have a certain aura and mystique (such as integral reality and objective illusion), 'production' is likely to strike the contemporary reader as lacklustre and humdrum. For Baudrillard, the term 'production' had particular purchase when western Marxism held sway over social theory. In Marxism, human beings are essentially productive, through their work and labour; human societies forge specific 'modes of production' such as feudalism and capitalism, each of which remakes the world in its own image; and human history unfolds discontinuously through the periodic and violent recasting of the irresolvable tension between the 'forces' and 'relations' of production, which manifests itself as an interminable struggle between those who are productive (for example, slaves and workers) and those who are parasitic (for example, masters and capitalists).

'Everywhere man has learned to reflect on himself, to assume himself, to *posit himself* according to [the] scheme of production which is assigned to him as the ultimate dimension of value and meaning,' observed Baudrillard (*MP*, 19). '[T]hrough this scheme of production, this *mirror* of production, the human species comes to consciousness *in the imaginary*' (*MP*, 19). Obviously, Marxism has not been alone in being absorbed by the 'unbridled romanticism of productivity' (*MP*, 17), through which 'everything is "produced" according to a "labor"' (*MP*, 17). It is, perhaps, our signature fantasy, through which our world and we ourselves are given meaning, purpose and – above all – value.

Now that western Marxism has largely faded from view, leaving little more than the spectre of a Gothic Marxism that is unlikely to spook anybody, production seems to have been left stranded. On the one hand, the notion that everything is produced is hardly contentious. 'Everywhere productivist discourse reigns' (*MP*, 18). Once we admit that everything is assembled, constructed, manufactured and fabricated, then production per se no longer has critical purchase. The critique of political economy touches only on the content of production, but it leaves the form of production – and its principle of reality – untouched. On the other hand, the contradictions that once threatened to revolutionise the world shaped in the image of production no longer seem to convulse the post-industrial world and its postmodern culture, which is more likely to be perturbed by the potentially catastrophic consequences of over-consumption, radical passivity and unbridled simulation – about which Baudrillard has had much to say.

Given that Baudrillard began his academic career in the shadow of Marxism, it is unsurprising that he worked through production, most notably in *The Mirror of Production* (1975 [1973]): not in order to leave it behind, but to arrive on the other side. What he found there was not consumption (a term that he had already exhausted), but seduction (a term that would fascinate him for the rest of his life). Consequently, while the notion of production may appear to hold a largely redundant place in Baudrillard's *oeuvre*, in actual fact it was a pivotal concept without which his thought may not have been so radically led astray: in his pursuit of production, he was drawn to seduction.

Baudrillard was especially adept at thinking through the implications of our centre of gravity shifting from production to consumption (see in particular *The System of Objects* (1996a [1968]) and *The Consumer Society* (1998a [1970])), and forging a 'general' political economy of the sign to supplant the 'restricted' labour theory of value (see especially *For a Critique of the Political Economy of the Sign* (1981 [1972])). His key insight was that the 'commodity law of value' (through which exchange value expropriates surplus value while debasing labour and eclipsing use value) has given way to the 'structural law of value' (through which the homology of the commodity form and the sign form – such that exchange value is to signifier as use value is to signified – ensures that both value and meaning flicker into and out of existence as simulacra). Production and finality have given way to reproduction and dissemination. '[A] commodity must function as an exchange-value in order better to hide the fact that it circulates like a sign and reproduces the code' (*SED*, 31). In short, the value of labour – which is meant to anchor the world of production – turns out to be a mirage occasioned by the play of signs. And when this mirage is mistaken for reality, it functions not as a centre of gravity around which the exchange relations of the social orbit, but as a black hole into which everything purportedly of value plunges and implodes.

While the mirror of production 'loaded' its commodity-signs 'with the burden of "utility," with gravity' (*SED*, 7), the models of simulation unloaded and unburdened them, enabling them to float freely and commute/consummate among themselves. Such is the great extermination of every system of reference: 'remove this "archaic" obligation to designate something and it finally becomes free, indifferent and totally indeterminate, in the structural or combinatory play which succeeds the previous rule of determinate equivalence' (*SED*, 7). Production simply came to an end – and in its wake seduction, symbolic exchange and death returned with a passion and a vengeance.

Since the mirror of production barely touches our own social formation – except in the imaginary – it is hardly surprising that Baudrillard should insist that it has no bearing whatsoever on other social formations: 'It is only in the *mirror* of production and history, under the double principle of indefinite accumulation (production) and dialectical continuity (history) . . . that our Western culture can reflect itself in the universal as the privileged moment of truth,' argues Baudrillard (*MP*, 114). 'Without this simulation, without this gigantic reflexivity of the concave (or convex) concept of history or production, our era loses all privileges. It would not be any closer to any term of knowledge or any social truth than any other' (*MP*, 114–15).

Accordingly, Baudrillard argued that the principle of equivalence, which is the very essence of the commodity–sign, corrodes the principle of ambivalence, exemplified by the gift and symbolic exchange: 'a *putting into value* opposed to all symbolic *putting into play*' (*MP*, 44). Baudrillard is one of only a handful of theorists to have fully appreciated the real, imaginary and symbolic violence of our compulsion to make everything submit to our (re)productive principle of equivalence: the promiscuous value of exchange and the indifferent exchange of values.

Baudrillard's encounter with production can be summarised by this fable. Once upon a time wealth was '*deduced*, from the grace (God) or beneficence (nature) of an agency which releases or withholds its riches . . . If there is a law here, it is . . . a *natural* law of value. A mutation shakes this edifice of a natural distribution or dispensing of wealth as soon as value is *produced*, as its reference becomes labour' (*SED*, 9). In the wake of this mutation, 'The critique of political economy begins with social production or the mode of production as its reference . . . Today everything has changed again. Production, the commodity form, labour power, equivalence and surplus-value . . . are now things of the past' (*SED*, 9).

Yet Baudrillard did not forget production entirely. For while production may well have ex-terminated itself, leaving only a trace of its alter ego – reproduction – in the imaginary play of simulations and simulacra, the principle of production persists, like the disembodied smile of the Cheshire Cat: not as a principle of labour, but as a principle of appearance: 'The original sense of "production" is not in fact that of material manufacture,' cautions Baudrillard (*FF*, 37). The original sense meant 'to render visible, to cause to appear and be made to appear: *pro-ducere* . . . To produce is to force what belongs to another order . . . to materialize' (*FF*, 37). This is why '*[s]eduction* is that which is everywhere and always opposed to *production*; seduction withdraws something from the visible order and so runs counter to production, whose project is to set everything up in clear view' (*FF*, 37).

With the coupling of production and seduction rather than of production and consumption, we finally come to understand that what is ultimately at stake is the 'forced realization of the world' (*BL*, 45). Everything that is produced is compelled to appear. The irony, of course, is not only that this is literally obscene, but that every appearance – forced or otherwise – is destined to disappear in its turn. '[B]y wishing the world ever more real, we are devitalizing it. The real is growing and growing; one day everything will be real; and when the real is universal, that will spell death' (*PC*, 46).

When all is said and done, our all-too-real world is ex-terminated by reproduction and executed by realisation. Hereinafter, we should forget modes of production, since only modes of disappearance will have been in play. 'It cannot be stressed enough: THERE IS NEVER ANYTHING TO PRO-DUCE' (*EC*, 64).

Passwords

Ambivalence
Consumption + Affluent society
Death
Disappearance
Gift
Political economy of the sign
Seduction
Symbolic exchange
Value + Structural law of value

PSYCHOANALYSIS

Victoria Grace

Baudrillard's work revolves first and foremost around a defiant critique and rejection of any form of productivist logic characteristic of western modernity. This logic, enshrined in semiology, is evident in its twin sibling sites, both of which spawn a lineage of positive objects and subjects: the two sites of political economy and psychoanalysis. Of the two, psychoanalysis most cunningly disguises its exclusion of seduction, is in fact strangely seductive in its prima facie refusal of reversion.

Throughout his work, Baudrillard most certainly makes plentiful use of psychoanalytic concepts and tropes, implicitly acknowledging its inevitable purchase on the constitution of the modern subject. But he is in the main always attempting to subvert its pre-eminent principles. In his references to psychoanalysis he vacillates between mildly ironic (psychoanalysis is for those who 'remain strapped in their Oedipal history' (*FS*, 172)) and searingly scathing (it has spun itself into 'a delirium of conceptual production' satisfying 'a sort of dizziness for explanations' (*BL*, 45)). Indeed, it is particularly with the work of Lacan that Baudrillard's pronouncements on the psychoanalytic enterprise intensify.

What observations provide the basis of Baudrillard's rejection? His is a critique of the political economy of the sign. Where Lacan builds his typology of the subject on an inevitable bar that positions the signified on the other side of the signifier, Baudrillard refuses the inevitability of this bar. For Lacan there can be no subject of language without a recognition of this positioning; such a subject is already 'subjected' to the order of signification; to take up an existence as a subject of language within the social world constituted as self and the Other is to concede to being constituted as a being who lacks (and therefore desires). The bar in Lacan's formulation is the bar of repression (taking Freud's process of negation as his point of departure); hence for something to exist, something must be negated (censored or repressed).

For Baudrillard this is absolutely not the case. The bar acts (intervenes) to establish the process of signification as positive, through a gesture of presence achieved through the parallel gesture of absence (denial, negation, exclusion, repression). According to Baudrillard, the fatal flaw in this structural model is its reliance on a fundamental positivity of the sign and its assumption of value (*CPS*).

Although Lacan builds a complex, critical theorisation of the psychic coordinates of the speaking subject in its imaginary misrecognition of itself, with its symbolic stakes, he begins and ends his psychoanalysis with the positivity of the sign and in particular the priority of the signifier. It is this beginning and end that Baudrillard confronts. Where Lacan cannot envisage any possibility outside the Law (of his symbolic order), apart from the exile of psychosis, Baudrillard precisely does envisage a very different and flourishing 'symbolic' exchange that is outside the register of value, not contained within it as semiology would prescribe. Language is not about establishing what exists, albeit in its imaginary formation within a structure of subject and object; Baudrillard's symbolic is, he writes, not inscribed anywhere: 'It is not what comes to be registered beneath the repression barrier (line), the Lacanian Sd. It is rather what tears all Srs and Sds to pieces, since it is what dismantles their pairing off (*appareillage*) and their simultaneous carving out (*découpe*)' (*CPS*, 162). As a non-place and non-value, symbolic exchange is not of the order of the sign with its bar establishing value or identity. Symbolic ambivalence (singularity outside of value) only emerges in the resolution of the sign, as an event we could say.

For Baudrillard, the demand that the world have meaning through signification is a demand that identity and equivalence be the basis for exchanging thought and world, exchanging the world for its meaning. The symmetry of the mirror relation that psychoanalysis inscribes between the world and its double, between subject and object, is enacted at the cost of the fundamental duality that is ambivalent, is outside any universal scale of value, is outside any point of reference for identity or equivalence. Baudrillard is for the 'dual relation', and this includes language insofar as it is a symbolic exchange and not a process of signification that inevitably institutes the master (and hence phallic) signifier as the universal exchange standard.

Baudrillard suggested that Lacan's seduction avenges Freud's foreclosure of seduction (*S*) but that this is an illusion of seduction; it remains unambivalently within the terms of the Law. Baudrillard was going to write *The Mirror of Desire* (a complement to his *The Mirror of Production* (1975 [1973])), both of which more than glance sideways at the symmetry of Lacan's mirror stage, but he decided it wasn't worth it. For Baudrillard, psychoanalysis was 'almost useless in relation to what was interesting' (*BL*, 58–9).

Passwords

Mirror
Political economy of the sign
Production
Seduction
Semiotics
Symbolic exchange

RADICAL ALTERITY

David Teh

For Baudrillard, 'difference' names the play of otherness (for example, gender or racial otherness) that is contained by the referential system of signification he calls 'communication', that is domesticated within the political economy of the sign. As the semiotic currency of 'psychological, intersubjective alienation or alterity' circulates within that economy alongside others, subject to an order of production, it is therefore a 'tainted' form of otherness (*RA*, 127). Baudrillard wishes to raise the stakes of the play of otherness beyond difference (which 'destroys otherness' (*TE*, 127)), to raise difference to a higher power, beyond the semio-economic realm and into the symbolic register outlined in his theory of symbolic exchange. Radical alterity is what the other summons to bolster itself against corrosion by the system of difference.

Radical alterity implies that we resist the empiricist urge to render everything in communicable forms of knowledge. It is not an analytic system, but a philosophical vocation – a fatal strategy – opposed to the rational understanding and valorisation of difference that underwrites the mainstream ideology of multiculturalism. It appears when communication is bypassed, frozen or short-circuited by an otherness that exceeds it, something incommensurable or uncommunicable, something inexchangeable. It may thus be compared to Derrida's notion of *différance*, in that it names an otherness that is irreducible or (in Bataille's terms) 'sovereign', with respect to the restricted economy of difference staked out by liberalism under the sign of tolerance. This mirrors Bataille's distinction between 'servile' discourse and sovereign writing – the latter consists in an excessive and supplementary relation to the former. While difference describes a production (of information), its radical shadow cannot and should not be made subject to production because its alterity underwrites the entire symbolic order of meaning. When all otherness has been assimilated (as difference), it has no choice but either to disappear or to turn the tables and take its revenge on rational systems of production and meaning (as on September 11, 2001). This reversibility is a hallmark of radical alterity, as it is of all forms of seduction (*RA*).

While it plays a greater role in Baudrillard's later work, radical alterity lurks throughout his *oeuvre*. It is anticipated in his early theorisations of the object – in certain limit cases where the logics of the commodity and value appear to unravel or collapse (for example, gadgets, the objects of the collection or the art auction). In the 1970s he attacked the notions of otherness found in anthropology (*MP*), in political economy (*SED*) and in Marxism's critique of it. Radical alterity could not emerge in its own right until Baudrillard had left these analytics behind, a departure more evident in his controversial critique of sexual difference (*S*). This phase also saw his concepts of death and symbolic exchange crystallise as figures of a radical excess opposed to rational systems of production.

By the 1980s, figures of radical otherness were multiplying, in Baudrillard's theories of the transpolitical/transeconomic, the 'fatal' and, in the sphere of objects, the crystal. A higher power of alterity now consistently denoted retaliatory condensations of symbolic otherness, erupting within the global system of exchange (for example, the absolute commodity, the hostage or the transpolitical figure of the hijacker). In the final stage of his career, Baudrillard recapitulates radical alterity (*RA*) as a response to the implosion of meaning in the era of 'orbital' capital, to a world fully discovered, where what is different is always already assimilated to the universal system of general equivalence. He proposes that we find another means of appreciating what is foreign, one that allows it to remain so. This means reintroducing a necessary distance between thought and its object, an agenda that serves as a guide to his aesthetic preoccupations as well, notably photography and exemplary artworks like Sophie Calle's (*SV*).

For this distantiation, Baudrillard finds a potent ally in the French traveller, doctor and writer Victor Segalen (1878–1919), whose 'exoticism' resisted both the superficiality of the colonial exot and the scientism of a thoroughgoing ethnography. Segalen dwells instead on the strangeness that grows the closer one gets to a foreign culture. ('That is the principle of exoticism according to Segalen: keep your distance' (*RA*, 70)). His call to preserve the other's 'eternal incomprehensibility' becomes a model for Baudrillard to reverse the inexorable appropriation of the world as knowledge under capitalism. This alterity principle has wide ramifications for his philosophy, demanding that we respect not just the other's otherness, but its indifference, or even its silence.

Passwords

Communication + Non-communication
Death
Excess
Fatal
Orientalism
Other + Otherness
Reversibility
Seduction
Symbolic exchange
Transpolitical

RANDOMNESS – see 'destiny' and 'pataphysics'.

REAL

Andrew Wernick

If 'the real' is one of Baudrillard's most elusive concepts this is in part because whatever 'the real' might refer to it has itself become elusive. The 'real', he insists, has disappeared, and that is the mystery. Why, he asks, turning philosophy's classic question upside down, is there nothing rather than something (*PC*, 2)?

What Baudrillard meant by 'the real' and its 'disappearance' is easily misunderstood. When he said 'the Gulf War did not happen' (*GW*) he did not mean that it was only a studio production, like the conspiracy theory version of the Moon landing. Nor, if he drew attention to the stage-managed video game version seen on our screens, was he denying that outside the televisual frame 'real' people were dying horribly and in great numbers. He *was* claiming though that the virtual and the real had become inextricably mixed, that this was only the simulacrum of war (not the *agon* of battle but the coolness of a technical operation) and that the one-sidedness of the contest was perfectly mirrored in the dominance of the virtual over the actual, including in the war room itself.

A subtler misunderstanding is built into *The Matrix*. In a climactic scene Morpheus shows Neo the ruined human world that underlies the virtual world (just like ours!) that the machines have wired into the humans they have turned into batteries. 'Welcome', he says, 'to the desert of the real'. The phrase had appeared in *Simulacra and Simulation* (1994a [1981]). However, Baudrillard's 'desert of the real' was not a bad reality as the truth underlying the illusion of a happy one; it was the evacuation of reality from what could no longer be called the real, the end of the real as something distinct from the apparent, or from its representational double. It is the ghastly immanence of a fully transparent world with no alterity and no outside.

Baudrillard's initial formulation of the reality problem in *For a Critique of the Political Economy of the Sign* (1981 [1972]) takes off from Guy Debord's (1983, 1) proposition that 'everything that was directly lived has moved away into a representation', and focuses on the merger of signs and commodities in an order of 'general exchange'. Expunged of ambivalence and stamped with the code of differential meaning (everything defined in terms of, and exchangeable with, everything else) the meanings attaching to signs float free of any external reference. Baudrillard's second and more definitive formulation, which he developed in the 1970s and 1980s (*MP*, *SED*, *FS*, *SS*) and explored in many works thereafter, concerns images and simulation. Here, taking off from Walter Benjamin on photography and film, de-realisation goes much further. As with Benjamin, the realness of the real is an aura that simulacra lack, but which they also compensate for by magically manufacturing reality as an effect. This hallucinated real – the hyper-real – is more real than real, with heightened reality effects that the merely existent cannot match.

However, the simulacra which have come to proliferate are not just mediatised, but embodied in objects, the built environment, bodies, everything. Through design, modelling and typifications, the tangible real of the human–made world becomes increasingly a blemish-free clone of itself. Correspondingly, what are marked as simulacra become an alibi for the simulation that is everywhere. The framing of Disneyland's Main Street as fake obscures the Disneyland character of Main Street outside the theme park. In addition, the emptiness and artificial aura of a reality that has become simulacral creates a nostalgia for the original and the pristine, which itself feeds the demand for compensatory simulacra, as in the museumification of the past and Baudrillard's possibly apocryphal story about the Tasaday, a 'lost' Phillipine tribe able to reproduce at will its stone-age authenticity for the benefit of tourists and ethnographers at its government protected reserve (*SS*).

That there is a metaphysical subtext in all this becomes increasingly evident in Baudrillard's later writings. His concern for reality is akin to Heidegger's concern with Being, and there are allusions to Descartes and Plato in Baudrillard's play with the Manichean figure of an evil demiurge. In effect, on the basis of his understanding of what advanced capitalism has brought about, Baudrillard has rewritten Nietzsche's (1987) fable about 'How the "Real World" at Last Became a Myth'. The 'real world' whose demise Nietzsche traces is that of Plato: a higher reality which is the repository of truth and of which the world of appearance is only a degraded copy. The imaginary power of this supersensory 'real' declines with the waning of religion, the rehabilitation of the senses and the rise of empirical science. Therewith comes a crisis in which the idea of a true reality behind the apparent collapses, together with its metaphysical and conceptualist residues. But with this step the apparent world has only taken the place of the real one, as objective, intelligible and its own foundation. So, to complete the process, the apparent world as itself now 'the real' is in turn abolished, and with it the grounding objectivity (reality itself!) with which it had been endowed.

Baudrillard takes all this over. However, in his re-rewrite the outcome is an ironic return to Plato. The apparent-as-reality has abolished itself only in the sense that it has disappeared behind a copy of itself that the machination of the world – the becoming machine of capital – has itself engendered. Hence what he calls 'the perfect crime' (*PC*): the disappearance of reality without trace. It is Baudrillard's version of the death of god, except that it is a disappearance, not a death; nor by the same token is it murder, resulting not from human agency but from an objective and seemingly autonomous process, the 'destiny of the object'. There remains, one might say, the 'real' process through which the real has disappeared.

But in one last Baudrillardian twist this process has delivered a result wherein the process itself has become inscrutable. In the age of simulation the 'perspectival space' within which there might be a logic for society and history has itself disappeared. What we used to call history and society have themselves become simulacra.

That is why, for Baudrillard, the old projects of liberation and transformation, together with all critical efforts to unmask the real, have become meaningless. Needed rather are 'fatal strategies' (*FS*) which challenge the system to challenge itself. In the realm of thought, correspondingly, he sees no point in furthering the 'glaciation of meaning'. 'The world was given to us as something enigmatic and unintelligible, and the task of thought is to make it, if possible even more enigmatic and unintelligible' (*IEx*, 151).

Passwords

Disappearance
Gulf War
Hyper-reality
Manichaeism
Perfect crime
Science fiction
Simulacra + Simulacrum
Simulation
Virtual

REALITY TV – see 'communication + non-communication', 'object' and 'obscene'.

REVERSIBILITY

Gerry Coulter

Reversion is an ancient concept in western thought. Herodotus speaks of those who were 'great long ago' but who have now 'become small' (Herodotus, *Book I*). At some points in our history we would have referred to what reversibility represents as poetic justice or the turning of the wheel of fortune. With the Renaissance, humanism, the Enlightenment and the stew of events and ideas which congealed, for a time, under the signs of modernity and progress, we have tended to downplay reversion. Indeed, many still see such a concept as a relic of previous determinisms. Baudrillard says that along with challenge and seduction reversibility is indestructible (*CA*) and that 'reversibility is the fundamental rule' (*LP*, 41). Determinism is not at work here, however, as for Baudrillard reversibility is important precisely because it is an 'absolute weapon' (*FS*, 82) against determination, against such notions as progress being the inevitable result of the passage of time (history).

Reversibility is a vital concept informing Baudrillard's reassessment of linear notions of progress that came to dominate the modern world. Reversibility is predicated on Baudrillard's belief, and his observation, that systems have within them a kind of built-in ability to undermine themselves by their very functioning. Hence, when advanced corporate and scientific medical systems develop antibiotics we find virulent viruses quickly develop which would not otherwise have done so. Our efforts to overprotect ourselves lead to a situation in which we are 'eminently vulnerable' (*EC*, 38). Similarly, computer viruses which can lead to the shutdown of the World Wide Web (such as the 'Love Bug' of 2003) proliferate along the very networks that computer systems use to function. This kind of reversibility was a source of great enjoyment for Baudrillard who deeply disliked systems. Reversibility thus fits into Baudrillard's Manichean dualism by which he understands evil to be every bit as powerful as good. It is in our attempt to do good (antibiotics, computer systems) that we create the possibility of reversion, in the form of human and machinic viruses.

In his distinctive poetic fashion Baudrillard deploys the concept of reversibility to broaden our intellectual horizons concerning development, progress and systems. He wonders in a cool memory (*CM3*) if the dinosaurs did not disappear as the result of a catastrophic *internal* process due to their very powers, and points out that our species may do the same thing precisely because of our superior powers (the ability to build systems which may well collapse or kill the natural environment we depend upon for life). In short, Baudrillard believed that systems tend to reverse at their apogee.

Against the likes of Noam Chomsky, Baudrillard wonders if the masses do not use the popular media to destabilise power by paralysing and immobilising everything (*CA*). In our time of hundreds of television channels and the Fox News motto 'We Report, You Decide', Baudrillard kept his cold eye on the power of the silent majority (*SSM*). His writing in this area helps us to understand that social scientists have a tendency to project their own assumptions on the masses through empirical data-gathering techniques. There is nothing more suspect in Baudrillard's mind than a questionnaire as such an instrument often amounts to little more than a menu of the researcher's preconceptions.

As for the great wave of 'liberation' which was the abandonment of colonial power in the 1950s through to the 1970s, Baudrillard wonders if the subaltern's liberation was not simply the best way the colonial masters could hand to them a bogus power and freedom (*P*). When we examine the crippling debt load carried by many of these countries in the post-colonial era of the World Bank we see one possible meaning of Baudrillard's assertion.

Baudrillard recently used reversibility to explain what has been happening to American power. When the images of abused Iraqi prisoners at Abu Ghraib were released to the world we soon discovered that the images originated from the digital cameras American troops are now outfitted with. These images were powerful examples of how far America had fallen from its promise to bring democracy and liberation to the peoples of the Middle East. Baudrillard pointed to the moment as one of reversibility as America, whose global status had so long lived by the image, was now dying by it (*CA*).

Reversibility is also important to Baudrillard's challenge to morality and ethics as for these concepts there must always be progress. Reversibility then is the concept which allows Baudrillard to look for ironies superior to morality. Terrorism too is also based in reversibility. In the case of 9/11 it was a reversal of humiliation.

From his first use of the term in a more analytical manner to his last (in a more ironic way), reversibility remains a quasi-spiritual entity in Baudrillard's thought – a kind of evil spirit that would ensure that every system will be overturned (*LP*). It is the concept which he deploys to argue that modernity is a mythology devoted to the irreversibility of time, production and history (*EC*). An irreversibility against which Baudrillard posits reversibility, one that is poetic and always already open to reversion itself (*AA*).

Passwords

Duality
Evil
Manichaeism
Masses
Media
Seduction
Terrorism

$$\boxed{\text{S}}$$

SAID, EDWARD (1935–2003) – see 'orientalism'.

SAUSSURE, FERDINAND DE (1857–1913) – see 'America', 'anagrams', 'hyper-reality', 'nihilism', 'poetic resolution', 'semiotics', 'sign', 'simulation' and 'value + structural law of value'.

SCIENCE FICTION

Catherine Constable

In a short chapter entitled 'Simulacra and Science Fiction' Baudrillard sets out three orders of simulacra which generate three modes of writing. The first order of 'natural' simulacra generates the 'imaginary of the *utopia*' (*SS*, 121), which sets up an absolute division between reality and fiction: 'the island of utopia stands opposed to the continent of the real' (*SS*, 122). The second order of 'productive' simulacra is the realm of science fiction, whose imaginary worlds are not 'qualitatively different' from the world of production, energy and machines, but rather a projection and 'multiplication of its own possibilities' (*SS*, 122). The third order obliterates the distinction between reality/fiction and the critical distance that distinguishes the real from its projected, fictional futures. The 'simulacra of simulation' (*SS*, 121) created through information systems and cybernetics marks a shift to the era of models. The model's capacity for infinite manipulation serves to anticipate and nullify the formulation of possible futures, because all possibilities are already contained within the model: 'it is not about a parallel universe, . . . or even a possible universe – neither possible, impossible, neither real nor unreal: *hyperreal*' (*SS*, 125). Contemporary science fiction, specifically J. G. Ballard's short stories and novels, captures and plays out the hyper-real erasure of all oppositional distinctions.

Baudrillard's argument concerning science fiction has a characteristically paradoxical formulation. Science fiction is writing that fictionalises the possibilities presented by science and new technologies. In undermining the opposition reality/fiction, the third order of simulacra brings about the end of reality, metaphysics and science fiction; however, the erasure of the opposition also marks the science fictionalisation of reality. Thus 'science fiction . . . is no longer anywhere, and it is everywhere, in the circulation of models . . . in the very principle of the surrounding simulation' (SS, 126). The disappearance of reality creates two different roles for science fiction. In the first, writers such as Phillip K. Dick are said to 'revitalize, reactualize, requotidianize fragments of simulation' in order 'to reinvent the real' (SS, 124). The second role is exemplified by Ballard's *Crash*, which reflects the hyper-real destruction of reality and fiction.

For Baudrillard, '*Crash* is *our* world, nothing in it is "invented"' (SS, 125). *Crash* is both hyper-real and 'hyper-functional' – beyond 'the old (mechanical and mechanistic) couple function/dysfunction' (SS, 125). The latter occurs through the presentation of automobile accidents throughout *Crash* in which bodies are 'confused with technology in its violating and violent dimension' (SS, 111). In this way the body is reconfigured as 'a semiurgy of contusions, scars, mutilations, wounds that are so many new sexual organs', thereby dispersing the traditional erogenous zones (SS, 112). At the same time, the psychoanalytic zoning of the body into surface versus depth, the latter taking the form of instincts and drives, is also obliterated. The body as a pure surface of wounding/scarification becomes a sign. While 'the anagrammatization of sex on the whole length of the body' (SS, 114) reconfigures sexuality as 'carnal abstraction' (SS, 112), it also abolishes traditional conceptions of sex and desire and the concomitant designations of sexual perversion and dysfunction. For Baudrillard, the obliteration of the binary functional/dysfunctional in *Crash* is crucial to its fascination. The moral and 'critical judgment that is still part of the functionality of the old world' is entirely absent from the text, which leads Baudrillard to laud *Crash* as an exemplary instance of 'hypercriticism' (SS, 119).

Baudrillard's reading of *Crash* is highly controversial. Numerous critics argue Ballard's work is a cautionary moral tale that therefore does not constitute a form of hypercriticism (Hayles, 1991; Sobchack 1991). Baudrillard is also said to misread Ballard's critique of a death-orientated male sexuality (Sobchack, 1991; Ruddick, 1992). More interestingly, such critics occasionally praise Baudrillard for being 'as skilled a fiction writer as Ballard, Dick, or Stanislaw Lem. More than describe the implosion into simulation, his works enact it' (Hayles, 1991: 323). Baudrillard's writing on science fiction takes up the tropes and terms utilised within the novels (Butler, 2003), blurring the boundary between theory and fiction, and thereby instantiating the breakdown between genres characteristic of the third order of simulacra (SS, 121). It is perhaps unsurprising that the theory/fiction of *Simulacra and Simulation* (1994a [1981]) should inspire *The Matrix* trilogy, a popular science fiction film series. While Baudrillard

(2004a) and other commentators (for example, Merrin, 2005; Smith, 2005) argue that the trilogy simply misrepresents his position, other critics (for example, Rovira, 2005; Constable, 2009) have argued that *The Matrix* trilogy adapts and transforms Baudrillard's work in interesting ways.

Passwords

Hyper-reality
Literature
Model
Sign
Simulacra + Simulacrum
Simulation
Utopia

SEDUCTION

Marcus A. Doel

Seduction plays a pivotal role in Baudrillard's conceptual universe and theoretical practice. It is a signature concept – even though he is much better known for his take on hyper-realism, postmodernism, and simulation. Yet seduction is also one of Baudrillard's most elusive, enigmatic and ambivalent concepts. To make things even more challenging for the unwary reader, seduction is not only a key component of Baudrillard's *oeuvre*. He aspired to render theory itself seductive.

Baudrillard locates seduction at the centre of a dense cluster of terms that includes production, realisation, obscenity, power, reversibility, play, symbolic exchange, disappearance and death. In keeping with the etymological derivation of seduction – from the Latin, *se-ducere*, 'to take aside, to divert from one's path' (*S*, 22) – Baudrillard gives seduction an explicitly spatial inflection rather than a sexual reference. This deflection – the exemplary form of which is the sign that differs and defers reference, the sign that is barred and devoid of meaning ('Only signs without referents, empty, senseless, absurd and elliptical signs, absorb us' (*S*, 74)) – has been the source of considerable confusion in the secondary literature, when writers mistake seduction for a referential concept (weighed down by a femme fatale) rather than a differential concept (splayed out through a manifold deflection). To be seduced is to be drawn towards something that constantly eludes us, like the inexhaustible face of the beloved, and to lose ourselves on its surface. So, although seduction is located at the centre

of a conceptual cluster, it offers neither stability nor balance nor security. To the contrary, precisely because it leads astray, seduction diverts,
deflects and unhinges the entire constellation of terms, including seduction itself. Aping the 'empty square' of structuralism or the '*différance*' of
deconstruction – both of which are always displaced and misplaced in relation to themselves, yet without which nothing would circulate – seduction
enables the conceptual cluster to hold together and compels it to fly apart.
As an ex-centric and ex-static enigma misplaced 'at the centre of things',
seduction not only diverts them from their 'right' and 'proper' path, it
also makes them curve in on themselves, spiralling towards the non-sense
whence they came, and the 'superficial abyss' into which everything of
value ultimately plunges. 'Things aspire to be straight, . . . but they all
have a secret curvature,' says Baudrillard. 'Seduction is that which follows
this curvature, subtly accentuating it until things, in following their own
cycle, reach the superficial abyss where they are dissolved . . . [I]n gambling money is *seduced*; it is deviated from the law of value and is transformed into a substance of bidding and challenge' (*EC*, 70).

Seduction, then, is a fatal attraction: labyrinthine, vertiginous and aporetic. It leads nowhere other than astray. Baudrillard's hunch is that all paths
ultimately lead astray – including those that ostensibly dedicate themselves
to directness, straightforwardness and irreversibility. When all is said and
done, only seduction will have been left in play: 'the destiny of signs is to
be torn from their destination, deviated, displaced, diverted, recuperated,
seduced' (*EC*, 80). Everything else is an illusion: from the Latin, *il-ludere*,
'in play, against play.' (Hence the almost absolute proximity of the 'play' of
seduction in Baudrillard and the 'play' of *différance* and dissemination in
Derrida.) This is why Baudrillard insists that 'The absolute rule of thought
is to give back the world as it was given to us – unintelligible. And, if possible, to render it a little more unintelligible' (*PC*, 105).

Baudrillard encountered seduction by way of production. While seduction
(*se-ducere*) diverts and leads astray, production (*pro-ducere*, to put forward)
'materialize[s] by force what belongs to another order' (*S*, 34). In other
words, 'Seduction removes something from the order of the visible, while
production constructs everything in full view' (*S*, 34). So, rather than situate
production and seduction within the seemingly incongruous domains of
industry and sexuality, which meld together in libidinal economy (Lyotard)
and desiring-production (Deleuze and Guattari), Baudrillard situates them
with respect to appearance and disappearance, and specifically the 'play'
– understood in a spatial sense – of appearances and disappearances.
Consequently, seduction comes to be figured twice: once in the lesser form
of disappearance, in the sense that all appearances are destined to disappear
in their turn ('everything wants to be exchanged, reversed, or abolished in

a cycle' (*FF*, 53)); and again in the greater form of the 'play' of appearances and disappearances, since this play is itself a form of seduction ('a circular and reversible process of challenge, one-upmanship, and death' (*FF*, 55)). This is why Baudrillard characterises the curvature of seduction as a double spiral: on the one hand, 'a spiral swerving towards a sphere of the sign, the simulacrum and simulation' (*EC*, 79), and, on the other hand, 'a spiral of the reversibility of all signs in the shadow of seduction and death' (*EC*, 79). Since the two spirals are always displaced and misplaced in relation to one another, their fate is to perpetually lead one another astray, without ever coming into contact with one another.

While one might expect a symmetrical relationship between appearance and disappearance, since they are two halves of the same cycle, western culture has nevertheless shown a systematic bias towards appearance, and a concerted effort to dissimulate disappearance. 'Everything is to be produced, everything is to be legible, everything is to become real, visible, accountable; everything is to be transcribed in relations of force, systems of concepts or measurable energy; everything is to be said, accumulated, indexed and recorded' (*S*, 34–5). According to Baudrillard, western culture has become increasingly fanatical about appearance and forced realisation: 'an *orgy of realism*, an orgy of *production*' (*S*, 32). We inhabit 'a pornographic culture *par excellence*; one that pursues the workings of the real at all times and in all places' (*S*, 34). Left to their own devices, however, this 'mad obsession with the real' (*FF*, 38), this 'rage to uncover the secret' (*EC*, 73), 'this compulsion to be rid of the world by realizing it, by forcing material objectivity upon it' (*PC*, 42), this desire 'to drive right through to the end, to exhaust all the possibilities' (*PC*, 48), is both obscene and suicidal: 'Obscenity begins when there is no more spectacle, no more stage, no more theatre, no more illusion, when everything becomes immediately transparent, visible, exposed in the raw and inexorable light of information and communication,' insists Baudrillard (*EC*, 21–2). 'It is no longer the obscenity of the hidden, the repressed, the obscure, but that of the visible, the all-too-visible, the more-visible-than-visible' (*EC*, 22).

For Baudrillard, obscenity is the destiny of modernity's long-standing project of effecting the 'destruction of appearances (and of the seduction of appearances) in the service of meaning' (*SS*, 160). Yet this project of dis-enchantment cannot but fail to be led astray by 'the immense process of the destruction of meaning, equal to the earlier destruction of appearances' (*SS*, 161), which Baudrillard associates with postmodernity.

Faced with obscenity and the consequent decomposition of meaning and reference into non-sense and undecidability, Baudrillard brings seduction back into play: '[T]he universe of seduction . . . stands out radically against the universe of production,' notes Baudrillard. It is 'no longer a question of bringing things forward . . . for a world of value, but of . . . diverting them from that value, and hence . . . to destine them for the play of appearances' (*PW*, 21).

Ordinarily, when theorists are faced with the appearance of a world, a reality or a theory, they undertake a critique by uprooting foundations, exploiting contradictions, displacing cornerstones, overturning structures and so on. However, every appearance 'can adapt to its subversion or inversion, but not to the reversion of its terms. Seduction is this reversible form' (*S*, 21). Baudrillard's key insight is to recognise that we are dealing with obscene modes of appearance and realisation that 'do not any more play on reversibility, on metamorphosis. And which have installed them-selves, on the contrary, in the irreversibility of time, of production, and things like that' (*BL*, 57). What this situation demands is the deployment of a strategy of seduction that 'dismantles the beautiful order of irrevers-ibility, of the finality of things' (*BL*, 57). Consequently, such a strategy needs to deflect irreversibility and restitute reversion. Accordingly, for Baudrillard, '[t]he principle of reversibility . . . requires that all that has been produced must be destroyed, and that which appears must disappear . . . Saturated by the mode of production, we must return to the path of an aesthetic of disappearance' (*EC*, 71). Such a manoeuvre returns the real 'to the great game of simulacra, which makes things appear and disappear . . . One could maintain *that before having been produced the world was seduced*, that it exists, as all things and ourselves, only by virtue of having been seduced' (*EC*, 71).

Seduction, then, is our culture's saving grace. For when everything has been forced to appear, when everything has been exhausted through reali-sation and rendered obscene, it will remain the case that 'the reversible form prevails over the linear form. The excluded form prevails, secretly, over the dominant form. The seductive form prevails over the productive form' (*S*, 17). When everything is given over, finally, to production and obscenity, its seduction will remain in play. Everything is destined to go astray. Seduction is 'an ironic, alternative form' that 'provides a space, not of desire, but of play and defiance' (*S*, 21).

Passwords

Disappearance
Double spiral
Obscene
Production
Reversibility
Symbolic exchange

SEGALEN, VICTOR (1878–1919) – see 'orientalism' and 'radical alterity'.

SEMIOTICS

Gary Genosko

The theory of value supporting structural linguistics is criticised by Baudrillard in *Symbolic Exchange and Death* (1993a [1976]) in an effort to move beyond all logics of value through the principle of symbolic exchange. This does not constitute a critical semiology because it entails that 'signs must burn' and thus is more destructively transgressive than constructive. Baudrillard posits a 'structural revolution of value' that combines convertible elemental relations from political economy and semiology in a political economy of the sign.

The general political economy of value developed by Baudrillard in *For a Critique of the Political Economy of the Sign* (1981 [1972]) is based on a homology between the linguistic sign and commodity form. The domain of value is for Baudrillard homogeneous and consists of a number of mutually convertible relations, at the base of which is the idea that two-sided forms (sign consisting of signifier and signified and commodity consisting of exchange value and use value) express relations of usefulness and equivalence: a thing may be exchanged for something dissimilar (money for a loaf of bread) or may be defined in relation to things of a similar kind (money of different face value in a national currency); likewise, exchange value is based on the expression of equality in abstraction between two similar things, whereas use value is realised by using a thing. Symbolic exchange is heterogeneous to such homogeneity and thus cannot be converted into any logic of value.

This claim of mutual structural implication between exchange value and signifier and use value and signified, once abolished in their specificities in being generalised, stops abruptly when considered in relation to symbolic exchange. The symbolic exchange of a thing as a use value is impossible for two reasons: Baudrillard claims that consumer society does not produce culturally significant differences through which one's needs may be satisfied; rather, use is metaphysical and meta-functional and always for others, hence produced for exchangeability, already social, and having taken the form of exchange value.

Symbolic exchange is a critique of use value's incomparability based on false one-to-one identities of paired forms: the signified has meaning not in relation to one signifier but as an effect of meaning generated through signifier relations of negative difference; likewise, needs are effects of industrially and artificially produced differences between objects; needs cannot be pinned down to specific objects that satisfy them since they are system elements.

Symbolic exchange is not equal to use value because it alone is incommensurable in its singularity, concreteness and ambivalence based on obligatory relations between persons. Symbolic objects are unlike signs and commodities. They embody non-economic relationships and do not acquire value in terms of differential relations in a system. Symbolic exchange realises the false promise of use value. It enters into the domain of value by breaking and entering and sets signification ablaze.

Why must signs burn? Signs are at the heart of Baudrillard's explanation of how the real is conjured up in a system of objects based on consumption. The manipulation of signs through consumption of differences between coded objects provides shelter from a real that is desperately signified by them. This is the precise meaning of the structural revolution of value: real referentiality is annihilated and simulation of the real wins out. The real is an effect of a structural system of value: 'The systems of reference for production, signification, the affect, substance and history, all this equivalence to a "real" content, loading the sign with the burden of "utility", with gravity – its form of representative equivalence – all this is over with. Now the other stage of value has the upper hand, a total relativity, general commutation, combination and simulation' (*SED*, 6–7).

However, at the heart of Baudrillard's theorisation of symbolic exchange is an anti-semiology advancing two claims. The first is that the linguistic sign described by Saussure as a two-sided psychical object encircling a signifier and signified whose necessary union is expressed by the bar mutually implicating them allows no foreign material to enter. Hence, there is no real referent, nothing extra-linguistic or extensional, of this kind of sign. It is 'free, indifferent and totally indeterminate' (*SED*, 7). This 'structural play' is supported by a second claim. In Saussure, the relation between signifying entities (signs) tends to dominate the relation internal to the sign just described. This is how Baudrillard understands the emphasis on the second principle of linguistic value (things related to similar things in a system): it results in a closed system of relations rather than an exchange against something dissimilar, namely the real. Ultimately, Baudrillard rejects signs altogether and subsumes them under the indeterminacy of the code.

Passwords

Code
Political economy of the sign

Real
Sign
Singularity
Symbolic exchange
Value + Structural law of value

SEX/GENDER

Victoria Grace

Sex as difference; this is the problem. Sex as identity is an artefact of this problem. The construct of sexual difference is one pivotal site through which Baudrillard exposes an economy of difference as one that is both rejecting of, yet haunted by, seduction. The construction of masculine and feminine as different within a dichotomous structure that marks individuals as one or the other is an example of the semiological reduction of what Baudrillard calls the symbolic. To be male or female is to be constituted within the order of identity; by contrast, Baudrillard is adamant, 'No being is assigned by nature to a sex' (*CPS*, 99). He is rather inclined to the view that each subject is traversed by the very ambivalence of activity and passivity that is of the order of the 'sexual', as 'sexual differentiation is registered as a difference in the body of each subject and not as an absolute term linked to a particular sexual organ' (*CPS*, 99). To insist on this linkage and its absolute quality is a form of violence that codifies and universalises a reference for the sexual. Furthermore, this semiologically instituted 'difference' or 'opposition', once established, serves a cultural logic whereby one sex has absolute privilege relative to the other.

Difference is structurally predicated on comparability. Sexual difference, sex as difference, has to be confronted by the ambivalence of the sexual, by a logic that is radically other than that based on comparability. Female and male become two incomparable terms; as Baudrillard writes, 'if there is [. . .] no sexual difference, this is because the two sexes are not opposable' (*PC*, 122). To posit the sexes as other to each other is not the same thing as positing difference: 'One might even say that difference is what destroys otherness' (*TE*, 127).

The two sexes constituted as different raises the question, as it indeed has in recent feminist theory, of why just two? Why not three or four or five or more? To introduce additional terms assumes a unit that can be added to or multiplied. Rather than representing a radical subversion of a binary logic, this proliferation of the number of sexes is simply more of the same, relying on a standard (what is 'sex') against which relations of equivalence and difference can be ascertained (this is another sex, and another, and so on). On the contrary, Baudrillard insists that sex does not have a calculable status; as well as the two sexes not being terms of a binary opposition, they equally cannot be added together, nor can they be part of a series (*SED*). The otherness of the sexes 'come into play' only in the dual relation: 'Only in duality are the sexes *fatal* to each other. In multiple relations they are merely mirrors of each other, and interlocking self-refractions' (*IEx*, 64). In this sense it is possible to see how Baudrillard's notion of the ambivalence of sex traversing each subject is different from Freud's polymorphous sexuality of the 'bisexual' infant, as the latter is still reliant on a calculus of two in one.

The American-derived term 'gender' is a relatively new invention and one that Baudrillard engages in its historical specificity. With the movement for 'sexual liberation' of the 1960s, the abstraction that is 'identity' becomes a 'choice', and as such sex becomes gender: 'once you are liberated, you are forced to ask who you are' (*A*, 46). The problematic of gender is 'now taking over from that of sex' and 'illustrates this progressive dilution of the sexual function' (*PC*, 117). This becomes the era of the transsexual.

Today it is less a matter of sexual difference and more a matter of sexual indifference (*P*). Ambivalence is replaced by bivalence, ambiguity and unisex. As Baudrillard writes in *The Perfect Crime* (1996c [1995a]), when otherness is in short supply, it becomes produced as difference, as is evident in the body, sex, social relations today: the other as 'different' is invented. In *America* (1988b [1986]), Baudrillard makes the observation that the outward signs of masculinity and femininity are trending towards zero. As this trend is pushed to its logical conclusion this would no longer render male and female as different, meaning the end of sexual difference, and we would see 'a slide towards a different system of values' (*A*, 47–8). This different system, he hazards, would see a 'dissemination of individual sexes referring only to themselves, each one managed as an independent enterprise' (*A*, 47), a trend that is possibly even more evident twenty-three years on from Baudrillard's writing of *America* (1988b [1986]). Sex in this sense becomes a mere vestige of that which has disappeared.

Passwords

Ambivalence
Body
Duality
Other + Otherness
Seduction
Transsexuality

SIGN

John Lechte

Marx developed a political economy based on a productivist and materialist metaphysic. He argued that the world of work and labour power were the key elements in understanding the 'fetishism' of the commodity form in bourgeois society. Baudrillard criticises Marx's materialism in the very name of political economy – a political economy of the sign, where the superstructure, against Marx, comes to claim its rights. For, in relation to production, 'nothing is *produced*, strictly speaking: everything is *deduced*' (*SED*, 9). Furthermore, the idea of universal needs, upon which Marx's theory is centred, is, says Baudrillard (*CPS*), ideological, not real. The same goes for the idea of scarcity in classical economics: it, too, is ideological.

The celebration of Ferdinand de Saussure's theory of the sign as the difference between the signifier and the signified will give Baudrillard's critique of all realisms its impetus, even if, ultimately, Saussure's linguistic theory also comes to bear the brunt of this critique.

Famously, Saussure, against the tradition of historical linguistics which had privileged a historical, or diachronic, theory of linguistic meaning, emphasises a synchronic and differential approach to meaning that defined the sign as being composed of the relationship between a signifier and a signified – a relationship that is arbitrary. In other words, there is no essential link between a given signifier and its signified (for example, between the word, 'tree' and the object designated). Furthermore, a synchronic approach to meaning implies that it is the relationship between signifiers, and not their intrinsic status, which is at issue. Relationships, and therefore difference as the code, govern the make-up of the Saussurian sign, not essential qualities that would be meaningful even in the event of the sign's complete isolation.

For Saussure, a signifier and a signified can never exist separately but only inextricably together. There is no signifier without its signified. And it is the signified that Baudrillard comes to view as problematic in his theory of the sign, where, ultimately, a sign becomes a simulacrum which means that it bears no relation whatever to reality (*SS*).

Saussurian linguistics also gave rise to semiotics (the theory of signs and significations) and the wide-ranging movement of structuralism in the social sciences. Thus during the 1960s all the talk in the circles that mattered centred on the importance of the differential nature of the sign. Such was the influence of this tendency in France and subsequently in the US and elsewhere that those thinkers experienced in traditions such as phenomenology or existentialism had to stand up and be counted. Merleau-Ponty made significant concessions to structuralism, while Sartre remained the same. Baudrillard, who wrote some of his most influential works in the late 1960s and early-to-mid 1970s (*SO, CS, CPS, MP, SED*), sought to think through it rather than take up the cudgels for structuralism. And nothing was more important to this rethinking than a reworking of the nature and significance of the sign.

If Baudrillard was able to unsettle Marxist theory by concentrating on the impossibility of ever proving that there existed essential needs to be satisfied – a point which had flow-on effects for the productivist metaphysic (if needs could not be proven, then neither could be proven the objective nature of production and labour power) – Baudrillard's target in Saussurian linguistics and semiotics was the apparently unshakable reality of the signified. Even Lacan in psychoanalysis had to resort to a theory of the '*points de capiton*' (anchor points) in order to prevent the signifier from floating out of the frame of rationality and meaning altogether.

Being beholden to the signified, and not just the signifier, was the weak link in the Saussurian theory of the sign. How does Baudrillard, for his part, proceed here? And how does his conception of the sign tie in with political economy? Part of the story is based on the transformation of use value into exchange value and exchange value into sign value. The latter remains in touch with political economy because it performs a political task – something the Saussurian notion of the sign bypassed altogether. Thus Baudrillard writes, 'Through objects, each individual and each group searches out his-her place in an order . . . Through objects a stratified society speaks' (*CPS*, 38). Ultimately, there are no objects if we mean by this elements of an external reality. There are only signs; but these are signs which mark out, as we can see, power relations in society; they cannot be exchanged for reality (*IEx*). While there is no essential external reality reflected in the sign, this does not mean that the sign is politically innocent. Thus the consumption of objects must be defined, '*not only structurally as a system of exchange and of signs, but strategically as a mechanism of power*' (*CPS*, 85). Through signs, politics plays itself out. Baudrillard thus continues to give a veiled salute to Marx.

Politics, however, is not symbolic. In a schema that illuminates the structure of Baudrillard's theory, the symbolic assumes the role of ambivalence: it does not participate in any essential link to reality, but neither is it constituted through difference, as is sign value. What is truly symbolic endures, unlike the fashion object which is entirely ephemeral and subject to the difference constitutive of sign value. The sign excludes the symbolic, banishes it from the centre of social and political life in the interest of maintaining the system of consumption and exchange itself (the basis of power relations). The equivalence of the sign value erases the ambivalence of the symbol (*CPS*).

Although the sign (as a system or code of differences) challenges naive realism, it is in Saussure's, then Benventiste's, version based in a metaphysic which privileges the signified-referent. Semiology, as the analysis of difference in the sign system, was not the answer and must also be transcended. For the arbitrary relation between signifier and signified is never experienced as such in a given social context, but rather as a moment of power where the two elements appear as resolutely fixed. In the end, it is a matter of restoring the symbolic, which is outside the code, to a position of pre-eminence. This, above all, Baudrillard seeks to reveal in going beyond semiology in his analysis of the sign. In other words, 'only total revolution, theoretical and practical, can restore the symbolic in the demise of the sign and of value. Even signs must burn' (*CPS*, 163).

Passwords

Fashion
Political economy of the sign
Production
Semiotics
Symbolic exchange

SIMULACRA + SIMULACRUM

William Pawlett

The notion of the simulacrum – meaning image, semblance or appearance – is explored throughout Baudrillard's *oeuvre*, from his work on the sign form (*CPS*) and the 'orders of simulacra' (*SED*), to his theorisations of seduction (*S*), impossible exchange (*IEx*) and the annihilation of simulacra in the virtual and integral reality (*LP*). The term simulacrum derives from the Latin *simulare* meaning to 'make like' or simulate (*OED*, 1989, plural form: *simulacra*) and is usually understood as constituting a problem for thought because it raises the issues of falsity and untruth. However, Baudrillard entirely rejects this (Platonic) understanding of simulacra. Influenced by Friedrich Nietzsche and Pierre Klossowski, he understands simulacra not as false images, nor as obscuring truth behind a facade, but as that which 'hides the truth's non-existence' (*S*, 35). In this sense the simulacrum is 'true'.

Baudrillard's early studies (*CPS*, *MP*) sought to understand the repudiation of symbolic exchange through the erection of the laws of value.

The signifier, considered as form rather than content, produces the effect of the real or referent as mirage, 'alibi' or simulation. The 'real' for Baudrillard is 'only the simulacrum of the symbolic, its form reduced and intercepted by the sign' (*CPS*, 162). In *Symbolic Exchange and Death* (1993a [1976]) Baudrillard turns to a speculative classification of the orders of simulacra. The first order dominates from the Renaissance to the Industrial Revolution, is based on the natural law of value and is characterised by the *counterfeit*. The second order of simulacra dominates through the industrial era, is based on the market law of value and is characterised by *production*. The third order dominates consumer society; it is governed by the 'structural law of value' and is characterised by *simulation*. The orders of simulacra are devices of social control, power structures which produce specific social relations based on binary disjunction. The first order severs or bars cycles of symbolic exchange and establishes the notion of the 'real'. The second order is distinctive in that it abolishes the notion of originality through the 'infinite series' of industrial production. With the third order goods, meanings and objects are not merely produced but are '*conceived according to their very reproducibility*' (*SED*, 56). Meaning or value is generated exclusively through affiliation to a model such that 'reality is immediately contaminated by its simulacrum' (*SED*, 74). This is the moment of implosion into hyper-reality, the loss of the 'sovereign difference' which created the illusion called 'reality'.

Baudrillard discusses simulacra in relation to sexuality in *Seduction* (1990a [1979]), arguing that pornography functions to maintain the simulacrum of sex, the illusion of an autonomous 'sexual' realm based on the physical satisfaction of desire. The notion of sexual liberation not only retroactively installs a principle of repression in order to function, it also props up the idea of sex as reality and truth. However, as truth has no foundation beyond the play of simulacra – the play of words and ideas – all 'truths' are at the mercy of seduction, the sudden diverting of signs into a play of appearance and disappearance. Linguistic signs are simulacra: they can play at signification or be seduced into nonsense, poetry or anagrammatic rituals. There is no hinterworld to ground a system of metaphysics: the world is a simulacrum.

In *Simulacra and Simulation* (1994a [1981]), Baudrillard sketches four successive phases of simulacra. Firstly, he argues, the image is taken as 'the reflection of a profound reality'. Then the image 'masks and denatures a profound reality'. The first phase Baudrillard associates with Platonism and the second with Marxism. Thirdly, following Nietzsche, Baudrillard contends that the image also 'masks the *absence* of a profound reality', and finally, with simulation, 'has no relation to any reality whatsoever: it is its own pure simulacrum' (*SS*, 6). These phases are not intended as historical stages but tendencies within the image. Baudrillard contends that the present media age is dominated by the 'pure simulacrum', giving a number of examples such as the media's love of political scandals and Disneyland which 'exists in order to hide that it is the "real" country, all of "real" America that *is* Disneyland . . . it is no longer a question of a false representation of reality (ideology) but of concealing the fact that the real is no longer real' (*SS*, 12–13). In other words, America, like Disneyland, is perceived and understood *through* simulacra: news and documentary images, tourist images, cinema and TV images, and the consumption of these images often precedes any 'real' experience of living in or visiting America. The simulacrum becomes the 'real'; there is no real that is more 'real' than simulacra, yet such simulacra are politically crucial because they obscure this fundamental absence of the real.

Baudrillard approaches the issue of simulacra from a different angle in *Impossible Exchange* (2001a [1999b]). Drawing upon Klossowski's notion of 'living currency', Baudrillard explores the curvature or spiralling together of the system (of simulation) with its 'absolute polar opposite' (*IEx*, 122) of singularities, such as impulses and emotions, creativity and death, which lack equivalents and are consequently impossible to exchange. The latter cannot be expressed directly, yet if they acquire a simulacrum or image they can be 'traded' or symbolically exchanged. That which is irreducible to the laws of value, in rare moments 'transfuses through the abstraction which denies it' (*IEx*, 122–3). In such moments, which cannot acquire duration or permanence, sign and thing are reversible; each is made volatile and cannot accumulate into abstracted or coded meaning. However, such moments become increasingly rare in the age of digital and virtual technologies. For Baudrillard computer-generated images are *not* simulacra because sign and thing, impulse and simulacra, are abolished by a total abstraction: the virtual. Digital technology becomes a fetish, a substitute for the world and for the sign which entered into relations with the world, sometimes designating the world, sometimes seducing it. Simulacra, reality and even human beings are now disappearing from the virtual world, Baudrillard speculates, yet this disappearance is not our death, it is our passion, our fascination and our art of disappearance.

Passwords

America
Code
Disappearance
Gulf War
Hyper-reality
Image

SIMULATION

Andrew Wernick

Simulation is a key Baudrillardian concept, and for many the one by which he is best known. In Latin, *simulare* (from the same Indo-European root as 'same' in English) means to copy. In modern English, simulation came to have the connotation of falseness and pretence. More recently it came to mean creating an analogue or mathematical model of something in order to study how it operates via artificially or abstractly producing its effects. With the advent of 'realistic' media (photography, film, sound recording, TV, digital media) it has also come to refer to an audio–visual experience that artfully mimics but otherwise has no connection with the reality it presents, as in a flight simulator used in pilot training and video games. Such an experience may at the same time heighten the senses and be more real than real: hyper-real.

All these meanings are present in Baudrillard's use of the term. But what ties them together is the notion of a kind of copy which is not merely indistinguishable from what it copies but in which the very distinction between copy and original disappears. The simulacrum, as the type of representation produced by simulation, is a copy without an original. In a world in which there are only simulations, or in which the form of the simulacrum predominates, the world itself is a copy of a copy and the very notions of authenticity and truth lose their reference point.

There is a crucial distinction in this respect between dissimulation and simulation. The latter is beyond truth and lies. As Baudrillard (*SS*, 3) puts it: 'to dissimulate is to pretend not to have what one has. To simulate is to feign to have what one doesn't have'. However, to simulate is not just to engage in pretence.

'Whoever simulates an illness produces in himself some of the symptoms' (Littré). Therefore, pretending, or dissimulating, leaves the principle of reality intact: the difference is always clear, it is simply masked, whereas simulation threatens the difference between the 'true' and the 'false', the 'real' and the 'imaginary'. (*SS*, 3)

Baudrillard's guiding hypothesis, first elaborated in *Symbolic Exchange and Death* (1993a [1976]) and further developed in *Simulacra and Simulation* (1994a [1981]), is that with the rise of post-industrial consumer capitalism (which he had earlier characterised as an order of 'general exchange' (*CPS*)) we have entered 'the age of simulation'.

One aspect of the change bringing this about has to do with media technology; Baudrillard's genealogy of simulation (he presents several) builds, in part, on Walter Benjamin's (2008) account of the transformation of art by visual media involving 'mechanical reproduction'. A first stage in the history of the simulacrum is as an individual artefact, for example a hand-made copy of a painting. A second, with photography and sound recording, is the mechanically reproduced copy in which all copies are identical with one another, but still retain a trace-connection with an original (light on silver oxide, soundwaves in wax). A third, the case of movies, is the production of a mechanically reproducible copy which has no original outside the composite process of its studio production. The shift from the production of serial copies to that of what is immediately (and only) mechanically reproducible takes us, in Baudrillard's language, from the second to the third order of simulation. He also came to speak of a fourth order of simulation, 'the fractal stage' (*TE*, 5), in which the mechanically reproducible product is not a unique series but an infinite array of possibilities generated by models. Here, simulacra become viral, they metastasise, and even the sense that referentiality is something lost disappears.

It is sometimes thought that Baudrillard's concept of simulation is confined to the world of media, particularly digital, where such a condition is fully realised. However, his application of the term is much wider, so that it becomes an enveloping metaphor for what has happened to the human-made world as a whole. Third-order simulation begins with serial (or mass) production, which became a generalised feature of industrial capitalism. With the 'design revolution' (*CPS*) and the rise of advertising, signs and commodities merged, which not only generated a vast media image factory, but extended simulation to the realm of objects as well as images. If a preliminary stage was captured in Debord's (1983) 'society of the spectacle' for Baudrillard the process of de-referentialism (in which images refer only to themselves and the line between image and reality is dissolved) that accompanied these developments has gone beyond the point of alienation, or even alienation from alienation. A critique in terms of disalienated labour and 'real needs' is itself based only on a simulacrum that mirrors a capitalist reality that belongs to a now obsolete phase in its development. Freudian psychoanalysis with its simulacral 'unconscious' and Saussure's semiology (which reproduces the late capitalist collapse of the symbolic into coded semiosis) are other instances of simulation in the realm of theory.

Entry into the age of simulation amounts, in fact, to a paradigm shift, and one so profound that it has made critical theory and practice as previously understood toothless, challenging us to mount an entirely different kind of response ('a move to the symbolic', 'seduction', 'theoretical terrorism', 'fatal strategies' and so on). Baudrillard's 'simulation', it should be noted, is also linked to a philosophical idea. The arrival of simulation corresponds, in Baudrillard's conceptual theatre, to the final stage in Nietzsche's (1987) 'How the "Real World" at Last Became a Myth'. Not only has the 'real world' (that is, the reality underlying or beyond appearances) been 'abolished', and with it the entire epoch of God and metaphysics, so too has the apparent world, itself the last in the succession of what are taken to be ultimate realities. However, whereas for Nietzsche this betokened the completion of nihilism and marked a liberating turning point, for Baudrillard the destruction of the difference between real and apparent by simulation betokens, for better or worse, the end of illusions about any redeeming end, including Nietzsche's. Nor, for Baudrillard, is the rise and predominance of simulation a primarily cultural process. It pertains not to any dialectic of the subject, which becomes a node in the network and an absorbent screen, but to the transformation of the object world which itself commits the perfect crime of making reality and its problem disappear.

Passwords

Hyper-reality
Image
Media
Model
Perfect crime
Real
Simulacra + Simulacrum

SINGULARITY

Jon Baldwin

In astrophysics a gravitational or space-time singularity refers to a point of infinite density and absolute uncertainty in which all laws collapse and from which anything can emerge. At the beginning of the Big Bang the initial state of the universe was a singularity. As with concepts such as strange attractors, paroxysm, metastasis, the viral and the fractal, Baudrillard's notion of singularity borrows terminology from the sciences, making a poetic and metaphorical application to the social mass and cultural universe.

Singularity receives no extended analysis or prime focus in a single text but haunts the later output such as *The Perfect Crime* (1996c [1995a]), *Impossible Exchange* (2001a [1999a]) and the dialogues *The Singular Objects of Architecture* (2002b [2000d]) and *Paroxysm* (1998b [1997]). If we follow Baudrillard's own version of a guide to his concepts, *Passwords* (2003b [2000c]), then we are alerted to his suggestion that 'we are in exchange, universally. All our conceptions lead back to it at some point or other' (*PW*, 73). What, then, is the relationship of singularity to exchange? Insofar as a singularity consists of uncertainty, the collapse of laws, and from which the new, or an event, can emerge, it is precisely that which, initially, has no equivalent. It is therefore not exchangeable. Singularity is a 'unique sign' (*IEx*, 130). The uniqueness of the singularity means it is impossible to exchange.

This resistance to exchange gives singularity its radical edge. In a world that wants to be universal, productive and cleansed of all ambiguity, in this 'culture of equivalence and calculation' (*CM3*, 128) a singularity stands as, and valorises, the unique, uncertain, unpredictable, incalculable, unrepresentable, untranslatable and unproductive. It threatens the drive towards a globalised, secure, neutralised sameness with a radical otherness. In this sense a singularity is analogous to the concepts offered by Baudrillard as antidotes to simulation, political economy, globalisation, monoculture, media–semiosis and the principle of equivalence, namely symbolic exchange, seduction, radical alterity, negativity and death – 'the most singular of singularities' (*SC*, 68).

Different implications are drawn, but Baudrillard's singularity is comparable with the discussion of singularities by Jacques Derrida as 'infinitely different and thereby indifferent to particular difference' (Derrida, 1997: 106) and Gilles Deleuze as 'non-exchangeable and non-substitutable' (Deleuze, 1994: 1). Baudrillard speaks of the possible singularity of events, beings and things. A singularity might take an ethnic, religious, linguistic or individual form (*P*). A work of art, worthy of the name, can be a singularity: indeed, the 'whole task of art is to bring language down to its singularity, to wrest it from the particularity and universality of meaning' (*F*, 80). A singularity is a resurgence or insurrection (*P*), a bursting-in, a breaking-in: 'It can come from a person, a group, an accident in the system itself' (*P*, 51).

Singularity is valorised as an existential attitude. Francis Bacon's singularity and 'touch of enchantment' (*P*, 99) is admired. Unlike most contemporary artists who are 'all too conscious of their place in the history of art' (*P*, 99) and exchangeable with art theory, the business of art, culture, value and aesthetics, Baudrillard's Bacon is retained as a singularity, 'a pure event'. Existence under the aegis of singularity is preferred to identity (and identity politics): 'each person should have an unyielding singularity' (*F*, 8). Singularity is sovereignty, a fight for glory, adventure, a mastery of existence: in 'a totalised, centred, concentric universe, only eccentric possibilities are left' (*F*, 9). On the other hand, identity is security, a mere reference, 'an existence label' (*P*, 49) in a 'bloodless, undifferentiated world' (*SC*, 65).

The singularity has 'a total autonomy, and exists only as such' (*P*, 51). Singularities may often assume 'monstrous forms' (*SA*, 21). From the viewpoint of 'enlightened' thought they may assume 'violent, anomalous, irrational aspects' (*P*, 13). This is certainly the 'enlightened' view of terrorism. Baudrillard defines the spirit of terrorism as 'the act that restores an irreducible singularity to the heart of a system of generalized exchange' (*ST*, 9). A singularity is, in this sense, antagonistic to 'a globality totally soluble in circulation or exchange' (*ST*, 58). Singularities do not resolve the antagonism with the system but exist in 'a symbolic dimension' (*ST*, 58) and function as 'a force of defiance'. Therefore singularities do not, in a traditional way, offer head-on resistance, but rather constitute 'another universe with another set of rules, which may conceivably get exterminated, but which, at a particular moment, represents an insuperable obstacle for the system itself' (*F*, 71). The antagonistic nature of a singularity means that it 'is made for a very rapid disappearance' (*P*, 51).

Science provides one further conception of singularity: the technological singularity. This is, in theory, a future point that occurs during a phase of unprecedented technological progress, sometime after the creation of a super-intelligence. This event of intelligence explosion could see the machine surpass human intellect and improve its design into far greater intelligences. The intelligence of man would be left far behind. The mathematician and science fiction author Vernor Vinge proposes that drastic changes in society would occur following such an intelligence explosion. This anxiety is often reflected in the science-fiction of Issac Asimov, Greg Bear, Phillip K. Dick and William Gibson, and in popular film and TV such as *The Terminator*, *The Matrix* and *Battlestar Galactica*. In summation, Baudrillard is for the interruption of singularities and against their violent incorporation. However, his work stands against the implications and pursuit of a technological singularity: cloning, artificial intelligence, virtuality, networks and other-world simulacrum. This technological goal is inhuman, against the human: 'in a world that wants absolutely to cleanse everything, to exterminate death and negativity . . . [thought must] remain humanist, concerned for the human' (*PW*, 92). Theory itself, to resist the artificial double, to resist assimilation, must be akin to a singularity, for 'in its singularity thought may be able to protect us' (*VI*, 29).

Passwords

Clones + Cloning
Death
Globalisation
Radical alterity
Science fiction
Seduction
Symbolic exchange
Terrorism
Universality
Viral

SITUATIONISM

Paul A. Taylor

A term that is used to describe the thought of the *Situationist International*: a loose grouping of radical artists, activists and theorists. Active in the heady days of 1960s Paris they were led by Guy Debord (1932–94) and popularly known as 'Situs'. Although Baudrillard was never directly linked with the group, there are clear parallels between his central concepts and those found within Debord's key work – *The Society of the Spectacle* (1983) – published in French in 1967.

Developing Lukács' notion of the commodity as advanced capitalism's defining feature, its universal concept, Debord argued that the spectacle had become the (il)logical conclusion of the commodity form. Marx famously observed that within capitalism, 'all that's solid melts into air' and mass media have exponentially furthered this process. Exchange value that stemmed from use value has, in its turn, morphed into the society-wide pervasive and invasive spread of 'sign value'. McLuhan argued that this creates a total environment that colonises and supplants traditional, non-mediated values. Both Debord and Baudrillard's work is characterised by the sustained, critical nature of their theoretical exploration of the full implications of this new totalising experience.

For Debord, the spectacle stands in the same relation to the commodity as the commodity did to the earlier forms of exchange it supplanted. Just as the commodity absorbed and abstracted the economic relations that pre-dated it, so the spectacle absorbs and abstracts the commodity form. Money as a medium of exchange permits a false equivalence to be established between two otherwise incommensurate objects. Money transforms and conflates distinctly different physical qualities into the sameness of a new medium. Capitalism extends this process to the point where it does not simply mediate prior forms of human experience, but begins to determine the fundamental nature of that very experience: 'The spectacle is the developed modern complement of money where the totality of the commodity world appears as a whole, as a general equivalence for what the entire society can be' (Debord, 1983: 49).

Baudrillard's notion of simulacra provides a Situationist-like appreciation of the extent to which mass media do not simply mediate reality, they now serve to hide the fact there is no longer a reality to be mediated. The total nature of the society of the spectacle is such that the individual has merely become a relay station, a medium among media. Baudrillard's notion of 'integral reality' (*LP*) describes the phenomenological experience of life in the resulting society in which our basic interactions are pre-enscribed with mediated values. Similarly, in his late essays 'Dust Breeding' and 'Telemorphosis' (*CA*), Baudrillard describes how genuine human relationships are replaced by a 'mirror of platitudes' (*CA*, 181) and social experience mediated by an endless chain of solipsistic screens in which mobile phone-wielding, über-networked contemporary citizens become denizens of an 'umbilical limbo' (*CA*, 191).

The Situationists saw the whole of society as a vital 'theatre of operations' and sought to develop corresponding forms of 'industrial action', the cultural equivalents of 'wildcat strikes' or 'work to rule', an 'aesthetic terrorism' to directly intervene in cultural production. Likewise, Baudrillard saw at least a partial counterpoint to the media's society of signs in street-level symbolic responses: 'Graffiti is transgressive, not because it substitutes another content, another discourse, but simply because it responds, there, on the spot, and breaches the fundamental rule of non-response enunciated by all the media' (*CPS*, 183). And:

There is no need for organized masses, nor for a political consciousness to do this – a thousand youths armed with marker pens and cans of spray-paint are enough to scramble the signals of urbania and dismantle the order of signs. Graffiti covers every subway map in New York, just as the Czechs changed the names of the streets in Prague to disconcert he Russians: guerrilla action . . . It is nevertheless astonishing to see this unfold in a Quaternary cybernetic city dominated by the two glass and aluminium towers of the World Trade Center, invulnerable meta-signs of the system's omnipotence. (*SED*, 80–2)

However, Situationist aesthetic terrorism is always vulnerable to being processed away and co-opted by the media system's 'mortal dose of pub-licity' (*CPS*, 174) so that the oppositional act merely becomes yet another spectacle. Under a capitalism dominated by exchange-value and crude industrial exploitation, at least workers still had their chains. In the society of the spectacle, alienated life itself forms the basis of the spectacle. Life thus becomes doubly alienated: in the society of the spectacle/simulacra we are alienated from alienation by alienation!

Passwords

City
Integral reality
Media
Simulacra + Simulacrum

SOCIOLOGY + THE END OF THE SOCIAL

Barry Smart

Jean Baudrillard's writings disrupt disciplinary order and defy con-ventional discursive designation. Nowhere is this more evident than in respect of his remarks on sociology and the concept of 'the social' (Smart, 1993). Situating Baudrillard is problematic: determining precisely what his narratives represent and where his deliberately provocative reflections belong are matters to which he was asked to respond in several interviews conducted over the course of his career. What emerged in most instances is that he considered himself not to be a sociologist. For example, asked whether he was a philosopher, sociologist, writer or poet, he replied that he was 'neither a philosopher nor a sociologist' and that his work was 'getting more literary' (*BL*, 43). In response to a description of his work as 'anti-sociology', Baudrillard responded that he was 'neither a sociologist nor an anti-sociologist', that while he began in sociology in the 1960s he left it for 'semiology, psychoanalysis, Marxism' and sought to develop a critique of both the discipline and its concept of the social:

It is postulated within sociology that there *is* a society, that there *is* a 'social' which is evident, and that you need do no more than conduct quantitative studies, statistical research, etc. Well, effectively, that is not the case. In that sense, yes, I want to go past working in sociology. (*BL*, 81)

Baudrillard's critical distance from sociology was reaffirmed in another interview conducted by Sylvère Lotringer in 1984–5 in the course of which he described himself as 'a metaphysician, perhaps a moralist, but certainly not a sociologist' and added that the 'only "sociological" work I can claim is my effort to put an end to the social, to the concept of the social' (*FF*, 85).

What emerges from Baudrillard's enigmatic remarks on sociology is a very limited understanding of the discipline and one that is not representative of the breadth of sociological approaches or the diversity of sociological analyses which do not employ quantitative methods or engage in forms of statistical research. But if we take Baudrillard at his word, it is to his observations on 'the end of the social' that analytic consideration needs to be directed to gain a clearer understanding of his 'sociology' and his view of the fate of the discipline's subject matter (*SSM*).

Baudrillard's late twentieth-century comments on sociology and the social take place in a specific historical context, one marked by the development of a neo-liberal, consumer-oriented, capitalism deploying 'post-industrial' information and communication technologies which have significantly transformed social life, cultural forms and practices, economic production and the world of work, as well the domain of politics (Smart, 1992, 1993). The view of the world that emerges from Baudrillard's narrative prioritises the impact of developments in communications media, in particular the way in which the increasing centrality of communication networks and information technology has led to the emergence of a new order of simulacra. Baudrillard distinguishes between four orders of simulacra denoting different relationships between simulacra and 'the real': (1) 'the counterfeit of the real' exemplified by the production of the copy as equivalent to the original in the period from the Renaissance to the Industrial Revolution; (2) the mass production of series of exact replicas or mass objects associated with the Industrial Revolution; (3) 'the disappearance of the referent' as the relationship between images, subjects and events is totally transformed as the world is constituted in and through models, codes and digitality; and (4) a fractal or viral order where in the absence of reference points culture and politics are characterised by uncertainty and non-equivalence (*SED*, *SS*, *EDI*, *TE*).

The media and the 'masses' are represented by Baudrillard as 'one single process' constitutive of a new age, a new era – '[m]ass(age) is the message' (*SSM*, 64) – one which is considered to precipitate the end of the social. For Baudrillard the extension of electronic communications and information media has transformed our experiences, dissolved meaning and signification in the 'space of simulation', undermined traditional forms of political strategy and while outwardly seeming to be producing 'more of the social' is in practice considered to be neutralising 'social relations and the social itself', in effect 'burying the social beneath a simulation of the social' (*SSM*, 80).

The social is not timeless or universal – in Baudrillard's view there have been 'societies without the social'. In outlining his argument on the social he suggests that 'its definition is empty . . . [that it] no longer analyses anything, no longer designates anything' (*SSM*, 80). In developing his thoughts on the fate of the social Baudrillard distinguishes between three possibilities, notably (1) the social has never existed; (2) it exists, is everywhere, 'invests everything' (*SSM*, 84); and (3) it did exist but '*does not exist anymore*' (*SSM*, 91). In a series of comments on each of these possibilities Baudrillard notes that the whole idea of the social is disintegrating, breaking down, as it is reabsorbed into 'an economy of extravagance and excess' (*SSM*, 91), transfigured and hyper-realised in its 'very simulation' (*SSM*, 94).

The dissolution of the social in its simulation is articulated with the demise of the political, the erosion of its specificity which follows, for Baudrillard, from the absence of anything to represent, the disappearance of such clearly delineated social referents as 'a people, a class, a proletariat, objective conditions' (*SSM*, 47) and its replacement by a media-constituted referent the 'silent majority' of public opinion whose mode of existence is not social but statistical. Baudrillard argues that politics now operates with an imaginary referent, the masses, which emerges through the survey rather than social expression, that 'there is no longer any social signified to give force to a political signifier' (*SSM*, 47).

As Baudrillard's narratives developed they moved further and further way from the terrain of sociology and political economy; indeed they ran in opposition to the goal intrinsic to modern sociology of cultivating informed individuals capable of rationally shaping their lives. As they did so, Baudrillard's analyses attracted increasing media attention, leading him to acquire the mantle of celebrity cultural polemicist.

Passwords

Masses
Media
Simulacra + Simulacrum
Simulation

SPORT

Gary Genosko

Baudrillard thought about sport in terms of failure. In *For a Critique of the Political Economy of the Sign* (1981 [1972]), value and symbolic ambivalence are mutually exclusive domains; in the latter desire is not satisfied through phantasmatic completion, and this entails that desire may ride failure to an ignominious counter-victory. Baudrillard found in the failure to react positively to an inducement like winning a race the principle of a radical counter-economy of needs. Citing Tony Richardson's 1962 film version of Alan Sillitoe's story *The Loneliness of the Long Distance Runner* (1959), in which a Borstal Boy throws a foot race to disgrace the reform school that exploits his talent, Baudrillard finds a truth preserved through losing against the competitive system of rewards. It is not only deliberate loss that interests Baudrillard, as he is equally attracted by athletes who cannot stop themselves from blowing it since this, too, foils exchange value.

During his travels throughout the United States while writing *America* (1988b [1986]), Baudrillard became fascinated by a wide-range of popular sporting activities: break dancing, marathon running, skateboarding, jogging, body-building and windsurfing. Many of these shared the attribute of self-reference ('blank solitude') towards death, often by seeking suicide ('sacrificial exhaustion') through extreme asceticism. The 'easy wear' of popular athletic costuming signified anorexia in fatigue and self-annihilation.

The prospect of the Los Angeles Olympic Games ('100 percent advertising event') on the horizon in 1984 stirred Baudrillard to mockingly redate it to 1989 as the Revolutionary Olympics that would celebrate the bicentenary of the French Revolution since everything that disappears in Europe resurfaces in California. Baudrillard also mocked the notion of a parallel Special Olympics, not for the paralympians, but for the 'sexually disabled' (*CM4*, 34). He found the 'gazes put out of play' (disjuncture between live performance and screen) in the television spectacle of the opening ceremonies of the 1992 Barcelona Olympics an update of the 'play of gazes' in *Las Meninas* (*CM3*, 48).

Baudrillard's most sustained sports writing concerned Formula One motor racing in 'The Racing Driver and his Double' (*SC*). Driver and machine are joined in a Möbius strip sitting atop a pyramid of investment and human capital: the single car and driver whose exploits are broadcast from the summit to millions of racing fans. The driver's double is his car, a projectile; the driver 'teleconducts' it on a 'screen of speed' and this for

Baudrillard takes all the pleasure out of driving and reduces victory to an 'operational passion'. Yet he also sees calmness in the high speeds and discovers symbolic stakes in the 'passion for accidents and death' whose randomness grips everyone involved in the sport.

The Formula One driver is a doubly mythic figure: a machinic element ('living prosthesis') integrated into a closed control circuit and a 'symbolic operator' risking death. In short, Formula One is a world of monsters whose disappearance in technical perfection concerns us because it would ruin competition and whose survival is equally worrying because they might pollute the everyday world of driving.

For Baudrillard, sporting violence is a diversion into the imaginary (*CM4*). Football interested him only as transpolitics. Hence Baudrillard's sustained reflection on the Heysel Stadium disaster in 1985 in *The Transparency of Evil* (1993b [1990a]). The consequences of football hooliganism in dozens of deaths and hundreds of injuries, and a European Cup match played before an empty stadium (Madrid in 1987) but televised, are evidence of an inversion of roles in which spectators take the initiative, displaying 'participatory hypersociality', because events have been emptied of meaning and surpassed by more dramatic acts of terror.

Passwords

America
Transpolitics

STRUCTURALISM – see 'city', 'consumption + affluent society', 'cool memories', 'object' and 'sign'.

SUBJECT – see 'anti-humanism + post-humanism', 'destiny', 'feminism/feminine', 'imaginary', 'metaphysics', 'mirror', 'modernity', 'object', 'photography', 'psychoanalysis' and 'sex/gender'.

SYMBOLIC EXCHANGE

Mike Gane

The concept of symbolic exchange is perhaps the most central of Baudrillard's terms and yet the most allusive. At bottom it is very simply a term derived from anthropological studies of the gift and gift exchange in so-called primitive societies. In classic anthropological studies, especially those of Marcel Mauss, gift exchange is not gratuitous and marginal, but obligatory and central to social life. Symbolic exchange is a broadening out of the terrain of obligatory exchanges of the same kind: from simple exchanges in conversation to sacred sacrifices, and the exchanges between the living and the dead (*SED*). These exchanges are not based on use values, and as such they stand in marked contrast to market exchanges mediated by money values. Baudrillard constantly reminds readers that the terms themselves are provisional since both 'symbolic' and 'exchange' give rise to misunderstandings if the anthropological background is not appreciated – 'the term is rather deceptive' (*BL*, 106). But what interests Baudrillard is the fact that gifts are obligatory, they are a form of empowerment through debt, and the counter-gift cancels this power and any accumulation. This counter-gift is conceived by Baudrillard as a kind of reversibility which annuls power, a reversibility that is founded on the fundamental dualism of the world. Through his writings it is clear that there is a feature of this way of analysing phenomena – the possibility of a gift which cannot be returned, a fundamental form of power. But this irreversibility is threatened by 'the violent resurgence of duality' (*LP*, 185). This is connected with Baudrillard's important idea of 'impossible exchange' derived from the idea of the 'accursed share' from the other key writer in this domain, Georges Bataille (*PW*, 74). That which cannot be exchanged forms a singularity and cannot be absorbed into the system. But with great subtlety Baudrillard in his later writings charts the accursed shares that can be put back into circulation 'like the devil who, having bought man's shadow, recycles it' (*PW*, 75).

Essentially, the concept of symbolic exchange is the basis of Baudrillard's critical thinking of contemporary societies, and in this sense is comparable to Marx's notion of communism. In his critique of Marx, Baudrillard holds that Marx's notion was not fundamental enough, and that it was trapped within the framework it sought to escape – it was a 'mirror of production' (*MP*). Symbolic exchange therefore is a strategic concept, conceived as providing the platform for a more radical critique of modern capitalist societies than developed by Marxists. Baudrillard often notes that modern societies are based on a different kind of exchange, commodity exchange, and modern cultures are similarly structured in a different way – on semiotic, modular structures – reflecting the way structural value (not symbolic exchange) permeates beyond the economy. Yet in charting these phenomena it is clear that symbolic exchange continues to haunt modern societies, and indeed Baudrillard suggests that it does continue to be the fundamental formation, 'has always been at the radical

base of things' (*PW*, 17). The difference with other societies is that previously symbolic exchange has been institutionalised in effective ritual
practices and reflected in poetic mythology. At this point it seems clear
that Baudrillard is based in an anthropological framework, and the terms
he uses are quite different from those developed in sociology which seems
trapped, like Marxism, in the semiotic order, in the 'real'.

The idea of the symbolic in this sense appeared clearly in Baudrillard's
essays from around 1970, and in one essay 'For a General Theory'
(*CPS*) he outlined a research programme that involved a critique of the
concept of use value, an extension of theory to the circulation of signs
and the development of the theory of symbolic exchange. The subsequent studies provide, then, first a critique of Marxism (*MP*), a theory of
symbolic exchange (*SED*) and then studies on death, fate, seduction, evil,
impossible exchange and so forth. On the other hand these studies are
complemented by further studies on simulacra, fashion, the body, jokes,
terrorism and contemporary politics and culture. Studies of the symbolic
order thus lie alongside those of the semiotic order and are used as a
basis for critique. But they go further than critique since on numerous
occasions Baudrillard refers to forms of mastery in the symbolic order,
an attempt to develop 'fatal theory'. This enigmatic proposition seems
to refer to mastery not of laws, but of the rules of the symbolic order. It
might seem that the fundamental rule is the obligation to return the gift,
but there seem to be more primordial ones relating to who we are, since in
the apparent world of the symbolic everything is challenged and seduced.
It is a rule, for example, that 'one cannot seduce others, if one has not
oneself been seduced' (*S*, 81). And these rules are related to Baudrillard's
basic hypotheses which outline the nature of the symbolic order itself.
The first is 'the hypothesis of the radical illusoriness of the world . . . the
impossibility of exchanging the world for any ultimate truth or purpose'
(*LP*, 32); the second is 'the world is given to us' (*LP*, 33). These propositions are a kind of metaphysical reflection on the anthropological studies
of Mauss and Bataille and form the frame for inferred rules such as '*things
exist because challenged, and because summoned to respond to that challenge*'
(*S*, 91).

The underlying fundamental principle is that of the world's dualistic
nature. It is this which all symbolic cultures recognise and master. In
order to grasp it, Baudrillard maintains, it is essential to get beyond the
(Christian) notion of the law in order to appreciate the more primordial
notion of the rule. Symbolic exchange itself rests within the context of that
which cannot be exchanged, the basic singularities, for example destiny
(*PW*). Yet it is clear that conceived in this sense exchange is, as Baudrillard
suggested, a misleading term – the gifts are not exactly exchanged but

given and received, and in turn given and returned. This ritual is rule-governed in many respects, for example when and what to give, when and what to return. Undertaking gift giving and receiving is thus a ritual governed by rules and obligations to be mastered by everyone entering the symbolic order.

Passwords

Accursed share
Death
Destiny
Duality
Evil
Fatal
Gift
Impossible exchange
Political economy of the sign
Reversibility
Seduction
Singularity

T

TELEVISION – see 'image', 'modernity' and 'politics'.

TERRORISM

Rex Butler

Baudrillard's response to the terrorist attacks on the World Trade Center on 11 September 2001, 'The Spirit of Terrorism', was published in *Le Monde* on 2 November. In his article, Baudrillard urges us not to rush to conclusions, to take time out before acting or responding to what had happened. Baudrillard cautions this because the attacks were a true 'event' that united within it 'all the events that have never taken place' (*ST*, 4). As a result, the usual 'calculations' regarding such acts of aggression no longer apply. Immediately striking back against the enemy – as Baudrillard notes the US already preparing to do in Iraq and Afghanistan – is to miss the true challenge of the strikes. Cutting down on civil liberties is to turn America itself into a terrorist state, in a continuation of the original logic of the hijackers. Even moral repulsion and condemnation is an 'abreaction', an attempt to deny the fascination of the terrorist act and its 'unforgettable' images (*ST*, 4). Against all of these, as he subsequently argues in an interview with the German magazine *Der Spiegel*, Baudrillard (2004b) emphasises simply attempting to understand what happened, which is not in the first instance to explain it or give it a meaning. The events of 9/11 undoubtedly constitute a true test for theory and its ability to think the world. At the heart of Baudrillard's engagement with the terrorist attacks is the problem of how to formulate a theoretical response that would be adequate to the event, that would capture it in its singularity without reducing it or comparing it to something else (*ST*).

If Baudrillard's series of responses to 9/11 – his original newspaper article, the books *Power Inferno* and *La violence du monde* (published in English as *The Spirit of Terrorism* (2003c [2002])) – represents a signal moment in his work, in fact terrorism was a constant subject of his theorising. Already Baudrillard's second book, *The Consumer Society* (1998a [1970]), concludes with a meditation on a terrorism – what Baudrillard calls there 'spectacular violence' (*CS*, 174) – that arises in response to the success of modern consumer society. Then in the later *Fatal Strategies* (2008a [1983]), undoubtedly in response to the Baader-Meinhof and Red Brigades terrorists of the 1960s and 1970s, Baudrillard theorises terrorism more explicitly. His first point – and this to go against all attempts to suggest that Baudrillard sympathises with the terrorists – is that the act of terrorism, if it is successful, necessarily goes beyond the aims and intentions of the terrorists themselves. They might think that they capture a hostage in order that someone is made to answer for society's failings or that their political grievances are heard, but there is no equivalence that can be made with the hostage in this fashion. Indeed, what the act of hostage-taking ultimately demonstrates is the very inexchangeability of the hostage, the inability of the terrorists to make demands upon society or even for the hostage to re-enter society when released. The social no longer works in terms of any personal liability of the form terrorists rely upon: there is no longer any single individual whom one can hold responsible for society's failings or with whom the terrorists could negotiate. There is on the contrary a general, floating system of regulation, in which at once everybody and nobody is held accountable. That is, the paradox played out by terrorism is that there is no exchange possible between the terrorist and the social, but only because the social itself is already terrorist: everything is organised as though a terrorist attack had already taken place and every-body is potentially a terrorist (*FS*).

It is just this 'impossible exchange' between society and terrorism that Baudrillard brings out in his analysis of 9/11. What Baudrillard empha-sises throughout is the fact that terrorism is not simply opposed to the West or even comes from somewhere outside of it. The very means of the terrorists are western: they secrete themselves in sleeper cells within the societies they attack, indistinguishable from ordinary citizens; they use the most advanced technologies of the West, like computers and airplanes, to plan and execute their attacks. But, more than this, the ter-rorist impulse, the secret jubilation at seeing the collapse of the Twin Towers and the injury inflicted upon the single power dominating the world, is also to be felt within the West itself. In Baudrillard's difficult and controversial words: 'At a pinch, we can say that they *did it*, but *we wished for* it' (*ST*, 5). This is what Baudrillard means by the 'spirit' of ter-rorism. It is nothing that can be geographically located or even culturally or ideologically specified. It is not to be reduced to a battle between Islam and America. It is not even exactly real, but takes place as a real that can be seen only through fiction or images. Rather, the 'spirit' of terrorism is an abstract limit to globalisation, the fact that any system pushed to its furthest extent will begin to reverse upon itself and produce the opposite effects from those intended. In this sense, Baudrillard is not repeating anything like the well-known 'clash of civilisations' thesis that became so popular after 9/11. Islamic terrorism is not opposed to western globalisa-tion, but arises as the necessary correlate of its historical triumph. It is for this reason that Baudrillard emphasises that the symbolic challenge of ter-rorism is not a matter of seeking any definitive victory over the west. The west must be kept alive exactly so that it can be 'targeted and wounded in a genuinely adversarial relationship' (*ST*, 26). But at this point a series of extremely complex questions emerges for Baudrillard's analysis. The first is, insofar as Islam and terrorism are only the 'moving front along which the antagonism crystallised' (*ST*, 15), to what extent does Baudrillard conceive of 9/11 as a limit occurring exclusively within the West itself? If any actual attack is only to take the place of an abstract 'spirit' of terrorism, can we say that this spirit can be seen only because of its earthly incarna-tion? And, along the same lines, is the symbolic exchange of terrorism, for all of Baudrillard's emphasis upon it as an act that risks its own death, not a true limit, insofar as both terms in a symbolic relationship are mutually dependent upon each other? Is any actual terrorist event only to stand in for another that has never 'taken place'? These are precisely the kinds of questions Derrida (1978) once put to Bataille and his attempts to theorise a certain non-dialecticisable 'terrorism'.

Passwords

Consumption + Affluent society
Fatal
Geopolitics
Gift
Globalisation
Impossible exchange
Reversibility
Singularity
Symbolic exchange

THE END

Richard G. Smith

Baudrillard's *oeuvre* is replete with a 'rampant Endism', or 'inverted millenarianism', littered throughout with 'the end' of this, that or the other. The end is a recurrent motif throughout his theoretical writings: the 'end of Marxism' (*MP*), the 'end of production' (*MP*, *SED*), the 'end of the social' (*SSM*), the 'end of the media' (*CPS*, *SSM*), the 'end of music' (*S*, *IE*, *CM*, *F*, *LP*), the 'end of sex' (*S*), the 'end of political economy' (*SED*; *TE*), the 'end of power' (*FF*), the 'end of ideology' (*SS*), the 'end of science fiction' (*SS*), the 'end of the subject' (*FS*, *WD*), the 'end of the political' (*GD*), the 'end of war' (*GW*), the 'end of history' (*IE*), the 'end of art' (*CA*) and so on. Indeed, Baudrillard's corpus appears to exemplify Derrida's observation in 1984 that much recent philosophy has an apocalyptic or eschatological tone:

Not only the end of this here but also and first of that there, the end of history, the end of the class struggle, the end of philosophy, the death of God, the end of religions, the end of Christianity and morals . . . the end of the subject, the end of man, the end of the West, the end of Oedipus, the end of the earth, *Apocalypse Now*, I tell you, in the cataclysm, the fire, the blood, the fundamental earthquake, the napalm descending from the sky by helicopters, like prostitutes, and also the end of literature, the end of painting, art as a thing of the past, the end of psychoanalysis, the end of the university, the end of phallocentrism and phallogocentrism, and I don't know what else. (Derrida, 1984: 21–2)

However, it is important to realise that despite all his talk of ends, Baudrillard does not use the word end to mean termination or full stop. He does not think that the numerous topics he says have reached their end are ending or have ended: the media continues, science fiction continues, production continues, music continues and so on. That is to say that by the word end he really means simulacrum: the media continues as simulacrum, wars continue as simulacra and so on. In other words, we are caught in a moment when things are bereft of their substance: history is without history, war is without warfare, sex is without sex, art is without art and so on.

Baudrillard rarely uses the terms postmodern/ism/ity in his body of writings (Gane, 1990) precisely because all his works are concerned with modernity, or rather with the 'end of modernity'. Thus the important point is that the multiplicity of ends scattered throughout Baudrillard's writings are all a part of modernity coming to an end (not a new postmodern beginning). In other words, Baudrillard's conceptualisation of the end belongs to a logic of dynamism and repetition:

Modernity is not a dialectic of history: it is the eventness, the permanent play of the present moment, the universality of news blurbs through the media . . . Modernity is not the transmutation of all values, it is the destruction of all former values without surpassing them, it is the ambiguity of all values under the sign of a generalized combinatory. There is no longer either good or evil, but we are not for all that 'beyond good and evil'. (Baudrillard, 1987: 71)

All the topics Baudrillard identifies as having 'ended' or 'vanished' – history, Marxism, music, war, political economy and so on – have done so because, within the model of modernity, they are simulations. In other words, nothing changes, all there is in the end is repetition in advance, endless recycling, an immanent unfolding in a closed space where everything becomes equivalent and idealised as signs in a code: 'Modernity, having inaugurated rupture and discontinuity, is now closed into a new cycle. It has lost the ideological drive of reason and progress, and confounds itself more and more with the formal play of change' (Baudrillard, 1987: 72). In other words, all of Baudrillard's ends are trapped in the hyper-real: a space with nothing beyond it, folded into an exterior (not an 'outside'), beyond transcendence and dialectical negation.

Passwords

Code
Gulf War
Hysteresis
Modernity
Music

Time + History
Simulacra + Simulacrum

TIME + HISTORY

Richard G. Smith

A voluble account of the w(h)ithering of history, *The Illusion of the End or Events on Strike* (1994b [1992]) is Baudrillard's major meditation on the shape and trajectory of time and history under conditions of hyper-reality. The essence of Baudrillard's argument is that, as a simulacrum, history cannot end with a final destination and purpose (*telos*). The time of hyper-reality, the 'end of history', is one of eternal return – not of no return as modernity supposes with its belief in linear and continuous time – and consequently has no 'end' precisely because its topology and logic is one that is curved and cyclical (and therefore endless):

The whole problem of speaking about the end (particularly the end of history) is that you have to speak of what lies beyond the end and also, at the same time, of the impossibility of ending. This paradox is produced by the fact that in a non-linear, non-Euclidean space of history the end cannot be located. The end is, in fact, only conceivable in a logical order of causality and continuity. (*IE*, 110)

Thus it is not that history has ended as such, but rather that, because the march of history has broken from its forward path, 'we have to get used to the idea that *there is no end any longer, there will no longer be any end*, that history itself has become interminable' (*IE*, 116). That is to say that history 'will continue to unfold slowly, tediously, recurrently, in that hysteresis of everything which, like nails and hair, continue to grow after death' (*IE*, 116). History is still moving – just like the *grande machine* in Alfred Jarry's novel *Le Surmâle* (1945) which was only granted motion through the cadaveric rigour of its cyclists – but it only does so as a simulacrum.

The 'end of history' for Baudrillard is not, then, Fukuyama's (1992) dream, but is rather a recognition of 'the radical failure of the whole Hegelian perspective which was the idea of the realisation of the Idea' (Baudrillard, 1992a: 236). That is to say that 'the Idea of history has vanished' and, therefore, to speak of the 'end of history' is an illusion, a mirage, because that end (qua goal) has already been lost in the endlessness of simulation – that is why Baudrillard could say in 1985 that 'The Year 2000 has already happened'.

History remains a journey that never ends because, as a simulation model, it is cyclical, caught in a loop so that it is always retracing its steps and raking over the past so that 'things are being replayed *ad infinitum*' (Baudrillard, 1987: 69). A movement that is evidenced by the way in which history, both before the *fin de millénium* and nowadays, is reduced to countless commemorations to the disappearance of the Idea of history as 'progress': 'The great ideological, historical or political events are on the wane. They are on their way to oblivion deep in memory and they re-emerge under another form – as commemoration' (Baudrillard, 1992a: 233). Thus history is never gone for good precisely because it is recycled and emptied of its substance to become nothing more than a play of images:

None of the 'retro' scenarios [commemorations] that are being got up has any historical significance: they are occurring wholly on the surface of *our* age, as though all images were being superimposed one upon another, but with no change to the actual course of the film. (*IE*, 117)

The 'end of history' is not its negation as Hegel supposed, but rather its recycling as a perpetual 'contemporaneity'. However, that said, just because the train of history has been derailed does not mean that nothing is happening, or will happen. Indeed, now history has no project, goal or end, anything can happen, be it good or bad: 'We can't live with the past, but neither do we have a project. Every day is rich with unpredictable happenings: terrorism, AIDS, electronic viruses . . . The course is uncharted' (Baudrillard, 1997: 220).

Passwords

Hyper-reality
Hysteresis
Modernity
Simulacra + Simulacrum
The end

TRANSAESTHETICS

John Armitage

That philosophical approach whereby Baudrillard considers questions of postmodern art as the inability of modern art to fulfil the utopian aesthetic of modernity. Baudrillard argues that postmodern art testifies to modern art's incapacity to surpass itself and become a perfect form of existence. He contends that, rather than being the source of an inspirational ideal, postmodern art has melted into the contemporary aestheticisation of everyday life, within the unadulterated flow of images or the transaestheticisation of banality. Baudrillard argues in *The Conspiracy of Art* (2005b) that the vital figure of modern art was Marcel Duchamp, whose art, by rejecting its own aesthetic laws, metamorphosed into transaesthetics or the banality of the image. What is at issue is the eruption of new transaesthetic forms into recognised cultural practices. Modern art thus engaged an established cultural tradition while its secrets inadvertently highlighted the initiatory nature of symbolic exchange.

Baudrillard proposes in *The Ecstasy of Communication* (1988c [1987b]) and *The Perfect Crime* (1996c [1995a]) that transaesthetic forms strive for 'culture' by creating spaces of initiation, types of exchange, semiotics and simulation in anticipation of critical or ironic reactions. Andy Warhol is significant for Baudrillard because Warhol's art communicates the innovation of the eruption of simulation while exploring new forms of seduction, the object and the event. In *Fatal Strategies* (2008a [1983]) and *The Conspiracy of Art* (2005b), Baudrillard suggests that Warholian visual pleasure is pure fascination with the eruption of the commodity as a new form of vertiginous obscenity. Postmodern artworks can thus be understood as novel and victorious fetishes that function to deconstruct their own conventional powers of illusion, to gleam magnificently in the untainted obscenity of the commodity. According to Baudrillard, Charles Baudelaire established the concept of the 'absolute commodity', motivating Baudrillard to characterise the contemporary object as that which must destroy itself as a recognisable object and become hideously alien. Such an absolute commodity burns with an absolute seduction that arrives from elsewhere, that arrives from having surpassed its own form and become pure object and event, where the only genuine aesthetic or metaphysical reaction is mocking and festive in the face of the challenge that the eruption of new transaesthetic forms symbolise.

Today it is a matter of posing fresh critical questions and of discovering appropriate confirmatory answers to them as Baudrillard believed that most contemporary answers were wide of the mark. Postmodern artworks must therefore be more than reappropriations of the artworks of days gone by, expressions of satirical wit or disenchantment, hoaxes or culled from advertising imagery; they call for an art beyond the irony of penitence and bitterness towards contemporary culture. Postmodern art is not just extreme cynicism. Expressions are not just history plundered in anticipation of salvation. For Baudrillard, one must oppose this apparently final phase of art history.

The trajectory taken by transaesthetics leaves us with Baudrillard's *The Transparency of Evil* (1993b [1990a]), with its move into indeterminacy, into reversibility and uncertainty that characterise the switch from the third to the fourth order of simulation. Advancing beyond alienation, transaesthetics pursues the object as strange attractor and as lack of determinancy as to the location of the subject concerning the other. As Baudrillard asserts, postmodern artworks signify the ending of the Marxian dialectic, bringing about fourth-order simulated aesthetic sequences and eternal replication, a new state of affairs that exceeds all previous aesthetic antagonisms. Once unchained from reality, then, postmodern artworks become more real than real: hyper-real.

It was in truth with pop art that transaesthetics began, that transaesthetics transformed into the ironic force of the hyper-real, of the hyper-real as the escalation of reality. In the transaesthetic of the real every aesthetic form becomes uninterested in itself, having left its own former authority behind. In the transaesthetic of the real, therefore, no aesthetic form clashes with any other. Consequently, while postmodern art movements continue on with a dazzling ability, they are simultaneously abandoned by the masses, and we encounter the demise of fixed aesthetic borders and the rapid immobilisation of postmodern artworks that function within a network of negativity, as an effect of their intensity, a perspective that arises from Warhol's 1962 work, *32 Campbell's Soup Cans*. As such transaesthetics evokes critical questions: how does Warhol liberate us from the requirement to choose between the genuine and the artificial? Or, finally, what is that radical fetishism outside alienation that ironically performs its own strangeness, elevated to perfection, making it possible, once more, for the spectacle of the void to emerge?

Passwords

Art
Hyper-reality
Object
Postmodernism/Postmodernity
Reversibility
Simulation

TRANSLATION

Brian C. J. Singer

Baudrillard's writings present singular difficulties for the translator, particularly once his work moves beyond the critique of the sign, of the real and of the truth that would bridge the two. It is not just a question of the invention of new words, or of new meanings for old words – though there is that too. The problem is that, as Baudrillard seeks to reformulate the relation of his work to the world, he must also reformulate its relation to language. Once the relation to some deeper truth, whether ascriptive or prescriptive, has been refused, all the modes of uncovering truth – science, interpretation or critique – that gave sense to the language of theory must be rejected. Baudrillard would seek to change the world rather than understand it. But the instruments of change are largely limited to words, and these words are denied the ability to represent, penetrate, contain or control the world. They have been loosened from much of the referential ballast that held them to the 'reality' of the world and loaded them down with their meaning. They cannot, to be sure, have lost all relation to meaning and reality – just enough to take on a lightness that causes them to circulate with considerable liberty and rapidity, thus the vertiginous conceptual shifts, the rapid succession of contrary hypothesis, the escalation to extremes, the iconoclastic provocations, the oft incantatory character of the prose and so on. With weightless words one does not seek to get a grip on the world, and mould it to one's will; one is obliged to resort to more playful strategies and try to either seduce or challenge the world. Baudrillard's writing is seductive and would seek to entrap the world in a veil of appearances, but it is increasingly relative to a world where there are only other appearances to seduce. His writing is also quite challenging, but to challenge the world is to make a game of it, even as one seeks to outdo that world at its own game. Games can be serious, but only within the terms set by the game. And games can be lost, the best wagers being the most desperate. The translator has to enter into the spirit of the game. Concretely, this means that whenever he has doubts about how to translate a section, he is obliged to choose the surface effect over the deeper meaning, form over content, and 'somnambular euphoria' over reasoned prose.

Passwords

Real
Sign

Translations
Writing

TRANSLATIONS

Richard G. Smith

Baudrillard began his career in 1956, teaching German at a provincial French high school (*lycée*). From 1966, Baudrillard was employed by the University of Paris X at Nanterre to teach sociology and rapidly established himself as an academic sociologist through the publication of a number of books that interrogated the culture of consumption in western societies. However, spanning this early period – between 1956 and 1971 – Baudrillard also translated a number of works from German to French.

The bulk of Baudrillard's translations are of plays by the late Peter Weiss (d. 1982). From 1964 to 1968, five translations of Peter Weiss's plays were published (1964, 1965, 1966, 1968a, 1968b). Weiss's plays of the mid-1960s are illustrative of his temporary commitment to revolutionary socialism, and it is telling that it is these particular plays that Baudrillard chose to translate. For example, Weiss's (1965) *The Persecution and Assassination of Jean-Paul Marat as Performed by the Inmates of the Asylum of Charenton under the Direction of the Marquis de Sade* is his most famous play, and is generally known as *Marat/Sade*. It involves a dialectical discussion of individualism and socialism, and his *Discourse on the Progress of the Prolonged War of Liberation in Vietnam and the Events Leading Up to It as Illustration of the Necessity for Armed Resistance Against Oppression and on the Attempts of the United States of America to Destroy the Foundations of Revolution* (1968b) is also staunchly Marxist, narrating both the historical antecedents to the Vietnam conflict and fiercely condemning the United States and France for warmongering.

As well as a translation of Bertolt Brecht's play *Dialogues of Exile*, Baudrillard also translated Mühlmann's *Messianic Revolutionaries in the Third World*, a sociological work on Third World messianic and millenarian movements which consists of a series of socio-psychological analyses of *Les movements nativestes*. Thus Baudrillard was at this time translating important works from the political Left. Indeed, he also translated in this period Marx and Engels' *The German Ideology* and Engels' *The Role of Violence in History*. Having translated ten (1956, 1961, 1964, 1965, 1966, 1968a, 1968b, 1968c,1968d, 1969) texts from German to French, taught German and provided the accompanying text for René Burri's *Germans* (1963) – a classic work of postwar European documentary photography

– it is evident that Baudrillard was, and remained throughout his life, a passionate Germanist. However, it is also clear through his translations, and his involvement with the journal *Utopie*, that Baudrillard was, in these early years, aligned intellectually with an oppositional climate in France that stood against the Arab–Israeli War (1967) and the Vietnam War, and which culminated in the protests of May 1968.

Passwords

May 1968
Photography
Politics
Utopie

TRANSPOLITICS

Diane Rubenstein

Transpolitics designates Baudrillard's recognition that 'Things have found a way of avoiding a dialectics of meaning that was beginning to bore them' (*FS*, 25). The transpolitical world is an extreme one of escalating and paradoxical potentialities; both *ecstasy* ('the quality proper to any body that spins until all sense is lost, and then shines forth in its pure and empty form' (*FS*, 28)) and *inertia* ('frozen forms proliferate, and growth is immobilized in excrescence' (*FS*, 31)). Each of these states has implications for Baudrillard's theory. Simulation is an 'ecstasy of the real'. Inertia provides the catastrophic form specific to an era of simulation in the earthquake; seismic events are poeticised as 'requiem[s] for the infrastructure' (*FS*, 40). As framed by these evocations of catastrophic inertia and ecstatic involution, the transpolitical marks a radicalisation of Baudrillard's analysis of the object world. Whereas earlier discussions (*SED*, *S*) stressed secrecy and the object's enigma, transparency irrupts in the transpolitical:

transparency and obscenity of all structures in a destructured universe, the transparency and obscenity of change in a dehistoricized universe, the transparency and obscenity of information in a universe emptied of event, the transparency and obscenity of space in the promiscuity of networks, transparency and obscenity of the social in the masses, of the political in terror, of the body in obesity and genetic cloning . . . (*FS*, 45)

Baudrillard's three transpolitical figures correspond to these disappearances and mutations. The obese stages the 'end of the scene of the body' (*FS*, 45), the hostage/terrorist marks the 'end of the scene of the historical' and 'of the political', the obscene is the 'end of the scene of fantasy' (*FS*, 45). But they also exemplify other paradigmatic aspects of transpolitics. The obese represent not just the disappearance of the body, but also a lack of limits characteristic of an anomalous quality. For Baudrillard, politics is anomic; there are crises, violence, madness, revolution and possibly (revolutionary) transcendence. Anomie is that which escapes the jurisdiction of a law. Baudrillard discussed modern forms of anomie in *The Consumer Society* (1998a [1970]), commenting on the Manson murders, serial killer Richard Speck and the Watts riot. Anomaly is that which escapes the norm's jurisdiction; its figures are less 'critical incidences' than 'mutants', exemplified by Andy Warhol and Michael Jackson. American obesity is exemplary of the lack of limits or transcendence to the external world that is literalised as a digestion of 'space in its own appearance'. There is a secondary (meta-level) obesity in the simulation of information systems 'bloated with information that they can never deliver'. Obesity is thus the figure for a social body that has lost 'its law, its scene and its stakes' (*FS*, 49).

The hostage also designates the victory of an anomalous (terror) over an anomic form (violence). For Baudrillard, hostages (and terrorists as their symmetrical figure) represent the transpolitical par excellence (*FS*). Objectively, '(w)e are all hostages' as we can all serve as a dissuasive argument as in nuclear deterrence. But in an era of increasing securitisation, we are also subjective hostages. The transpolitical spaces of terrorism are 'fractile' zones: airports, and especially the embassy, an 'infinitesimal space in which a whole country can be taken hostage' (*FS*, 59). Terrorism and hostage taking as a generalised activity ('on the part of all nations and all groups') is no longer the political act of a determinate 'desperate oppressed'. Many of Baudrillard's transpolitical examples are from Reagan's America (the US holding the Olympic Games hostage) and the former Soviet Union (USSR taking Sakharov and Afghanistan hostage). These work via a mechanism of dissuasive blackmail ('If you don't do it . . .') far more effective than interdiction and sanctions as it substitutes the suspense that is peculiar to terror.

Terror underwrites Baudrillard's last transpolitical figure, the obscene. The hostage is a prototype of the pure object we will see in Baudrillard's later writings (*IEx*, *LP*) as well as what was already prefigured in the masses. A pure object is one that is torn from the circuit of exchange. Hostage taking thus experimentally stages an impossible exchange or the 'historical loss of the scene of exchange . . . and the social contract' (*FS*,

73). Paradoxically, this loss of scene is concomitant with both media over-representation and the disappearance of a necessary minimal illusion that could frame a politico-historical event of consequence.

Baudrillard made two important specifications to this presentation in his lecture, 'Transpolitics, Transsexuality, Transaesthetics'. The transpolitical is recoded as a 'fractal stage of value' (Baudrillard, 1992b: 15). As in *America* (1988b [1986]), Baudrillard also evaluated the transpolitical as an 'achieved utopia'.

Passwords

America
Masses
Object
Obscene
Terrorism
Transaesthetics
Transsexuality

TRANSSEXUALITY

Victoria Grace

Baudrillard frequently invokes the figure of the transsexual, of transsexuality, along with the transeconomic, the transpolitical and the transaesthetic, as particular manifestations of a generalised state of 'trans'. 'Trans' means movement between, a confusion of boundaries, of being neither here nor there, a contagion across states; this loss of specificity he associates with the fractal stage of value when there is no reference point for value at all. Possibly there is no longer any value at all. With this loss of reference there is also a loss of relationality; instead of reproduction in the spheres of sex, art, politics, etc. occurring through any relational encounter in which another form is produced through a simultaneous cancelling out, there is a shift into a self-replicating logic that Baudrillard argues is a metastatic mode of self-reproduction. Transsexuality is of this order.

The state of 'trans' as a contagion, or promiscuity across terms comes to mean that everything is sexual, everything is political, everything is aesthetic. Nothing is 'not'; what is, is all in the positive. This means that sex becomes generalised, and can effectively be modelled and signified in all sorts of ways. This commutability of the terms of sex is more to do with sexual indifference than sexual difference. The flotation of the signs of sex mean the sexual body has been assigned an artificial fate of transsexuality. In other words, whether we choose to change the signs of sex or not, it is the mere fact that sex is now constituted through commutable signs that makes us transsexual. We are now all transsexuals, therefore (*SC*).

In this way, Baudrillard's references to transsexuality are less those partaking of a medicalised discourse (premised on a sex and gender distinction) of the individual who feels that their gender orientation is trapped within the wrongly sexed body, but is rather more to do with the transsexual as s/he who is attracted to playing with the signs of sex, with lack of differentiation, with the simulation of difference. Transsexuality is thus underpinned by artifice (*TE*), which Baudrillard associates with the state of sexual indifference rather than sexual difference. This sexual indifference emerges with the loss of sexual otherness, as an ambiguity of the sexes supersedes the ambivalence of sex. Where playing with the signs of sexual difference is about jouissance, playing with the signs of sexual indifference is about artifice:

After the orgy [of liberation], then, a masked ball. After the demise of desire, a pell-mell diffusion of erotic simulacra in every guise, of transsexual kitsch in all its glory. A postmodern pornography, if you will, where sexuality is lost in the theatrical excess of its ambiguity. (*TE*, 22)

Long after any real alterity of the sexes has disappeared, this self-replicating manipulation of signs of an indifferent and ambiguous sex continues its empty kind of rehearsal. It's as if sex has been resolved into its 'part objects' or 'fractal elements'.

The transsexual is in this sense the subject become fully self-identical; s/he has no double, no other, no shadow. Inscribed fully within the order of a virtualised identity, '*[h]e [sic] no longer differs from himself*, and is, therefore, indifferent to himself' (*IE*, 108). And hence indifferent to others similarly encapsulated within their own self-identical, undivided, unseducing and unseducible existence. 'It is my right to be a man or a woman!' As for desire, Baudrillard is clear, with an implied reference to Deleuze, that the era of the transsexual (and transpolitical, transaesthetic) is one in which 'desiring machines become little spectacle machines, then quite simply bachelor machines, before trailing off into the countdown of the species' (*VI*, 38). So what about 'the end'? Precisely, '"our destiny is the end of the end"' (*BL*, 163); to be living in the functionality of a 'trans' state is a kind of tragedy marking a passing beyond our own finitude as human beings. Consequentially, 'it would no longer even be possible to live or confront our own end' (*BL*, 163).

Is it possible that the site of transsexuality could rather be seductive in its play of the interchangeable signs of sexual (in)difference? Baudrillard certainly notes that by virtue of the transsexual fate of the sexual body, transsexuality becomes 'the site of seduction' (*SC*, 9), a site, however, that is one of artifice rather than jouissance. The figure of the transsexual is, in Baudrillard's writing, not at all the radical and emancipatory form that deconstructs the m/f binary. Rather, as he writes in *Cool Memories* (1990b [1987c]) 'Transsexuality is not seductive, it is simply disturbing' (*CM*, 76).

Passwords

Seduction
Sex/Gender
The end
Transaesthetic
Transpolitical

TRAVERSES

Richard G. Smith

Baudrillard was a founding editor – with Michel De Certeau, Gilbert Lascault, Marc Le Bot, Louis Marin and Paul Virilio – of the periodical *Traverses*, published by the Georges Pompidou Centre (a.k.a. the Beaubourg) in Paris. Between 1976 and 1989, Baudrillard contributed some eighteen articles to the journal, thirteen of which were subsequently reprinted as book chapters (*SED*, *S*, *SS*, *FS*, *A*, *TE*, *IE*).

The journal emerged on the French intellectual scene in the mid-1970s, just as Baudrillard could no longer see a meaningful role for the journal *Utopie* to which he contributed and served as an editor. Consequently, Baudrillard shifted his energies from *Utopie* which was forged in the spirit of Lefebvre's urbanism and an anticipation of the events of May 1968 to *Traverses* because it was 'based on a kind of transversality, not any more a transgression, in order to find a negativity of another type, more interstitial, more floating, semi-institutional' (*BL*, 64). In other words, Baudrillard saw in *Traverses* the possibility of a critical distance to liberalism and socialism that was of a different type to that afforded by *Utopie*. While *Traverses* was published by the Pompidou Centre it was nevertheless anti-Beaubourg in the sense that its view of culture was intellectual rather than public. However, for Baudrillard the journal was effectively finished as a critical force in the early years of the 1980s because 'there was a political ultimatum to the journal, via the Beaubourg, to widen its social base, to become a "social" review, to take account of the requests of the people and not to be intellectual' (*BL*, 65). That is to say that, there was an attempt to turn the periodical into a socialist journal that ultimately compromised the autonomy and foundations of the journal so that, for Baudrillard speaking in 1983, '*Traverses* is virtually finished in my opinion, although it will continue for the time being' (*BL*, 65). Indeed, looking back on the journal in an interview in 1997 Baudrillard noted that, 'for a time, a journal like *Traverses* was the locus of a collective activity, a structure of reception, but never my unique center of gravity. It was a thematic journal that invested in the world, but even this kind of journal was already no longer possible on the fringes of the 1980s . . .' (*UD*, 20).

Passwords

Beaubourg
May 1968
Situationism
Utopie

TWIN TOWERS – see 'double' and 'terrorism'.

UNIVERSALITY

David B. Clarke

'The universal', Baudrillard declares, is 'on its way out' (*P*, 11) – a fast-fading hope, long past its sell-by date, and in any case a chimera, modernity's founding myth. In its place, globalisation has taken hold, its ascendancy intimately related to the demise of the modern ambition crystallised in universality.

Globalisation and universality are not equivalent terms; in fact they could be considered mutually exclusive. Globalisation pertains to technologies, the market, tourism and information. Universality pertains to values, human rights, freedoms, culture and democracy. Globalisation seems to be irreversible; the universal on the other hand seems to be disappearing, at least in so far as it constitutes a system of values for Western modernity with no counterpart in any other culture. (Baudrillard, in Grace et al., 2003: 23)

'Other cultures . . . have never laid claim to universality. Nor did they ever claim to be different – until difference was [foisted upon] them' (*TE*, 132). Today, however, 'triumphant globalisation is levelling out every difference and every value, ushering in a perfectly indifferent (non)culture' (Baudrillard, in Grace et al., 2003: 26). Where universality instituted difference in place of singularity, globalisation instates indifference.

As Lyotard (1992: 30) insightfully argued, 'the project of modernity (the realisation of universality) has not been forsaken or forgotten, but destroyed, "liquidated".' It is not simply the 'legitimacy' of universality that has been put in question, but its very *possibility*; not merely the wilful abandonment of modernity's hopes and dreams (the realisation of the universality of values, rights, liberty, democracy), but the dissolution of modernity's ambition from within. Modernity was founded on 'an idea (of freedom, of wisdom, of justice, of equality, or whatever) which is universal but whose universality lies in the future' (Bauman, 1992: 40–1). But this teleological myth contained its own undoing. 'There is a kind of reversible fatality for systems', says Baudrillard, 'because the more they go towards universality, towards their total limits, there is a kind of reversal which they themselves produce, and which destroys their own objective' (*BL*, 91). Modernity's dogged pursuit of universality inevitably induced such a reversal: 'By crossing into a space whose curvature is no longer that of the real . . . the era of simulation is inaugurated by a liquidation of all referentials' (*SS*, 2). It is necessarily the case that 'Every universal form is a simulacrum, since it is the simultaneous equivalent of all the others – something it is impossible for any real being to be' (*IE*, 64). By virtue of the same process, a universality infinitely postponed until the end of history has witnessed its dissolution, along with that of the end of history. Accordingly, one should not expect an end to the discourse of universality – to claims registered in the name of freedom, justice and democracy. Given that 'in a non-linear, non-Euclidean space of history the end cannot be located' (*IE*, 110), one may expect an ever-increasing clamour of claims to universal rights, which are progressively hollowed out by the self-same process. Today, the 'universal itself is globalized; democracy and human rights circulate just like any other global product – like oil or capital' (*ST*, 90).

As the forces unleashed by globalisation proliferate at the expense of a rapidly diminishing universality, the outcome remains uncertain. Unlike universality, globalisation 'is not really a concept . . . it is a fact, a state of things, an apparently irresistible one, but one that, precisely because no—one has a monopoly on it, runs the risk of becoming a fact at everyone's expense' (Baudrillard, in Grace et al., 2003: 28). Whereas universality was a statement of intent, globalisation is a catalogue of consequences. But, fortunately:

the die has not yet been cast, even if, for universal values, all bets are definitely off. The stakes have risen and globalisation is by no means a sure winner. In the face of globalisation's dissolving and homogenising power, everywhere heterogeneous forces are arising that are not only different but antagonistic and irreducible. (Baudrillard, in Grace et al., 2003: 26)

'What must be opposed to globalisation is not an effective universal instance but a radical singularity', Baudrillard proposes, offering the following apposite image of thought:

We . . . have spoken of the violence done to the singular by the universal and the violence done by the global to the universal. We must think of the game of Paper, Scissors, Stone. The scissors break on the stone, but the paper covers the stone and the scissors cut the paper. There are three terms. Each overtakes the other in a ceaseless cycle and it is the same with the global, the universal and the singular. But I will leave you to guess which is which. (Baudrillard, in Grace et al., 2003: 35)

Passwords

Globalisation
Modernity
Singularity

URBAN – see 'architecture', 'Beaubourg' and 'city'.

UTOPIA

David B. Clarke

'Utopia *puts an end to the real*,' claims Baudrillard (*SED*, 188), indicating the concept's pivotal status as a symbolic entity. Indeed, the symbolic '*is the u-topia that puts an end to the topologies of the soul and the body, man and nature, the real and the non-real, birth and death.* In the symbolic operation, the two terms lose their reality' (*SED*, 133). Noting that 'Western thought cannot bear, and has at bottom never been able to bear, a void of signification, a *non-place* and a non-value' (*SED*, 234), Baudrillard enlists the notion of utopia as precisely such a non-place, ellipsis of value and eclipse of meaning. 'Utopia is that which, by the abolition of the blade and disappearance of the handle, gives the knife its *force de frappe*,' wrote Baudrillard (*UB*, 59), adapting an aphorism of Lichtenberg's.

Utopia does not, then, represent a transcendent state, where present inadequacies are overcome. Indeed, '*utopia . . . would have nothing to do with the concept of alienation.* It regards every man and every society as already totally there, at each social moment, in its symbolic exigency' (*MP*, 165). Likewise, even though 'the psychoanalytic (Lacanian) real is no longer given as substance, nor as a positive reference' (*SED*, 188), it is no closer to grasping utopia's challenge to the real. For 'The idea of the unconscious, *like the idea of consciousness,* remains an idea of discontinuity and rupture . . . [I]t substitutes the irreversibility of a lost object and a subject forever "missing" itself, for the positivity of the object and the conscious subject' (*SED*, 143).

However decentred, the subject remains within the orbit of Western thought, with its successive 'topologies' (hell/heaven – subject/nature – conscious/unconscious), where the fragmented subject can only dream of a lost continuity. It will never get back to, or catch up with [*rejoindre*] utopia, which is not at all the phantasm of a lost order but, contrary to all the topologies of discontinuity and repression, the idea of a duelling order, of reversibility, of a symbolic order. (*SED*, 143–4)

This, however, marks a fateful turn in the history of utopia as that which puts an end to 'the reality principle which is only the phantasm of the system and its indefinite reproduction' (*MP*, 167). For utopia has itself fallen prey to the 'limitless operation of the real' (*LP*, 72). 'The utopia of another society – as one could have dreamed of at the time of production – is literally impossible, since it is already here' in an era of simulation (Baudrillard, 1992a: 241). In a world where 'Everything belonging to the order of dream, utopia and phantasm is given expression, "realized"' (Baudrillard, 2004a: unpaginated), utopia has, paradoxically, been achieved. 'But is this really what an achieved utopia looks like? . . . Yes indeed! . . . There is no other' (*A*, 98). As Baudrillard (1998: 6) resignedly observes, 'From this point on, the problem in hand is not one of changing how life is lived, which was the maximal utopia, but one of survival, which is a kind of minimal utopia.'

Passwords

America
Modernity
Simulation
Symbolic exchange

UTOPIE

Richard G. Smith

Baudrillard published dozens of articles in the topical and political journal *Utopie (Revue de sociologie de l'urbain)*, many of which were subsequently republished as chapters in his books of the 1970s and 1980s, appearing in *CPS, MP, SS, S, GD* and *SSM*. In 2006, many of Baudrillard's *Utopie* articles were finally collected together in English as *Utopia Deferred: Writings for Utopie, 1967–1978* (2006b).

From 1966 Baudrillard taught sociology at the University of Paris X at Nanterre, and it was in that year that the *Utopie* group was established: '*Utopie* truly began at Lefebvre's place at Navarrenx, in the Pyrenees, in 1966. I got to know the group. In fact, just before 1968. All of this really began right before 1968 . . .' (*UD*, 16). The first issue of the periodical *Utopie* appeared in May 1967 with Hubert Tonka, an architect and Henri Lefebvre's assistant, as its managing editor. The publication brought together 'a few architects and young intellectuals' (*UD*, 13): the sociologists Jean Baudrillard, René Lourau and Catherine Cot, the architects Jean Aubert, Jean-Paul Jungmann and Antoine Stinco, and the landscape architect Isabelle Auricoste. The journal's membership fluctuated around the first issues until a principal group, including Baudrillard, remained. In the 1990s there was initially some confusion as to the history of the journal, with Genosko (1994: 166) only examining 'the first seven issues up to August–September 1973'. However, it is now established that the journal was, in fact, published for a decade, the final issue being that for December 1977–January 1978 (Number 17). In an interview Baudrillard comments that *Utopie* ended around this time because, with 'the appearance of the Giscardian type of liberalism in 1975–6, it suddenly became evident that these small journals were doomed because they no longer had anything to say that mattered' (*RC*, 32–3), 'They did not speak to anyone any more, they no longer had an impact' (*BL*, 64), consequently Baudrillard shifted his energies to co-found the journal *Traverses*.

Baudrillard had a central role in the establishment and success of *Utopie*

whose collective aim – nourished by the thought of Henri Lefebvre – was
to advance a radical ultra-left critique of architecture, urbanism and everyday life: 'the intention was to surpass architecture as such, just as urbanism as such had been surpassed and as the Situationists had liquidated
the space of the university as such . . . Everyone was trying to liquidate
his own discipline' (*UD*, 13). While *Utopie* was 'a minor radical review,
of a situationist type' (*BL*, 64), 'a little on the margin' (*UD*, 17), that sold
few issues, it nevertheless flourished for just over a decade as its founders
and contributors had, if not a common project, then at least a clear sense
of what they were opposing, 'society, power are on the other side' (*BL*,
64), and were also energised by having a sense that they were speaking
to a movement and atmosphere of revolt that existed in some sections of
French society around the events of May 1968: 'The 1968 event came,
in some way, to "realize" the project, though also, in the same blow, to
extinguish a little of its potential' (*UD*, 15).

Passwords

Architecture
May 1968
Sociology + The end of the social
Traverses

VALUE + STRUCTURAL LAW OF VALUE

David B. Clarke

The term 'value' has currency not only in political economy – use value,
exchange value, surplus value – but also in terms of 'the great humanist
criteria of value, the whole civilisation of moral, aesthetic and practical
judgement' (*SED*, 9). Value's stratagem is to arrange the world into 'distinctly opposed terms between which a dialectic can then be established'
(*PW*, 15). Aesthetic value establishes an opposition between the beautiful and the ugly; moral value between good and evil; and so on. Such
oppositions appear symmetrical – no beauty without ugliness; no ugliness
without beauty – but this symmetry is deceptive. The positively charged
term asserts and controls the distinction, defining its opposite as lacking

what it possesses, anticipating its demise in a generalised system of equivalence. All systems of value postulate 'the possibility of balancing out value, of finding a general equivalent for it which is capable of exhausting meanings and accounting for an exchange' (*PW*, 9). Value, then, 'grounds our morality, as does the idea that everything can be exchanged, that the only thing that exists is what can assume value' (*PW*, 73).

On this basis, Baudrillard is as interested in what value excludes as in value itself: 'there is in our system of values no reversibility: what is positive is on the side of life, what is negative is on the side of death; death is the end of life, its opposite' (*PW*, 16). Death, in our society, is afforded no value and no meaning: we would be better off without it. Yet life and death are characterised by reversibility rather than opposition. 'In the symbolic universe, life and death are exchanged. And, since there are no separate terms but, rather, reversibility, the idea of value is cast into question' (*PW*, 15). However much a society predicated on value might attempt to eliminate the individual causes of dying, it cannot escape the fact that 'Death is an aspect of life' (*SED*, 188). Insofar as it is premised on the resolution of opposed terms, value can only ever feign its status as a self-sufficient principle. By attempting to force that which cannot be exchanged to disappear, all systems of value are destined to see their ambition humiliated: 'All that lives by value will perish by equivalence' (*P*, 4). Just as all forms of physical energy dissipate into the state of maximal entropy known as thermic death, a kind of metaphysical entropy has led everything to dissipate into the value-form, and thence to the dissipation of value itself. 'The great Nietzschean idea of the transvaluation of all values has seen itself realized in precisely the opposite way: in the involution of all values . . . For the transmutation of values we substituted the commutation of values, for their reciprocal transfiguration we substituted their indifference to one another and their confusion' (*P*, 2).

Evidently, Baudrillard's conception of value and its fate differs starkly from Marx's. From the perspective of symbolic exchange, Baudrillard sees Marx's critique of political economy as a woefully inadequate reflection of its object, already caught in the mirror of production through which 'the human species comes to consciousness [*la prise de conscience*]' (*MP*, 19). The imaginary, 'through which an objective world emerges and through which man recognizes himself objectively', is determined solely by 'production which is assigned to him as the ultimate dimension of value and meaning' (*MP*, 19). Production, however, is blind to the challenge of seduction, which draws us 'beyond the reality principle' (*EC*, 58). It is in this context that Baudrillard's identification of a 'structural' law of value assumes its significance. For Marx, it is the additional dimension of exchange value, over and above use value, that defines the commodity. Unlike use value, exchange value is marked by the relativity of its form. Yet as far as Marx was concerned, this does not detract from the sense in which the value form expresses an underlying substance – 'a congelation of homogeneous human labour' (Marx, 1954: 46). Abstracting from use value, £10 of cheese is worth ten times more than £1 of chalk. How much cheese or chalk one gets for £1, however, is determined by the abstract social labour 'congealed' in the commodity. Such is the classical law of value: the abstract labour time socially necessary to produce a commodity under prevailing social and technological conditions is conserved in the sphere of exchange. Drawing on Ferdinand de Saussure's analysis of linguistic value, however, Baudrillard historicises Marx's concern with the substance of value. Marx privileged the role of use value as 'the horizon and finality of the system of exchange-values' (*SED*, 6), failing to detect that use value is subject to precisely the same 'logic of equivalence' as exchange value, and mistakenly 'maintaining use value as the category of "incomparability"' (*CPS*, 134) when it is merely the alibi of exchange value and subject to the same law of equivalence.

For Saussure (1959: 115), 'To determine what a five-franc piece is worth one must . . . know: (1) that it can be exchanged for a fixed quantity of a different thing, e.g. bread; and (2) that it can be compared with a similar value of the same system, e.g. a one-franc piece.' The first dimension corresponds, by analogy, to the functional capacity for a linguistic sign to refer to something; the second corresponds to the structural system of differential terms capable of allowing such reference in the first place. Saussure held that language as such inheres in its structural dimension, in purely differential terms, defined by 'their *relativity*, internal to the system and constituted by binary oppositions' (*SED*, 6). The substance happened upon by language – vocal chords and sound waves, paper and ink – is wholly incidental. Yet under 'classical' conditions, the structural and functional dimensions of language mesh and cohere. Just as 'the commodity law of value is a law of equivalences, . . . it equally designates . . . equivalence in the configuration of the sign, where one signifier and one signified facilitate the regulated exchange of a referential content' (*SED*, 8), presiding over a dialectic between the sign and the real. Yet 'a revolution has put an end to this "classical" economics of value, . . . *Referential value is annihilated, giving the structural play of value the upper hand*' (*SED*, 6). Such is the *structural* revolution of value, which entails that, 'from now on, signs are exchanged against each other rather than against the real' – indeed, 'the real has died of the shock of value acquiring this fantastic autonomy' (*SED*, 7). It is in this technical sense that Baudrillard intends the term 'simulation'.

Passwords

Ambivalence
Death
Political economy of the sign
Production
Reversibility
Semiotics
Simulation
Symbolic exchange

VEBLEN, THORSTEIN (1857–1929) – see 'consumption + affluent society' and 'fashion'.

VIRTUAL

William Pawlett

The virtual is an important term in Baudrillard's later work, used frequently as a noun and also as an adjective in his notions of virtual events, virtual war and virtual power. The most important dimensions of the virtual or 'virtuality', for Baudrillard, are information technology and the news media, artificial intelligence and cloning. Baudrillard associates the virtual with the 'fourth order' and 'integral reality', that is with a new phase or tendency beyond that of simulation, or alternatively simulation's 'highest stage' (*LP*, 44). Virtuality consists of 'an identical copy of our world, a virtual artifact that opens up the prospect of endless reproduction' (*VI*, 8). In a sense the virtual is the ultimate system of control because instead of exerting control over the world it attempts to jettison it and produce a substitute, double or clone of the world. Yet Baudrillard insists there is also a more benign potential within the virtual, one that hints at a 'new freedom'.

For Baudrillard the notion of 'virtual reality' is an 'oxymoron' (*PW*, 39); he contests the commonplace neo-liberal perspective which contrasts 'the real world' with 'the virtual world' of new technologies and the information superhighway. For Baudrillard 'the real has only ever been a form of simulation' and the virtual 'is merely a hyperbolic instance of this tendency to pass from the symbolic to the real' (*PW*, 39). The 'real' and the 'hyper-real' are both orders of simulacra (*SED*), that is they are generated by images or signs, firstly through representation and then simulation.

The fundamental distinction, for Baudrillard, is not then between real and virtual, but between the symbolic and the successive attempts to neutralise it – the real, the hyper-real and the virtual.

The term virtual has a long history. Firstly associated with the spiritual and divine, in modern usage it referred to potentiality, to that which might become real or actual. Today the term becomes more restricted, 'no longer the potentially real', the Virtual is 'non-referential – orbital and exorbital – it is never again intended to meet up with the real world. Having absorbed the original, it produces the world as undecidable' (*IEx*, 15). Virtuality is 'the reality that [is] . . . perfectly homogenised, digitised and "operationalised" . . . verifiable and non-contradictory' (*PW*, 39). The virtual is not unreal; it is more 'real' than the hyper-real: 'more real than what we have established as simulacrum' (*PW*, 39). The virtual then is not of the order of images, it is not a simulation because it 'murders the sign': 'if the phase of simulation is indeed that of the murder of the real, the virtual, for its part, is the phase of the murder of the sign' (*ExD*, 76). More devastating than the murder of reality; the murder of the sign is also the 'murder of illusion' (*F*, 46) and the final elimination of the 'symbolic dimension' (*LP*, 68).

The virtual replaces the sign as its 'final solution', a term Baudrillard adopts from the German *Endoslung*, the term used for the final annihilation of the Jews under the Nazis. The virtual, he suggests, may be catastrophic in its annihilation of both symbolic forms and the sign. The virtual tends to make historical, political and critical analysis impossible 'in the sphere of the Virtual . . . nothing is representable . . . neither distance nor a critical or aesthetic gaze: there is total immersion . . . not of the order of representation, but of decoding and visual consumption . . . it is impossible to work back from them to some tangible reality' (*LP*, 77). Virtuality then has dire consequences for the understanding of historical events, such as war: '[War] is no longer representable, and to the ordeal of war is now added that of the impossibility of representation . . . [f]or there to be critical perception and genuine information, the images would have to be different from the war' (*LP*, 77). But the images are the war, 'the specificity of the Virtual is that it constitutes an event *in* the real *against* the real and throws into question all these categories of the real, the social, the political and history – such that the only emergence of any of these things now is virtual' (*LP*, 83). The virtual threatens the very possibility of critical thinking by producing information to such an excess that it becomes impossible to contextualise, digest or apply. This produces virtual or 'non-events', and because 'we shall never get back to pre-news and pre-media history' (*IE*, 6) we cannot know how events would be had they not been mediated.

Yet Baudrillard suggests, frequently in his later work, that the virtual may bring some surprisingly 'happy consequences'. While the screen's virtuality 'screens out any dual relation' (*LP*, 78) it also falls prey to 'objective irony', to a sudden reversal. For example, far from being spellbound into passivity by the media, people increasingly disbelieve everything they see on a screen, which, in a way, confers a 'new freedom'. The virtual, for Baudrillard, is a mode of disappearance: 'the disappearance of the real in the virtual, the disappearance of the event in information, the disappearance of thought in artificial intelligence, the disappearance of values and ideologies in the globalisation of trade' (*IEx*, 121). And disappearance may even 'clear the way for the exercise of a thinking freed from all purpose, all "objectivity", and restored to its radical uselessness' (*IEx*, 111). Writing on artificial intelligence, Baudrillard suggests 'leaving intelligence to machines is, in the end, relinquishing the responsibility of knowing, just as leaving it to politicians to govern us relieves us of the responsibility of power' (*IEx*, 114). Virtual technology may be an 'ironic strategy' on the part of the species, involving 'a superior intuition of the illusoriness' of the world; indeed, virtuality 'is perhaps all we have left of the original illusion . . . [and] preserves us from any temptation one day to possess the truth' (*LP*, 85).

Baudrillard's comments are clearly highly speculative and he does not explore the notion of a digital divide, of cyber-serfdom, which is unfortunate given that the liberation into purely experimental thought 'free to lead nowhere' (*IEx*, 120) is likely to be the preserve of the elite. However, Baudrillard certainly does not claim that such a positive outcome is imminent and emphasises that other 'catastrophic' outcomes are perhaps more likely. The situation is rather one of radical uncertainty; virtual technology may be what 'frees us from the world of value' and 'liberates us from technology' (*PW*, 42) or it may be what destroys us, or helps us destroy ourselves.

Passwords

Code
Disappearance
Hyper-reality
Integral reality
Real
Simulacra + Simulacrum
Simulation

WARHOL, ANDY (1928–87) – see 'America', 'art', 'artists', 'hyper-reality', 'transaesthetics' and 'transpolitics'.

WATERGATE – see 'architecture' and 'politics'.

WORLD TRADE CENTER – see 'architecture' and 'terrorism'.

WRITING

Gerry Coulter

Baudrillard was a writer at odds with the universe. Writing was for him a kind of abreaction, an acting out: 'you push your life out . . . into your writing' (*PH*, 146–7). He often wrote of everyday events in a way that sought an escape velocity from so-called 'traditional academic discourse' and his *oeuvre* is an interesting example of the way in which theory and literature begin to communicate with greater affection in the late twentieth century. It serves as a kind of proof of his notion that 'Theory is never so fine as when it takes the form of a fiction or a fable' (*CM5*, 11). When his writing produced 'meaning' it was 'to play that meaning against the system itself' (*ED*, 41). Faced with an indifferent universe and a world given to us as unintelligible and enigmatic, why should writing attempt to clarify or simplify? For Baudrillard 'we must make that world even more unintelligible, even more enigmatic' (*VI*, 83).

By working and reworking mysterious paradoxes into the lyrical complexity of writing, Baudrillard took his revenge on the universe, a revenge on notions such as the 'Real', 'Truth' and 'Meaning' to argue that theory precedes the world – and writing brings it into existence (*F*). For Baudrillard, writers 'cause things to exist, not by producing them in the material sense of the term, but by defying them, by confronting them' (*BL*, 44). He avoided ideological or moral critique because he felt these were forms of writing 'obsessed with meaning and content' and with the 'political finality of discourse' (*PC*, 103). For Baudrillard such forms do

violence to 'the act of writing, the poetic, ironic, allusive force of language
. . . the juggling with meaning' (*PC*, 103) that is so vital. Writing was
Baudrillard's politics (*BL*). Writing concerned the production of illusion
for Baudrillard (*BL*), and when it accomplishes this, writing is truly a form
of art. For Baudrillard, the job of art is to assist us in understanding the
vital illusion behind everything – that the real hides behind appearances.
If all art can do is become entangled in the real (such as writing that adds
meaning to the world), it loses its way as art and becomes something else.
The absolute conspiracy of art for Baudrillard is in its giving up on illusion
and seeking the real (*P*).

For Baudrillard, writing is also 'an inhuman and unintelligible activity
– one must always do it with a certain disdain, without illusions, and leave
it to others to believe in one's own work' (*CM*, 68). Writing (theory) for
Baudrillard was to observe a fatal strategy – to go to extremes. He mainly
wrote in fragments or short essays. 'I just write for myself', he wrote; 'I
no longer pretend to that privileged position of a person who has the right
to know and to write' for others (*BL*, 182). Writing for Baudrillard was a
precious 'singularity', 'a resistance to real time', 'something that does not
conform', 'an act of resistance', the 'invention of an antagonistic world'
rather than a 'defence of a world that might have existed' (*P*, 32). Writing,
he wrote, 'is the living alternative to the worst of what it says' (*CM5*, 43).

Writing was for him a form of challenge and always a provocation
(*ED*). It held a seductive power (*PC*) and was a kind of theory fiction
where things in the end simply fall apart on their own into fragments
separated only by the play of correspondence between them (*BL*). Behind
Baudrillard's writing was not what we would call a form of hope but he
was very optimistic in his own way. This came from a deep understanding of reversibility and the self-destructive logic of systems from the
small scale to the global (*P*). The reason theory and writing are so closely
related for Baudrillard is that for him writing is closer to thinking than to
speaking.

Baudrillard wrote about our world of illusion – one in which truth,
meaning and the real exist only along local and restricted horizons, as
partial objects (*SS*). He was critical of the death of politics and the proliferation of simulation and virtuality – but he did postulate a way to thrive
in these bleak conditions while continuing to think and write: 'We no
longer have any standards of truth or objectivity, but a scale of probability
. . . The space between the true and the false is no longer a relational space,
but a space of random distribution . . . The uncertainty principle does not
belong to physics alone; it is at the heart of all our actions, at the heart
of "reality"' (*SC*, 85 and 86). Writing was a source of deep pleasure for
Baudrillard.

Passwords

Art
Fatal
Fragments
Illusion
Literature
May 1968
Singularity

$$\boxed{Z}$$

ŽIŽEK, SLAVOJ – see 'communication + non-communication' and 'politics'.

Bibliography

JEAN BAUDRILLARD, BOOKS IN ENGLISH

This section is of book-length works available in the English language by Jean Baudrillard and is arranged in order of appearance in the original French (where applicable). It provides a key to almost all references to Baudrillard's works in the individual entries. These are standardised so that any citation of one of Baudrillard's books is either spelt out, as in 'Symbolic Exchange and Death (1993a [1976])' (where the first date refers to the publication of the English translation, while the second, in square brackets, refers to the original French publication date), or is abbreviated so that, for example, '(SED)' refers to Symbolic Exchange and Death and (SED, 17) refers to a specific page in Symbolic Exchange and Death. This list contains works that are not solely by Baudrillard and some that are originally English-language publications.

[SO]   Baudrillard, J. (1996a [1968]) *The System of Objects*, trans. J. Benedict. London: Verso.

[CS]   Baudrillard, J. (1998a [1970]) *The Consumer Society: Myths and Structures*, trans. C. Turner. London: Sage.

[CPS]   Baudrillard, J. (1981 [1972]) *For a Critique of the Political Economy of the Sign*, trans. C. Levin. St Louis, MS: Telos.

[MP]   Baudrillard, J. (1975 [1973]) *The Mirror of Production*, trans. M. Poster. St Louis, MS: Telos.

[SED]   Baudrillard, J. (1993a [1976]) *Symbolic Exchange and Death*, trans. I. H. Grant. London: Sage.

[FF]   Baudrillard, J. (2007a [1977]) *Forget Foucault*, trans. N. Dufresne, 2nd edn. New York: Semiotext(e).

[SSM]   Baudrillard, J. (2007b [1978]) *In the Shadow of the Silent Majorities or The End of the Social*, trans. P. Foss, J. Johnston, P. Patton and A. Berardini, 2nd edn. New York: Semiotext(e).

[S]   Baudrillard, J. (1990a [1979]) *Seduction*, trans. B. Singer. London: Macmillan.

[SS]   Baudrillard, J. (1994a [1981]) *Simulacra and Simulation*, trans. S. F. Glaser. Ann Arbor, MI: University of Michigan Press.

[FS]   Baudrillard, J. (2008a [1983]) *Fatal Strategies*, trans.
                P. Bietchman and W. G. J. Niesluchowski. London:
                Pluto.

[SV]   Baudrillard, J. and Calle, S. (1988a [1983]) *Suite vénitienne/
                Please Follow Me*, trans. D. Barash and D. Hatfield. Seattle,
                WA: Bay Press.

[A]   Baudrillard, J. (1988b [1986]) *America*, trans. C. Turner.
                London: Verso.

[ED]   Baudrillard, J. (1987 [1987a]) *The Evil Demon of Images*,
                trans. P. Patton and P. Foss. Sydney: Power Institute.

[EC]   Baudrillard, J. (1988c [1987b]) *The Ecstasy of Communication*,
                trans. B. Schutze and C. Schutze. New York: Semiotext(e).

[CM]   Baudrillard, J. (1990b [1987c]) *Cool Memories*, trans.
                C. Turner. London: Verso.

[RC]   Baudrillard, J. (1990c) *Revenge of the Crystal: Selected
                Writings on the Modern Object and its Destiny, 1968–1983*,
                trans. P. Foss and J. Pefanis. Sydney: Power Institute.

[TE]   Baudrillard, J. (1993b [1990a]) *The Transparency of Evil:
                Essays on Extreme Phenomena*. Trans J. Benedict. London:
                Verso.

[CM2]   Baudrillard, J. (1996b [1990b]) *Cool Memories II, 1987–90*,
                trans. C. Turner. Cambridge: Polity.

[GW]   Baudrillard, J. (1995 [1991]) *The Gulf War Did Not Take
                Place*, trans. P. Patton. Sydney: Power Institute.

[IE]   Baudrillard, J. (1994b [1992]) *The Illusion of the End*, trans.
                C. Turner. Cambridge: Polity.

[BL]   Baudrillard, J. (1993c) *Baudrillard Live: Selected Interviews
                (1982–1993)*, ed. M. Gane. London: Routledge.

[RA]   Baudrillard, J. and Guillaume, M. (2008b [1994]) *Radical
                Alterity*, trans. A. Hodges. New York: Semiotext(e).

[PC]   Baudrillard, J. (1996c [1995a]) *The Perfect Crime*, trans.
                C. Turner. London: Verso.

[CM3]   Baudrillard, J. (1997a [1995b]) *Fragments, Cool Memories
                III, 1991–1995*, trans. C. Turner. London: Verso.

[AA]   Baudrillard, J. (1997b) *Art and Artefact*, ed. and trans.
                N. Zurbrugg. London: Sage.

[P]   Baudrillard, J. (1998b [1997]) *Paroxysm: Interviews with
                Philippe Petit*, trans. C. Turner. London: Verso.

[PH]   Baudrillard, J. (1999a [1999a]) *Photographies, 1985–1998*.
                Ostfildern-Ruit: Hatje-Cantz.

[IEx]   Baudrillard, J. (2001a [1999b]) *Impossible Exchange*, trans.
                C. Turner. London: Verso.

[LA] Baudrillard, J. and Delahaye, L. (1999b [1999c]) *L'Autre*, trans. C. Turner. London: Phaidon.

[VI] Baudrillard, J. (2000) *The Vital Illusion*. New York: Columbia University Press.

[SC] Baudrillard, J. (2002a [2000a]) *Screened Out*, trans. C. Turner. London: Verso.

[CM4] Baudrillard, J. (2003a [2000b]) *Cool Memories IV, 1995–2000*, trans. C. Turner. London: Verso.

[PW] Baudrillard, J. (2003b [2000c]) *Passwords*, trans. C. Turner. London: Verso.

[SA] Baudrillard, J. and Nouvel, J. (2002b [2000d]) *The Singular Objects of Architecture*, trans. R. Bononno. Minneapolis, MN: University of Minnesota Press.

[UB] Baudrillard, J. (2001b) *The Uncollected Baudrillard*, ed. G. Genosko. London: Sage.

[F] Baudrillard, J. (2004 [2001]) *Fragments: Conversations with François L'Yvonnet*, trans. C. Turner. London: Routledge.

[ST] Baudrillard, J. (2003c [2002]) *The Spirit of Terrorism and Requiem for the Twin Towers*, trans. C. Turner. London: Verso.

[LP] Baudrillard, J. (2005a [2004]) *The Intelligence of Evil or The Lucidity Pact*, trans. C. Turner. London: Berg.

[CA] Baudrillard, J. (2005b) *The Conspiracy of Art: Manifestos, Texts, Interviews*, ed. S. Lotringer. New York: Semiotext(e)/MIT.

[CM5] Baudrillard, J. (2006a [2005a]) *Cool Memories V (2000–2005)*, trans. C. Turner. Cambridge: Polity.

[UD] Baudrillard, J. (2006b) *Utopia Deferred: Writings from Utopie (1967–1978)*, trans. S. Kendall. New York: Semiotext(e).

[ExD] Baudrillard, J. with Noailles, E. V. (2007c [2005b]) *Exiles from Dialogue*, trans. C. Turner. Cambridge: Polity.

[WD] Baudrillard, J. (2009 [2007]) *Why Hasn't Everything Already Disappeared?*, trans. C. Turner. London: Seagull.

[CC] Baudrillard, J. (2010 [2008]) *Carnival and Cannibal, or the play of Global Antagonism*, trans. C. Turner. Chicago: Chicago University Press.

JEAN BAUDRILLARD, BOOKS IN FRENCH

Books in French that are not available as full free-standing English translations are listed here.

[AS] Baudrillard, J. (1978) *L'Ange de Stuc*. Paris: Galilée.

[GD]   Baudrillard, J. (1985) *La Gauche Divine: Chronique de années*
                   1977–1984. Paris: Bernard Grasset.
[JJ]   Merzeau, L. and Baudrillard, J. (2004) *Au jour le jour*. Paris:
                   Descartes & Cie.

JEAN BAUDRILLARD'S TRANSLATIONS FROM
GERMAN TO FRENCH

Baudrillard, Jean (translation). Bertolt Brecht: *Dialogues d'exiles*, traduit
   par Jean Baudrillard et Gilbert Badia. Paris: L'Arche, 1956.
Baudrillard, Jean (translation). Karl Terzaghi and Ralph Brazelton Peck:
   Mécanique des sols appliquée aux travaux publics et au bâtiment, traduit
   par Jean Baudrillard et Claude Meunier. Paris: Dunod, 1961.
Baudrillard, Jean (translation). Peter Weiss: *Point de fuite, roman traduit de*
   l'allemand par Jean Baudrillard. Paris: Éditions du Seuil, 1964.
Baudrillard, Jean (translation). Peter Weiss: *La Persécution et l'assassinat*
   de Jean-Paul Marat: représentes par le groupe théâtral de L'hospice de
   Charenton sous la direction de Monsieur de Sade: drame en deux actes.
   Paris: Éditions du Seuil, 1965.
Baudrillard, Jean (translation). Peter Weiss: *L'Instruction: oratorio en onze*
   chants. Paris: Seuil, 1966.
Baudrillard, Jean (translation). Peter Weiss: *Chant du fantoche lusitanien*.
   Paris: Seuil, 1968a.
Baudrillard, Jean (translation). Peter Weiss: *Discours sur la genèse et le*
   déroulement de la très longue guerre de libération du Vietnam: illustrant la
   necessité de la lutte armée des opprimés contre leurs oppresseurs ainsi que la
   volonté des États-Unis d'Amérique d'anéantir les fondements de la révolu-
   tion. Paris: Seuil, 1968b.
Baudrillard, Jean (translation). Wilhelm E. Mühlmann: *Messianismes révo-*
   lutionnaires du tiers-monde. Paris: Gallimard, 1968c.
Baudrillard, Jean, Gilbert Badia (introduction, annotations) et al. (translation). Karl Marx and Friedrich Engels: *L'Idéologie allemande, critique de*
   la philosophie allemande la plus récente dans la personne de ses représentants
   Feuerbach, R. Bauer et Stirner, et du socialisme dans celle de ses différents
   prophètes. Paris: Editions Sociales, 1968d.
Baudrillard, Jean et al. (translation). Friedrich Engels: *Le Rôle de la vio-*
   lence dans l'histoire; Violence et économie dans l'établissment du nouvel
   Empire allemand. Paris: Editions Sociales, 1969.

OTHER BAUDRILLARD CITED

Baudrillard, J. (1962a) 'Uwe Johnson: La Frontière', *Les Temps Modernes*, 1094–107.

Baudrillard, J. (1962b) 'Les Romans d'Italo Calvino', *Les Temps Modernes*, 1728–34.

Baudrillard, J. (1962c) 'La Proie des Flammes', *Les Temps Modernes*, 1928–37.

Baudrillard, J. (1963) *Les Allemands. (Textes réunis et présentés par Jean Baudrillard. Photographies de René Burri).* Paris: Delpire.

Baudrillard, J. (1978) 'La Précession des Simulacres', *Traverses* 10: 3–37.

Baudrillard, J. (1985) 'The Masses: The Implosion of the Social in Media', *New Literary History*, 16(3): 577–89.

Baudrillard, J. (1987) 'Modernity', *Canadian Journal of Political and Social Theory*, 11(3): 63–73.

Baudrillard, J. (1988) 'L'Objet Pur', in A. Mariani (ed.) *Façades* (Catalogue of an Exhibition held at Georges Pompidou). Rio de Janeiro: Nova Fronteira.

Baudrillard, J., Gadamer, H.-G., Jameson, F., Kristeva, J., Lyotard, J.-F., Marin, L., Perniola, M., Sloterdijk, P., Sollers, P., Virilio, P. and West, C. (1991) *Art and Philosophy*. Milan: Giancarlo Politi Editore.

Baudrillard, J. (1991a) 'When Bataille Attacked the Metaphysical Principle of Economy', *Canadian Journal of Political and Social Theory*, 15: 135–8.

Baudrillard, J. (1991b) 'Charles Matton ou l'illusion objective', in *Charles Matton*. Paris: Editions Hatier, pp. 5–8.

Baudrillard, J. (1992a) 'Revolution and the End of Utopia', in W. Stearns and W. Chaloupka (eds), *Jean Baudrillard: The Disappearance of Art and Politics*. London: Macmillan, pp. 233–42.

Baudrillard, J. (1992b) 'Transpolitics, Transsexuality, Transaesthetics', in W. Stearns and W. Chaloupka (eds), *Jean Baudrillard: The Disappearance of Art and Politics*. London: Macmillan, pp. 9–26.

Baudrillard, J. (1995a) *Andy Warhol: Paintings, 1960–1986*. Ostfildern: Hatje Cantz Publishers.

Baudrillard, J. (1995b) 'Vivisecting the 90s: An Interview with Jean Baudrillard'. Online at: CTheory.net/articles.aspx?id=66.

Baudrillard, J. (1997) 'After Utopia: The Primitive Society of the Future', in N. Gardels (ed.), *At Century's End*. Dublin: Wolfhound, pp. 214–20.

Baudrillard, J. (1998) 'The End of the Millennium or the Countdown', *Theory, Culture and Society*, 15(1): 1–9.

Baudrillard, J. (1999) 'Truth or Radicality? The Future of Architecture', *BluePrint*, January, pp. 30–5.

Baudrillard, J. (2001) 'Sanctuary City', *TATE: The Art Magazine*, 24: 38–41.

Baudrillard, J. (2002) *Power Inferno*. Paris: Galilée.

Baudrillard, J. (2003) 'Dust Breeding', *Quaderns d'Arquitectura i Urbanisme*, 236: 13–15.

Baudrillard, J. (2004a) 'The Matrix Decoded: *Le Nouvel Observateur* interview with Jean Baudrillard', *International Journal of Baudrillard Studies*, 1(2): July. Online at: http://www.ubishops.ca/baudrillardstudies/vol1_2/genosko.htm.

Baudrillard, J. (2004b) 'This Is the Fourth World War: The *Der Spiegel* Interview with Jean Baudrillard', *International Journal of Baudrillard Studies*, 1(1): January. Online at: http://www.ubishops.ca/BaudrillardStudies/spiegel.htm.

Baudrillard, J. (2004c) 'Interview with Jean Baudrillard', in P. Hegarty, *Jean Baudrillard: Live Theory*. London: Continuum, pp. 134–49.

Baudrillard, J. (2005) 'Holy Europe', *New Left Review*, 33: 24–5.

Baudrillard, J. (2007) 'Hetero-da-fe', *International Journal of Baudrillard Studies*, 4(2): July. Online at: http://www.ubishops.ca/BaudrillardStudies/vol4_2/v4-2-baudrillard-hetero-da-fe.html.

BOOKS ON BAUDRILLARD

Almond, I. (2007) *The New Orientalists: Postmodern Representations of Islam from Foucault to Baudrillard*. London: I. B. Tauris.

Bishop, R. (ed.) (2009) *Baudrillard Now: Current Perspectives in Baudrillard Studies*. London: Polity.

Butler, R. (1999) *Jean Baudrillard: The Defence of the Real*. London: Sage.

Clarke, D., Doel, M., Merrin, W. and Smith, R.G. (eds) (2009) *Jean Baudrillard: Fatal Theories*. London: Routledge.

Constable, C. (2009) *Adapting Philosophy: Jean Baudrillard and 'The Matrix Trilogy'*. Manchester: Manchester University Press.

Cormack, P. (2002) *Sociology and Mass Culture: Durkheim, Mills, and Baudrillard*. Toronto: University of Toronto Press.

Florian, T. (2004) *Bonjour . . . Jean Baudrillard*. Paris: Éditions Cavatines.

Frankovits, A. (ed.) (1984) *Seduced and Abandoned: The Baudrillard Scene*. Glebe, NSW: Stonemoss.

Gane, M. (1991a) *Baudrillard: Critical and Fatal Theory*. London: Routledge.

Gane, M. (1991b) *Baudrillard's Bestiary: Baudrillard and Culture*. London: Routledge.

Gane, M. (2000a) *Jean Baudrillard: In Radical Uncertainty*. London: Pluto.

Gane, M. (ed.) (2000b) *Jean Baudrillard, Volumes 1–4*. London: Sage.

Genosko, G. (1994) *Baudrillard and Signs: Signification Ablaze*. London: Routledge.

Genosko, G. (1999) *McLuhan and Baudrillard: The Masters of Implosion*. London: Routledge.

Grace, V. (2000) *Baudrillard's Challenge: A Feminist Reading*. London: Routledge.

Grace, V., Worth, H. and Simmons, L. (eds) (2003) *Baudrillard West of the Dateline*. Palmerston, New Zealand: Dunmore Press.

Gundersen, R. and Dobson, S. (1996) *Baudrillard's Journey to America*. London: Minerva Press.

Hegarty, P. (2004) *Jean Baudrillard: Live Theory*. London: Continuum.

Horrocks, C. (1999) *Baudrillard and the Millennium*. Cambridge: Icon Books.

Horrocks, C. and Jevtic, Z. (1996) *Baudrillard for Beginners*. Cambridge: Icon Books.

Kellner, D. (1989) *Jean Baudrillard: From Marxism to Postmodernism and Beyond*. Cambridge: Polity.

Kellner, D. (ed.) (1994) *Baudrillard: A Critical Reader*. Oxford: Blackwell.

Kershaw, B. (1999) *The Radical in Performance: Between Brecht and Baudrillard*. London: Routledge.

L'Yvonnet, F. (ed.) (2004) *L'Herne Baudrillard*. Paris: Éditions de l'Herne.

Lane, R. J. (2009) *Jean Baudrillard*, 2nd edn. London: Routledge.

Leonelli, L. (2007) *La Séduction Baudrillard*. Paris: École Nationale Supérieure Des Beaux-Arts.

Levin, C. (1996) *Jean Baudrillard: A Study in Cultural Metaphysics*. Hemel Hempstead: Prentice Hall.

Majastre, J.-O. (ed.) (1996) *Sans oublier Baudrillard*. Brussels: La Lettre Volée.

Merrin, W. (2005) *Baudrillard and the Media*. Cambridge: Polity.

Pawlett, W. (2007) *Jean Baudrillard: Against Banality*. London: Routledge.

Pefanis, J. (1991) *Heterology and the Postmodern: Bataille, Baudrillard and Lyotard*. Durham, NC: Duke University Press.

Poster, M. (ed.) (2001) *Jean Baudrillard: Selected Writings*, 2nd edn. Cambridge: Polity.

Proto, F. (ed.) (2006) *Mass Identity Architecture: Architecture Writings of Jean Baudrillard*, 2nd edn. Chichester: John Wiley & Sons.

Rajan, T. (2002) *Deconstruction and the Remainders of Phenomenology: Sartre, Derrida, Foucault, Baudrillard*. Stanford, CA: Stanford University Press.

Redhead, S. (ed.) (2008) *The Jean Baudrillard Reader*. Edinburgh: Edinburgh University Press.

Rojek, C. and Turner, B. S. (1993) *Forget Baudrillard?* London: Routledge.

Schuster, M. (2008) *Don DeLillo, Jean Baudrillard, and the Consumer Conundrum*. Amherst, NY: Cambria Press.

Scott, D. (2004) *Semiologies of Travel: From Gautier to Baudrillard*. Cambridge: Cambridge University Press.

Stearns, W. and Chaloupka, W. (eds) (1992) *Jean Baudrillard: The Disappearance of Art and Politics*. London: Macmillan.

Toffoletti, K. (2009) *Baudrillard Reframed: A Guide for the Arts Student*. London: I. B. Tauris.

Woodward, A. (2009) *Nihilism in Postmodernity: Lyotard, Baudrillard, Vattimo*. Aurora, CO: Davies Group.

Zurbrugg, N. (ed.) (1997) *Jean Baudrillard: Art and Artefact*. London: Sage.

OTHER TEXTS CITED

Allberry, C. R. C. (ed. and trans.) (1938) *A Manichaean Psalm-book (Part 2)*. Stuttgart: W. Kohlhammer.

Artaud, A. (1958 [1938]) *The Theatre and Its Double*. New York: Grove Press.

Barthes, R. (1982) *Camera Lucida: Reflections on Photography*. London: Jonathan Cape.

Bataille, G. (1985a) 'The Notion of Expenditure', in A. Stoekl (ed.), *Visions of Excess: Selected Writings, 1927–1939*. Minneapolis, MN: University of Minnesota Press, pp. 116–29.

Bataille, G. (1985b) 'Base Materialism and Gnosticism', in A. Stoekl (ed.), *Visions of Excess: Selected Writings, 1927–1939*. Minneapolis: MN: University of Minnesota Press, pp. 45–52.

Bataille, G. (1991a) *The Accursed Share, Volume I*. New York: Zone.

Bataille, G. (1991b) *The Accursed Share, Volumes II and III*. New York: Zone.

Bataille, G. (1995) 'Formless', in G. Bataille, M. Leiris, M. Griaule, C. Einstein and R. Desnos, *Encyclopaedia Acephalica*. London: Atlas Press, pp. 51–2.

Bauman, Z. (1992) *Mortality, Immortality and Other Life Strategies*. Cambridge: Polity Press.

Benjamin, W. (2003) 'On the Concept of History', in H. Eiland and M. W. Jennings (eds), *Selected Writings: Volume 4, 1938–1940*. Cambridge, MA: Harvard University Press, pp. 389–400.

Benjamin, W. (2008) *The Work of Art in the Age of Its Technological Reproducibility, and Other Writings on Media*. Cambridge, MA: Harvard University Press.

Bonnal, M. (1986) *Passage*. Paris: Editions Galilée.

Borges, J. L. (1970) *Labyrinths*. Harmondsworth: Penguin.

Bridges, J. (1979) *The China Syndrome*. IPC Films.

Butler, A. (2003) 'Postmodernism and Science Fiction', in E. James and F. Mendlesohn (eds), *The Cambridge Companion to Postmodernism*. Cambridge: Cambridge University Press, pp. 137–48.

Carrier, D. (1988) 'Baudrillard as Philosopher or, The End of Abstract Painting', *Arts Magazine*, 63(1): 52–60.

Coppola, F. F. (1979) *Apocalypse Now*. Zoetrope Studios.

Coulter, G. (2007) *Never travel on an aeroplane with God*. Online at: http://www.ubishops.ca/baudrillardstudies/Book-Index.html.

Debord, G. (1983) *The Society of the Spectacle*. Detroit, MI: Black & Red.

Deleuze, G. (1994) *Difference and Repetition*. New York: Columbia University Press.

Deleuze, G. and Guattari, F. (1983) *Anti-Oedipus: Capitalism and Schizophrenia*. Minneapolis, MN: University of Minnesota Press.

Derrida, J. (1978) *Writing and Difference*. Chicago: University of Chicago Press.

Derrida, J. (1979) *Spurs/Éperons*. Chicago: University of Chicago Press.

Derrida, J. (1984) 'Of an Apocalyptic Tone Adopted in Recent Philosophy', *Oxford Literary Review*, 6(2): 20–1.

Derrida, J. (1997) *Politics of Friendship*. London: Verso.

Dick, P. K. (1977) *A Scanner Darkly*. New York: Doubleday.

Dyakov, A. (2009) 'Baudrillard, Gnosticism and the Beginning of Simulation', *International Journal of Baudrillard Studies*, 6(1): January.

Foster, H. (ed.) (1983) *The Anti-Aesthetic: Essays on Postmodern Culture*. Port Townsend, WA: Bay Press.

Foster, H. (1986) 'Signs Taken For Wonders', *Art in America*, June: 80–91 and 139.

Foucault, M. (1970) *The Order of Things: An Archaeology of the Human Sciences*. London: Tavistock.

Foucault, M. (1977) *Discipline and Punish: The Birth of the Prison*. New York: Pantheon.

Foucault, M. (1978) *The History of Sexuality: Volume 1. An Introduction*. New York: Random House.

Freud, S. (1953–74 [1919]) 'The Uncanny', in *The Standard Edition of the Complete Works of Sigmund Freud, Volume XVII*, ed. J. Strachey. London: Tavistock, pp. 219–52.

Freud, S. (1953–74 [1919]) *The Standard Edition of the Complete Works of Sigmund Freud, Volume XVII*, ed. J. Strachey. London: Tavistock.

Fukuyama, F. (1992) *The End of History and the Last Man*. London: Hamish Hamilton.

Gane, M. (1990) 'Ironies of Postmodernism: Fate of Baudrillard's Fatalism', *Economy and Society*, 19(3): 314–34.

Giraudoux, J. (1983) *The Trojan War Will Not Take Place*. London: Methuen.

Gottdiener, M. (1994) 'The System of Objects and the Commodification of Everyday Life: The Early Baudrillard', in D. Kellner (ed.), *Baudrillard: A Critical Reader*. Oxford: Blackwell, pp. 25–40.

Grant, R. M. (ed. and trans.) (1996) *Irenaeus of Lyons (The Early Church Fathers)*. London: Routledge.

Green, M. (1993) *The Dada Almanac*. London: Atlas.

Greenlees, D. (1956) *The Gospel of the Prophet Mani*, World Gospel Series, Vol. 12. Madras: Theosophical Publishing House.

Halley, P. (1986) 'Frank Stella and the Simulacrum', *Flash Art*, 126: 32–5.

Hayles, K. (1991) 'The Borders of Madness', *Science-Fiction Studies*, 18(3): 321–3.

Heartney, E. (1987) 'Reluctant Prophet (Jean Baudrillard)', *Art News*, 86(7): 18.

Hughes, R. (1989) 'The Patron Saint of Neo-Pop', *New York Review*, 1 June, pp. 29–32.

Isenberg, W. W. (trans.) (1981) 'The Gospel of Philip', in J. M. Robinson (ed.), *The Nag Hammadi Library in English*. New York: Harper & Row.

Jakobson, R. (1960) 'Closing Statement: Linguistics and Poetics', in T. A. Sebeok (ed.), *Style in Language*. New York: Wiley, pp. 350–77.

Jameson, F. (1991) *Postmodernism, Or The Cultural Logic of Late Capitalism*. London: Verso.

Jarry, A. (1945) *Le Surmâle*. Paris: Fasquelle.

Jonas, H. (1963) *The Gnostic Religion: The Message of the Alien God and the Beginnings of Christianity*, 2nd rev. edn. Boston: Beacon Press.

Kester, G. (1987) 'The Rise and Fall? Of Baudrillard', *New Art Examiner*, November, 20–3.

Laclau, E. and Mouffe, C. (1985) *Hegemony and Socialist Strategy: Towards a Radical Democratic Politics*. London: Verso.

Le Roy Ladurie, E. (1979 [1978]) *Montaillou: The Promised Land of Error*. New York: Vintage.

Lotringer, S. (2008) 'Remember Foucault', *October*, 115: 19–20.

Lyotard, J.-F. (1986) *The Postmodern Condition: A Report on Knowledge*. Manchester: Manchester University Press.

Lyotard, J.-F. (1992) *The Postmodern Explained to Children: Correspondence 1982–1985*. London: Turnaround.

Lyotard, J.-F. (1993) *Libidinal Economy*. London: Athlone Press.

Marx, K. (1954) *Capital: A Critique of Political Economy, Vol. 1*. London: Lawrence & Wishart.

Mauss, M. (1966) *The Gift: Forms and Functions of Exchange in Archaic Societies*. London: Routledge & Kegan Paul.

McLuhan, M. and Fiore, Q. (1967) *The Medium is the Massage*. Harmondsworth: Penguin.

Merrin, W. (2009) 'Floral Tributes, Binge-Drinking and the Ikea Riot Considered as an Uphill Bicycle Race', in D. B. Clarke, M. A. Doel, W. Merrin and R. G. Smith (eds), *Jean Baudrillard: Fatal Theories*. London: Routledge, pp. 61–82.

Miller, J. (1987) 'Baudrillard and His Discontents', *Artscribe International*, 63: 48–51.

Morson, G. S. (2003) 'The Aphorism: Fragments from the Breakdown of Reason', *New Literary History*, 34(3): 409–29.

Nietzsche, F. (1987) *Twilight of the Idols / The Anti-Christ*. Harmondsworth: Penguin Books.

Norris, C. (1992) *Uncritical Theory: Postmodernism, Intellectuals and the Gulf War*. Amherst, MA: University of Massachusetts Press.

Rank, O. (1971 [1914]) *The Double. A Psychoanalytic Study*. Chapel Hill, NC: University of North Carolina Press.

Rorty, R. (1979) *Philosophy and the Mirror of Nature*. Princeton, NJ: Princeton University Press.

Rovira, J. (2005) 'Subverting the Mechanisms of Control: Baudrillard, *The Matrix Trilogy*, and the Future of Religion', *International Journal of Baudrillard Studies*, 2(2). Online at: http://www.ubishops.ca/BaudrillardStudies/vol2_2/rovira.htm.

Ruddick, N. (1992) 'Ballard/Crash/Baudrillard', *Science Fiction Studies*, 19(3): 354–60.

Runciman, S. (1947) *The Medieval Manichee: A Study of the Christian Dualist Heresy*. Cambridge: Cambridge University Press.

Said, E. (1979) *Orientalism*. New York: Vintage Books.

Saussure, F. de (1959 [1916]) *Course in General Linguistics*. London: Peter Owen.

Sillitoe, A. (1959) *The Loneliness of the Long Distance Runner*. London: Pan.

Sim, S. (ed.) (2004) *The Routledge Companion to Postmodernism*. London: Routledge.

Smart, B. (1992) *Modern Conditions, Postmodern Controversies*. London: Routledge.

Smart, B. (1993) *Postmodernity*. London: Routledge.

Smith, R. G. (2003) 'Baudrillard's Non-representational Theory: Burn the Signs and Journey Without Maps', *Environment and Planning D: Society and Space*, 21: 67–84.

Smith, R. G. (2005) 'Lights, Camera, Action: Baudrillard and the Performance of Representations', *International Journal of Baudrillard Studies*, 2(1): 1–9.

Smith, R. G. with Doel, M. A. (2001) 'Baudrillard Unwound: The Duplicity of Post-Marxism and Deconstruction', *Environment and Planning D: Society and Space*, 19(2): 137–19.

Sobchack, V. (1991) 'Baudrillard's Obscenity', *Science-Fiction Studies*, 18(3): 327–9.

Surya, M. (1987) *Georges Bataille, La Mort à l'œuvre*. Paris: Editions Garamont.

Tester, K. (1994) *Media, Culture, and Morality*. London: Routledge.

Vine, R. (1989) 'The Ecstasy of Baudrillard', *New Criterion*, 7/9: 39–48.

Vizenor, G. (1997) *Hotline Healers*. Hanover, NH: Wesleyan University Press.

Wachowski, A. and Wachowski, L. (1999) *The Matrix*. Groucho II Film Partnership.

Wenders, W. (1984) *Paris, Texas*. Road Movies Filmproduktion.

Zurbrugg, N. (1994) 'Baudrillard, Modernism, and Postmodernism', in D. Kellner (ed.), *Baudrillard: A Critical Reader*. Oxford: Blackwell, pp. 227–55.

Notes on Contributors

John Armitage is Principal Lecturer in Media and Communications at Northumbria University, UK.

Jon Baldwin is Lecturer in Media and Communications at London Metropolitan University, UK.

Malcolm Barnard is Lecturer in Visual Culture in the School of Art and Design at Loughborough University, UK.

Matthias Benzer is Lecturer in Sociology at Manchester University, UK.

Ryan Bishop is Associate Professor in the Department of English Language and Literature at the National University of Singapore.

Rex Butler is Associate Professor in the School of English, Media Studies and Art History at the University of Queensland, Australia.

Alan Cholodenko is Honorary Associate in the Department of Art History and Film Studies at the University of Sydney, Australia.

David B. Clarke is Professor of Human Geography at Swansea University, Wales, UK.

Catherine Constable is Associate Professor in the Department of Film and Television Studies at Warwick University, UK.

Patricia Cormack is Associate Professor in Sociology at St Francis Xavier University, Canada.

Gerry Coulter is Professor of Sociology at Bishop's University in Lennoxville Quebec, Canada.

Marcus A. Doel is Professor of Human Geography at Swansea University, UK.

Mike Gane is Professor of Sociology at the University of Loughborough, UK.

Gary Genosko is Professor of Sociology at Lakehead University, Canada.

Graeme Gilloch is Reader in Sociology at Lancaster University, UK.

Victoria Grace is Professor of Sociology and Gender Studies at the University of Canterbury, New Zealand.

David J. Gunkel is the Presidential Teaching Professor of Communication Technology at Northern Illinois University, USA.

Paul Hegarty is Lecturer in Philosophy and Cultural Studies in the Department of French, University College Cork, Ireland.

Richard J. Lane is Professor in the Department of English at Vancouver Island University, Canada.

John Lechte is Professor in the Department of Sociology at Macquarie University, Australia.

William Pawlett is Senior Lecturer in Cultural Studies at the University of Wolverhampton, UK.

Francesco Proto is an architect and a part-time lecturer in Visual Culture (Nottingham Trent University) and History and Theory of Architecture (DeMontfort University, Leicester), UK.

Diane Rubenstein is Professor of Government and American Studies at Cornell University, USA.

Marc Schuster is an author and novelist who teaches English at Montgomery County Community College in Blue Bell, Pennsylvania, USA.

Stuart Sim is Professor in the Department of English at the University of Sunderland, UK.

Laurence Simmons is Associate Professor in the Department of Film, Television and Media at the University of Auckland, New Zealand.

Brian C. J. Singer is Associate Professor in Sociology at Glendon College, York University, Canada.

Barry Smart is Professor of Sociology at the University of Portsmouth, UK.

Jonathan Smith is Lecturer in Philosophy and Research Methods within the School of Media and Communication at RMIT University, Melbourne, Australia.

Richard G. Smith is Senior Lecturer in Human Geography at Swansea University, UK.

Paul A. Taylor is Senior Lecturer in the Institute of Communication Studies at the University of Leeds, UK.

David Teh is Assistant Professor in the Department of English Language and Literature at the National University of Singapore.

Kim Toffoletti is Lecturer in Gender Studies at Deakin University, Australia.

Andrew Wernick is Professor of Cultural Studies and Sociology at Trent University, Canada.

Ashley Woodward is a member of the Melbourne School of Continental Philosophy, Australia.